Whoever wishes to investigate medicine properly should proceed thus: in the first place, consider the seasons of the year, and what effect each of them produces...

Hippocrates

THE HIBERNATION RESPONSE

This is a book about human adaptation in its oldest form, adaptation to the periodic nature of our planet. That we live in such a changing environment is something that we have partially forgotten but that our bodies and brains remember. A better understanding brings fascinating insights into ourselves. We are extraordinarily adaptive beasts; I firmly believe that with some creative introspection we can improve our adaptation to the seasons and temper our natural response to the challenges of winter—that of hibernation.

Peter Whybrow, M.D.

The Hibernation Response

WHY YOU
FEEL FAT,
MISERABLE,
& DEPRESSED
FROM OCTOBER
THROUGH
MARCH—AND
HOW YOU CAN CHEER UP
THROUGH THOSE
DARK DAYS OF WINTER

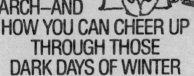

PETER WHYBROW, M.D., AND ROBERT BAHR

AVON BOOKS ◢◣◥◤ NEW YORK

AVON BOOKS
A division of
The Hearst Corporation
105 Madison Avenue
New York, New York 10016

First Avon Books Printing: November 1989

AVON TRADEMARK REG. U.S. PAT. OFF. AND IN OTHER COUNTRIES, MARCA
REGISTRADA, HECHO EN U.S.A.

Printed in the U.S.A.

RA 10 9 8 7 6 5 4 3 2 1

Preface

As a child growing up in England, I sometimes found it impossible to get to sleep on a summer's night. The sun never seemed to go down, and I would lie awake pondering the irrational nature of adults who sent me to bed according to the dictates of a brainless timepiece. It was probably my first experience with the seasonal variation of behavior.

England is a good deal higher in the hemisphere than Philadelphia, Pennsylvania, about the same latitude as Labrador, so there were many long summer days of playing—and eventually working—in the hayfields. By contrast, the winters were dark, very wet, with shiny pavements and gray skies. It's just impossible to avoid the weather in England. It's everybody's first topic of conversation; there are even radio programs devoted to the seasons and the poetry that they have spawned.

When in my late twenties I migrated permanently to America, it is not surprising that I was lured to the country and eventually to working a small family farm in New England. There at Blow me down Brook Farm, Ruth, Kate, Helen, and I together enjoyed, wondered, and learned about the seasons for well over a decade: We increased the egg supply by keeping the chicken house lights on a timer that created eternal springtime, we watched the coats of the cows and the horses fall out in the spring and grow back in the fall, and the newborn lambs always came in March and April. We noted, too, the folklore of the place: the winter blahs; the cabin fever; the New England soul in winter. It was on this latter topic that in the winter of 1977–78 I was asked to speak to the Dartmouth alumni, together with Lou Renza, a professor of English. I provided the physiology, he the poetry, and it worked very well. In the audience was the editor of *Yankee Magazine*. The following year I wrote a small piece for him on adapting to winter, "Where There Is Mud There Is Momentum," which appeared in the April 1979 edition.

The article led to a flurry of invitations to appear on TV and radio shows and to give interviews to the press. Everybody wanted to know about the seasons and what they did to us. In fact, nobody knew very much—at least not about the behavioral aspects. The details of animal and human physiology, especially in response to cold, had been fairly well worked out, but it was thought that humans, extending their days through artificial means, stood apart from the seasonal changes of sunlight. It took the genius of Al Lewy of the National Institute of Mental Health to determine that the photoperiod which we knew so much about in animals was also important in human beings. I was a visiting scientist at NIMH that winter, and while working with Lewy, Norman Rosenthal, and Tom Wehr, I decided to study *normal* behavior through the seasons in a New England population. When I returned to Dartmouth after my sabbatical year, thanks to the generous support and kindness of Posey Fowler and the Fowler Fund, I was able to conduct that research and

6

learned that normal people do have a distinct seasonal cycle in behavior. Indeed, in pattern it was not dissimilar to those being described by the NIMH researchers in Washington and dubbed "seasonal affective disorder," or SAD. The normal experience appeared the same but was not so severe. The whole subject fascinated me; it seemed to integrate my love of the countryside, my avocation in farming, the experience enjoyed with my family through the changing seasons, my professional interest in endocrinology and behavior, and the psychological and physiological adaptation that as human beings we have made to our environment. It was clearly the case that human beings have a hibernation response.

We are imperial as a species, we humans. Many of us seem to have forgotten our natural habitat: that we are attuned to nature's laws just as are all other animals. Many have forgotten—but not all. In New England there is still an acute awareness. That sort of thing tends to get reinforced when you can't get down your driveway without digging for three hours in the morning. But in the big cities, too, I have discovered that there remains a nagging awareness that the weather has something to do with the way we feel.

Hence, when Robert Bahr sought me out and suggested that we write a book together explaining these phenomena and giving some advice on how best to survive winter, it sounded like a natural idea. It has been an exceptionally interesting and easy book to put together, thanks to the ease of our collaboration.

There are many people to thank for those special experiences along the way: in particular Ruth, Kate, and Helen, for the wonderful years farming together in New England; Al Lewy, Anna Wirz-Justice, Norman Rosenthal, and Tom Wehr, for their insights into rhythmicity and the seasons; Eva Redei, for her scientific curiosity and the creative insights she provided regarding stress hormones and the brain; Jeanne Blackman, and particularly Lenore Stiber, who put this manuscript together, and Peter Alahi, who did a lot of the library research.

This is a book about human adaptation in its oldest form, adaptation to the periodic nature of our planet. That we live in such a changing environment is something that we have partially forgotten but that our bodies and brains remember. A better understanding brings fascinating insights into ourselves. We are extraordinarily adaptive beasts; I firmly believe that with some creative introspection we can improve our adaptation to the seasons and temper our natural response to the challenges of winter—that of hibernation.

PETER WHYBROW, M.D.
Philadelphia, 1988

For thirteen days in January 1977 the thermometer outside our woodland cabin in Upper Milford, Pennsylvania, registered 13 degrees below zero. The indoor temperature that month never climbed above 62 degrees. We wore coats to dinner, slept fully dressed.

The water pipes froze, and we collected drinking and cooking water from a stream behind the cabin. Snow avalanched into that stream, froze, and forced the water over its banks, across ten feet of ice, and into our basement window. While the water climbed the carpeted steps to the living room, we drove through blowing snowdrifts to the hardware store, bought a sump pump, and set it up in two feet of basement water so cold that a skin of ice had formed across the surface. The pump held its own, and a day later we dug open the streambed.

The winter of 1977 is historic. Records tumbled from Milwaukee to Miami. Power lines fell; municipal sewage pipes froze; factories closed; crops and livestock perished. And thirteen thousand residents of Buffalo, New York, whose story I later told in *The Blizzard*, found themselves stranded downtown for up to five days during the city's worst snowstorm ever.

The heating bill for that tiny five-room cottage quickly approached two thousand dollars that year, but it wasn't the money—or even that particular winter—that drove me to hating winters in the northern United States.

From my mid-twenties until 1981 I remember each autumn and winter:

—Listening to disgustingly cheerful voices sing, "Let it snow, let it snow, let it snow," and commenting to myself, "Oh, shut up!"

—Sitting at the typewriter on many a gray afternoon intending to organize my thoughts and realizing suddenly that I had devoted two hours to discovering that I had no thoughts whatever.

—Cramming food in my mouth virtually nonstop, not because I was hungry but because I was simply *compelled* to do it. I earned thereby a wondrous physical transformation from a tautly muscular 165 pounds at five feet eleven inches to an impressively puffy 192 pounds.

—Loving TV football, although any sport played in the autumn probably would have sufficed if accompanied by the requisite gin and tonic and potato chips. Even a blank screen might have done the job.

—Recognizing a quite inexplicable change in all my friends, relatives, and the world at large. They became unworthy of me. They grew intentionally irritable, petty, and quarrelsome. I gave fleeting thought to leaving them in the lurch, departing for the great beyond, which would certainly have taught them a lesson or two.

It was in 1981, after I'd written three books and several articles about blizzards, that I realized I truly hated winters. All my research on winter weather had been an unconscious effort to confront the enemy. At that time the work of Dr. Norman Rosenthal and his colleagues at the National Institute of Mental Health on seasonal affective disorder began to appear in the medical literature. I knew immediately that I had discovered at least part of my problem.

Subsequently I found that millions of people around the world respond in similar fashion to the shorter days and colder temperatures of autumn and winter. But their complaints go well beyond those of SAD; the range of symptoms is much broader for most of us than can be explained simply by seasonal depression.

As long ago as 1979, while he was professor and chairman of the Department of Psychiatry at the Dartmouth Medical School, Dr. Peter Whybrow was perhaps the first authority ever to suggest that humans, like many other animals, have a natural hibernation response. Because our modern, civilized life-styles don't permit it and, perhaps more significantly, because of evolutionary changes in our body chemistry, humans—with the possible exception of one tribe in Australia—are not now able to enter into a true hibernating state. And it's that conflict between the tendency to hibernate and the impossibility of doing so which makes autumn and winter a disastrous time for many millions of us around the world.

Dr. Whybrow's innumerable medical journal reports have concerned, for the most part, his specialty of psychiatric endocrinology, the ways in which our hormones dictate our moods. Specifically he's a leading authority on the thyroid gland, which, as you'll see, plays a major role in the hibernation response. Few individuals could have

11

brought to this book the broad yet detailed knowledge of human psychology and endocrine physiology which Dr. Whybrow has contributed.

For my part, there are others to thank as well. And just as the truck driver who fills your empty oil tank at midnight in the depths of winter is, at that moment when the heat kicks on, more important than any President ever was, so the following people have provided indispensable assistance: Carol Nippert and her staff at the Lehigh Valley Hospital Center library, Patricia Ann Sacks, Scherelene Schatz, Christine Fiedler, Neal Owens of the SunBox Company, and Barbara Eastland.

Particular thanks to Barbara Erich for both typing and deciphering illegible notations. And to my best researcher, best friend, and only wife, Alice Harrison Bahr, Ph.D., my deepest gratitude.

ROBERT BAHR
Macungie, Pennsylvania, 1988

Contents

The Hibernation Response

The Sleep That Never Comes: Hibernation in Its Many Forms

*The climatic influence runs deep . . . at the deepest
level of the subconscious mind of all those
descended from Ice Age people, there swirls
the genetic memory of an unending snowstorm.*
                              —LOREN EISELY

We are now living through the fourth major ice age of the past billion years. Fortunately ice ages are divided into glacial and interglacial periods, and we are now in an interglacial phase. But if the calculations of the widely respected Yugoslavian geophysicist Milutin Milankovich are correct, a mere fifteen thousand years ago the earth, and what there was of the human race, faced extinction in the grip of profound cold. During that last glacial age all of upper America lay under a gleaming slab of ice, some of it, including the area now known as Chicago, a mile deep. According to David O. Woodbury, author of *The Great White Mantle*, 25 percent of the earth was buried under ice; today ice covers only about 8 percent of the globe, and all but 15 percent of that is in the Antarctic.

That last glacial period, the Wisconsin Glaciation, began with a gradual cooling some seventy-five thousand years ago. For twenty thousand years the snow fell and pressed into ice, the ice weighing heavier and heavier upon the earth, rising like a mountain until across the entire northern part of the globe the individual crystals slipped imperceptibly forward, an inch, a foot, not more than two feet a year. From many directions the ice oozed south, chilling the air, sucking moisture from furious blizzards on which the glaciers continued to nourish. For fifteen thousand years the glaciers covered all of Canada and the United States as far south as Kentucky. They cut deep into the south-central states, swept east to Long Island, buried Buffalo, Ireland, and most of England. Scandinavia was covered with a solid ice cap more than a mile thick and thousands of square miles wide. Ice covered Russia to the Urals, blanketed eastern Asia. All of northern Europe was an unbroken ice cap.

With the descending cold, glaciers formed in the mountains of the equator. Snow fell in South America and in the deserts of Africa. All across the earth, the air surrendered its moisture in herculean gales of snow and rain, forming an island sea over most of Utah, Nevada, and Idaho. Lakes appeared in the world's deserts. An ice bridge joined Australia and Tasmania. The Baltic was a small bowl of ice.

The Wisconsin Glaciation lasted for seventy-five thousand years, ending only a hundred centuries ago. Many species perished: those unable to migrate to the narrow belt of warmth girding the earth; those lacking, too, a dense pelt of hollow hairs to preserve body heat or, possessing that, unable to find food in the ice or in the sea.

A few endured, living on the brutal tundra and ice that covered much of the earth. Many were small, furry animals, but there were also the caribou and wolves and mastodons and woolly mammoths, all perfectly adapted for combat against the cold.

And there was the Cro-Magnon—man—who had long since lost any fur that he might have had. The mammoths and the mastodons grew extinct, but humankind survived, hurling themselves puny and naked against those awesome beasts, wrapping their bodies in the skins, filling their stomachs with the flesh. And when there was neither food nor warmth, they huddled with their kind against the elements, and they survived. Their body temperature a mere few degrees above that of the tiny cave or burrow to which they retreated, their metabolism almost at a standstill, they drew stingily on their ample reserves of body fat and slept away the bad times.

The Many Faces of Winter Sleep

Every autumn, in fields and forests and ponds and bays, plants and virtually all living creatures are stirred into response. The shorter days—not the cold—trigger a primordial instinct in many bird species. Using the stars to guide them, they take to the air in dense and noisy flocks, fleeing the darkness. The broad-winged hawks and warblers take flight as early as August and do not cease until they reach South America. The swallows are gone quickly, also, followed by bluebirds and some of the forty sparrow species. Robins and finches fly south, too, reluctantly. They are the last to leave and the first to reappear in the spring.

Some toads, mice, squirrels, and bears enter a state of torpor, or shallow hibernation. Their body temperatures drop, but not profoundly. They sleep away the winter but arouse themselves frequently to eat, urinate, give birth, and confront intruders. They may awaken once a week— or a couple of times a day. The Manitoba toad burrows into the soft earth and grows torpid as winter approaches. But plunging temperatures and encroaching frost will awaken it and it'll dig deeper before resuming its seasonlong snooze.

Snakes and lizards seek a safe hideaway, well protected

17

from the cold winds and ice to come. They huddle there while their own body temperatures drop along with the surrounding air, a state called hypothermia. They do not hibernate, or enter into torpor, but grow dormant, with no capacity to warm their bodies, and will remain in this peculiar state of living death until the spring sun heats the air around them or until they freeze.

Sea turtles grow lazy and inactive, finally sinking to the floor of a sandy bay to sleep through the cold months of winter, like the snakes and lizards, in a state of dormancy. Many fish do the same. Others, like their avian relatives, undertake an exhausting southern migration to warmer water.

Among some birds and mammals the intrusion of autumnal darkness triggers a profound response. Such creatures include the poorwills and nighthawks, koalas and other marsupials, spiny anteaters, platypuses, bats and other rodents, woodchucks (groundhogs), and hedgehogs (porcupines). The change is both physical and mental. By mid-December they are not at all the creatures they were in mid-July.

In the first phase the darting, streamlined, promiscuous woodchuck of early spring grows lazy and rotund, with no interest in sex or play or adventure, only with interest in more food. To all intents it is virtually asleep on its feet.

As autumn progresses with ever-shorter days and increasing cold, the woodchuck enters the second phase. It gives up the fight, crawling into its secret cave or burrow to pass the winter in hibernation. It appears that it is not at all happy about sleeping much of its life away, for it struggles fitfully to sustain consciousness. But its own body chemistry has dealt it a knockout punch against which it is powerless.[1]

If the woodchuck does indeed struggle against the narcotic drowsiness that envelops it, it is just that miracle of hibernation that has spared it and its species from extinction. Nature has not prepared it to scavenge for food during the frigid winter. At its normal metabolic rate it would burn up the energy stored in its body fat in short order. It would no longer be capable of generating body heat, and it would freeze. Or it would starve. Entire species have perished for such reasons.

Others adapted. Some developed a hibernation response. In the process the heart rate drops; the heart of a flying bat will beat a thousand times per minute during the summer, but only ten while hibernating.

Oxygen consumption plummets. Porcupines may take only a single breath in two and a half hours.

Depending upon the animal, body temperature falls sharply, as much as 50 or 60°F, until it is only a degree or two above the surrounding temperature.

Brain waves become extremely slow and regular; the hibernator's sleep is dreamless. Blood vessels in the extremities constrict, reducing demand on the circulatory system, allowing the severely limited oxygen and energy to be shunted directly to the heart and brain.

In such fashion, many species of the cold and temperate regions, unsuited for migration, incapable of finding food beneath the snow and ice and frozen earth, have survived. Their mode of entering the hibernating state, its depth, the length of time between arousals all vary— not only between species but among subgroups of species and even individuals within subgroups. For example, Syrian hamsters store food in their nests and arouse themselves every few days for a snack, while some bats refuse to stir for more than a month. Ground squirrels remain inactive for a couple of weeks at a time, but squirrels in tropic zones never hibernate.

Swallows have been reported to hibernate all winter,

the hummingbird for fewer than twelve hours, and some birds not at all. There are animals that pass into hibernation within minutes, and others that require weeks. It appears that an individual animal's capacity to experience the hibernation response is dependent upon both its own environment and that in which its forebears lived. Animals whose ancestors survived cold winters and food shortages through deep hibernation will themselves, as the days grow shorter, enter deep hibernation. Those whose lineage populated tropical climates will respond only subtly to reduced photoperiods. They may grow sluggish, fat, and irritable, but even when limited to very brief periods of light and subjected to profound cold, they will not hibernate. Like all mammals—including humans—and many birds and rodents, they experience the first, or preparatory, phase of hibernation. Lacking the capacity to actually achieve hibernation or having lost that function during eons in which survival did not require it, they react to artificially reduced photoperiods and cold by preparing for the sleep that never comes.

That preparatory phase is a biochemical response. Here's how it works: All mammals, along with snakes and lizards, possess what was once called a third eye. In the lizard the pineal gland[2] actually resembles an eye protruding from the center of the forehead. And like an eye, it includes a miniature cornea, lens, and retina. One of its functions is to register the amount of darkness to which the reptile is exposed. In response to the darkness, it secretes a hormone called melatonin.

The human, too, possesses a pineal gland. It weighs only a few thousandths of an ounce and resides on the upper surface of the thalamus between the two halves of the cerebral cortex. Unlike the lizard's pineal, the human gland is buried under a more or less thick skull and senses darkness through light receptors in the eyes. The same is true of many other animals, although light actually does penetrate the skulls of sheep, dogs, rabbits, and rats. In some creatures the pineal begins producing melatonin at dusk and keeps on until the onset of light. In others, including humans, melatonin levels in the blood usually increase after an hour or more of darkness—to five times that of daytime levels—and begin dropping again after six to eight hours.

Melatonin is a tranquilizer. That nightly dose prepares us for sleep. Our reaction time slows. We become fatigued. Since we were infants, melatonin has been sending us the same message: early to bed and early to rise—even on weekends, to the consternation of parents everywhere. Perhaps that day-after-day, year-after-year ebb and flow of melatonin in our blood actually established the endogenous circadian sleep/wake cycle, the daily inner rhythm that keeps us functioning spontaneously on an almost twenty-four-hour schedule even when we have no access to sunlight or time cues for weeks at a time.

The Human Hibernation Response

Every autumn millions of people living in temperate and cold climates undergo measurable physiological and psychological changes. During the spring and summer they played tennis and jogged and swam and pursued life with vigor, but with the onset of shorter days they slow down. Some react as early as July; most, by October or November. They become moody, depressed. They don't work as well as they did during the summer months; they make more mistakes, accomplish less, withdraw.

This is true of all of us who live in a markedly seasonal climate, essentially normal folks who go to work every day and enjoy productive, healthy lives. While at the Dartmouth Medical School in Hanover, New Hampshire,

I (Whybrow) undertook a careful study of the behavior of normal individuals through the seasons. New England is well known for its changeable weather: frigid winters and hot summers separated by cool weather in the spring and the fall. The marked seasonal differences in temperature and the length of the daylight period provide ideal conditions for testing theories about the effects of seasons on behavior. In 1983 we signed up about a hundred normal people who had never seen psychiatrists or taken any medications for mood troubles. They agreed to fill out detailed daily records of their sleep, energy, appetite, and mood for approximately fifteen months. These people lived in northern New England at a latitude of approximately 48 degrees. We did the study in cooperation with Norman Rosenthal at the National Institute of Mental Health (NIMH). When we analyzed the vast volume of information, we found that indeed, normal people do have a markedly seasonal pattern in their activity. The variation in behavior through the year was very real. People tended to sleep more in the winter, for example. The amount of time they spent in bed at night was essentially the same as in the summer. They also got up at the same time since they had to go to work. However, they began taking naps, usually after supper, apparently compensating for a general decrease in energy compared with the summer months. They also reported less drive and a lower mood during the winter, eating more carbohydrates and gaining weight.

During the spring and the fall, when the march of the seasons is most recognizable, people were at their most restless. This was the time of greatest subjective tension, while the peak of energy and optimism was found in the late summer.

These responses are well recognized outside the scientific field. The columnist Erma Bombeck has made some very important observations about our reaction to them: "The trouble with humans is that they carry on in winter with 'business as usual.' If snow covers their driveway, they remove the snow. If ice threatens their car, they cover it with a blanket. If there is a life-threatening blizzard, they get a snow plow to take them to the beauty shop. I say humans are not physically or mentally prepared for winters."

In the winter, says Bombeck, ordinary people become irritable. "Having a stranger say, 'Have a good day,' is grounds for assault. What do they know about you? What is good? What is day? If you wanted advice from them, you'd ask for it."

For others, the mental depression associated with winter becomes almost intolerable. In the diary of Samuel Marchbanks created by the novelist Robertson Davies, Marchbanks complains, "It is this time of year that I begin to think seriously about suicide. My interest in the matter is not practical; I never reach for the bread-knife or the poison bottle. But I begin to understand what it is that people see in suicide and why they do it. They have seen too many Februaries; they have lugged too many cans of ashes; they have shivered on too many bus stops."

Until the early 1980's most psychiatrists would have diagnosed such people as typical depressives. Yet, rather than suffer insomnia as most depressives do, the seasonally depressed person will sleep 17 percent more in winter months than he or she did during the rest of the year; while typical depressives lose their appetites, seasonal depressives gain ten to fifteen pounds every fall and winter. However, until recently there have been very few reports of such cases in the professional psychiatric journals. In the late 1800's Richard von Krafft-Ebing told of a thirty-five-year-old woman who suffered depression between the fall and spring of each year. Since then only a handful of additional cases had been described, one by Emil Kraepelin in 1921: "Repeatedly I saw in these cases moodiness set in in autumn and pass over in the spring, 'when the sap shoots in the trees,' to excitement, corresponding in a certain sense to the emotional changes which come over even healthy individuals at the changes of the seasons."

Until 1980 few researchers recognized or considered important the seasonal depression sometimes associated with the hibernation response and how it differed from typical depression. They treated these patients—and many still do—with drugs, psychotherapy, and hospitalization. For the most part the traditional approaches fail to prevent recurrence, and such individuals continue to spend every autumn and winter preparing for the sleep that never comes and the depression frequently associated with it. For milder cases, one reason traditional therapy has failed is that it has been based on a false assumption: that the slowdown of the hibernation response is an abnormal condition. In fact, it is *perfectly* normal, significantly responsible for the survival of the human species and probably present to a greater or lesser degree in all humans. Seasonal depression is a very severe form of the hibernation response afflicting the smaller percentage of people who find it impossible to respond to personal and cultural expectations during the winter months.

To paraphrase Shakespeare, the problem is not within the stars but in our modern life-styles. While growing darkness for Cro-Magnons ushered in sex and sleep, for moderns, color television and strobe lights introduce the fun part of the day. While our cave-dwelling ancestors responded to shorter, colder days with increasing torpor, we condemn ourselves for that natural biological response and attempt to continue life as usual.

As one woman hibernator put it, "I should have been a bear. Bears are allowed to hibernate, but humans aren't." She was entirely correct. The fault was not with her but with an incompatible life-style.

Managing the Hibernation Response: The First Step

Our very first step in controlling the hibernation response must be taken in our heads, and it might as well be taken now. We've seen that hibernation is an animal's response to its environment. We must begin by getting it clear in our minds that the urge to hibernate is a response of the human as animal and that our vaunted intellects have precious little to do with either the problem or the solution. For some, recognizing our animal natures comes easily. Others resist strenuously the fact that, in the words of zoologist Desmond Morris (*The Naked Ape*), "we are, despite all our great technological advances, still very much a simple biological phenomenon. Despite our grandiose ideas and our lofty self-conceits, we are still humble animals, subject to all the basic laws of animal behavior." Adds Morris: "Optimism is expressed by some who feel that since we have evolved a high level of intelligence and a strong inventive urge, we shall be able to twist any situation to our advantage; . . . that our intelligence can dominate all our basic biological urges. I submit that this is rubbish. Our raw animal nature will never permit it."

Day upon day, season upon season, we exist not merely *in* the environment but as part and parcel of it. Without giving it a single thought, we are constantly reacting to environmental stimuli—sounds; airborne particles; humidity; barometric pressure; the wind and its direction; its speed. That is our nature. That is what we do, whether from a penthouse on Fifth Avenue or a log cabin in Montana.

The single most dominant environmental influence upon life on earth is the sun. It has always been so, and humankind has always recognized the fact. Until just the other moment (according to the evolutionary clock), the sun dictated the ebb and flow of our lives like a rigorous, inflexible taskmaster. In its heat we hunted and gathered and feasted, and in its retreat we rested. Our lives evolved around temperature and around the photoperiod, or length of daylight.

Although we humans are as adaptable as the rat (a highly adaptable creature indeed), we can no more shed these natural responses to temperature and sunlight than we can dismiss hunger and the sex urge. But there is much you *can* do to cope with the hibernation response.

First, you can embrace it. That's right. If your life-style allows such flexibility, you can surrender to your natural biological impulse and spend the winter in a state of relative torpor. And you needn't feel guilty. Most of human society until the last two hundred years was agrarian. We lived off the land and worked hard in the spring, summer, and fall. But after the harvest and the thanksgiving feasts we rested and did not feel that the compulsion to do so was abnormal or a symptom of mental illness.

Another alternative is to relocate to a latitude at which the photoperiod is relatively constant and the hibernation response is not triggered. Chapter 11 will help you to identify such locations.

A third choice is to remain where you are and adapt your environment to that of spring and summer. That's what this book will help you accomplish. In the following chapters you will discover how to:

—Regain summertime energy and enthusiasm all winter long

—Keep your weight under control with the Anti-hibernation Diet

—Design an Eternal Springtime room in your home

—Identify the negative factors at work and at home which reinforce the hibernation response

—Find the ideal time to take a healing vacation and the vacation spots around the world that offer the most effective exposure to the sun

—Prepare your personal chronobiology chart so that you can understand your daily and seasonal rhythms of sleep, sexuality, intellectual and creative peaks

—Use cold temperatures to trigger an endocrine response that will give you more pep and energy

—Identify an often-neglected part of your body which, if protected from the cold, can dramatically improve bodily comfort and emotional stability during the winter

—Make the fall and winter as happy a time of life as any other season

That's just a hint of what this book can do for you. And because many of you who are reading these pages are already in a desperate slump, we'll tell you almost immediately what you need to know to get back on your feet. But first, are you really a hibernator?

Are You A Hibernator?:
How to Recognize the Winter Depression

*Indeed, for more than 2,000 years
physicians believed that . . . depression was
caused by cold and was most
prevalent in the autumn.*
— THOMAS A. WEHR, M.D.

It was the first week in December 1980. The sun had risen at 7:00 A.M., although in Washington, D.C., the hometown of sixty-three-year-old Larry Pressman (a pseudonym), a gray dome of clouds obscured it during the day. At 5:00 P.M. dusk preceded another frigid evening.

For Pressman, festive holiday preparations that year were a painful burden, as they had been for almost half his life—since he was thirty-five years old. He had spent every Christmas since then withdrawn, self-critical, and anxious. He'd had no energy, had been afraid to go to work, and had lost interest in life.

Like thousands of others, he'd been told he suffered from "Christmas depression syndrome," the "holiday blues," the "winter woes." Perhaps he'd read popular articles tracing the ailment to childhood disappointment during the Christmas season or the stress incurred during those hectic weeks of celebration or the financial pressures of gift buying.

But Larry Pressman had an analytical mind, and none

of those answers ever satisfied him. He had already recognized the seasonal nature of his mood changes. Usually they began in late June or early July, just as the days started growing subtly shorter. With a sensitivity found only among extreme hibernation responders, he began by feeling anxious. By midsummer he had become reluctant to go to work, feared interacting with people, lost the creativity required for his job. His interest in sex all but vanished. Getting out of bed every morning became a monumental struggle. Offered job promotions, he turned them down because he felt inadequate.

His depression grew deeper day by day until the end of January, when over a two-week period he became almost excessively cheerful. By March he was getting by on three hours of sleep a night and working feverishly with great enthusiasm.

After fourteen years of suffering, Larry sought psychiatric help. He received various antidepressants—amitriptyline, tranylcypromine, and lithium carbonate—but even on low doses he suffered unpleasant side effects. What's more, the drugs didn't relieve the depression. He discontinued the medication and began keeping both a daily log of his work accomplishments and a diary of his mood state. He had no idea that anyone would ever find those notes of interest. Ironically they became the catalyst for a revolution in diagnosing and treating a form of emotional depression now known as seasonal affective disorder, or SAD. It's a depression with major symptoms and the most severe complication of the hibernation response.

How Common Is Depression in the Hibernation Response?

Even some of those at NIMH who successfully treated Pressman back in 1980 thought his condition was relatively rare. They soon learned otherwise. After a simple article on SAD appeared in the Washington *Post*, the NIMH researchers were bombarded with letters from more than two thousand people claiming that they, too, suffered seasonal mood changes.

In fact, a great many more of us than previously suspected suffer changes in behavior from the reduced photoperiod of autumn and winter. In addition to our own studies in New Hampshire that showed increased sleep and decreased energy, one report presented at the American Psychiatric Association's 140th annual meeting in Chicago in 1987 estimated that perhaps one in four of us is *troubled* by the change in photoperiod.

That's not surprising. We are among the first generation in human history to live most of our lives in comparative darkness. Those of us who work indoors are rarely exposed to sufficiently intense light to curtail melatonin production, and that's particularly true if we work in windowless offices or on evening shifts which require that we sleep during daylight hours. From late fall to early spring most of the work force in northern latitudes commutes in darkness.

We don't know much about how life in this twilight zone affects us physically and emotionally, but there is sufficient concern among the experts that in November 1984 the New York Academy of Sciences gathered researchers from around the world to discuss that question, among others. In the absence of completed research, prudent individuals, whether professional or not, would do well not to dismiss too quickly any plausible link between light starvation and symptoms of the hibernation response.

Even in the spring and summer months—when the days are at their longest—some sensitive people suffer a hibernationlike response. According to Hugh Ridlehimber, M.D., of San Mateo, the depression seen frequently in San Franciscans during the summer has been linked by researchers to the dense fog that frequently smothers the city then, often blocking out the sun for days at a time.

In fact, Norman Rosenthal of NIMH writes, "Reduction in environmental light for any reason, for example, a spell of cloudy weather . . . in the summer . . . is frequently followed by deterioration in mood." He points out that even so apparently benign an act as moving from a brightly lit office to a dimmer one can mimic the symptoms of seasonal affective disorder.

We personally suspect that virtually all humans—along with other living things, including many plants and creatures of the sea—respond to the seasonal variation in photoperiod. And while many are not even consciously aware of the changes in their moods and behavior, there is good evidence from our New England studies that these changes indeed take place, affecting our daily lives.

Recognizing the Depression of Hibernation

The most prominent feature of the hibernation response that is troublesome is depression. Occasional sadness and low energy are ubiquitous; everybody suffers from them from time to time. Usually they're associated with some obvious event in our lives that presents a knotty problem or something that's difficult to get used to. A new job, a disappointment, a broken love affair—all of us experience a reaction to such situations and feel down from time to time.

But such sorrows occur randomly throughout the year, are very short-lived, and usually disrupt sleep, not increase it.

Seasonally related sadness, however, that can be part of

the hibernation response is just that—*seasonal*. It returns annually. What's more, it can be severe and has a characteristic set of associated feelings and behaviors which are almost always present.

Here are the characteristics of the depression most commonly associated with the hibernation response (seasonal affective disorder, SAD):

—The majority of SAD sufferers (86 percent) are women whose seasonal symptoms typically begin in their twenties. However, in 42 percent of cases, symptoms first surface in childhood or adolescence.[3]

—For most people depression begins between October and December and ends in March. A few report "anticipatory anxiety" as early as July or August.

—Almost half experience a negative change in their cycles over the years, more than 60 percent attesting that the depression had become more severe or of longer duration as they got older.

—Almost 80 percent report carbohydrate craving—for sweets, chocolate, and starchy foods. They speak of "a compulsion," "a craving," and "pressure to eat," in order to keep warm. In three-fourths of the cases weight increases by ten pounds or more during the autumn and early winter.

—Virtually all hibernators sleep longer in the fall and winter, yet many never feel refreshed. Typically, their energy and mood levels hit their lowest ebb late in the afternoon.

—About 70 percent lose interest in sex.

—Almost all participants report problems in getting along with others and suffer poor performance at work. Their ability to concentrate, feel motivated, and initiate projects plummets. Many take sick leave. Others, irritable and suspicious, withdraw into themselves.

Here's how one sufferer, Steven Molello, of Toms River, New Jersey, describes it: "Since 1982 I noticed a marked tendency to gain from ten to fifteen pounds from late October (usually around the time the clocks are set back) to early January." Weight gain is one of the sure signs of the hibernation response, even when depression is not present. By contrast, those suffering other forms of depression usually lose their appetites along with some weight.

Molello continues: "I notice during the period of weight gain extraordinary periods of almost insatiable appetite; decreased will to exercise; increased need for sleep; reduced self-esteem as weight climbs."

Not everybody who has a seasonal slowdown gets all the symptoms of SAD, of course, but by the time the dark days are here those with a clear hibernation response will have noticed a *seasonal marked decrease in energy* with a *downturn in mood* and an overwhelming *desire to sleep longer*, making it difficult to get up in the morning. Weight gain results from succumbing to the urge to go to the refrigerator at night for that extra helping of ice cream and such.

Major Depression and the Depression of Hibernation (SAD)

There are many causes of depression besides that associated with hibernation, and serious ones, too. Major depression, as opposed to SAD, is not only a very common ailment but a serious illness, one that needs to be carefully distinguished from seasonal slowdown or the hibernation response. About 15 percent of the American population experience a serious depression during their lifetimes, serious enough, that is, to take them to a hospital or psychiatrist. While for some the illness may strike only once, for the majority it's a recurrent disorder, attacking women more frequently than men (about two to one) and running strongly in families, suggesting that it has a genetic component.

Serious or major depression, as it's called by psychiatrists, is also called melancholia, endogenous depression, and biological depression, all of which imply that the illness frequently starts without any apparent external trigger and may become severely incapacitating, with symptoms of bodily disturbance as well as changes in thinking and behavior.

There are two basic forms of depression recognized by doctors. In unipolar illness the victim suffers only depression, while the sufferer of bipolar illness experiences not only depression but periods of excitement or mania as well. The two illnesses have distinctly different natural histories, tend to occur at different ages, and have different family histories.

Unipolar major depression is more common than bipolar major depression and is about twice as frequent in women as in men. It may start, although not always, with a disappointment or loss of an important person or goal. Soon the sufferer experiences overwhelming sadness, an inability to feel any pleasure (sometimes called anhedonia). The sorrow is so deep as to be unjustifiable, yet it's totally beyond the individual's control. Characteristically the depressed person sleeps poorly, wakes early in the morning, usually about two hours before his or her normal time, and just cannot get back to sleep. Victims lie tossing and turning and ruminating about the day, unable to make decisions and having great difficulty concentrating. They're reduced to worrying about the details of life and are usually preoccupied with morbid thoughts and memories. As the illness progresses, they become preoccupied with their past behaviors, sometimes believing them to be sinful. Sometimes people even develop the idea that the depression is some sort of punishment. They lose their appetite, their energy, their sexual interest, they avoid social interaction, and frequently they become constipated and lose a considerable amount of weight.

Although all this can happen quite suddenly, it usually progresses slowly, often making it difficult for family and friends to recognize at first that anything serious is happening. However, as the illness develops and the sufferer becomes submerged by it, withdrawing from family and friends and sometimes becoming preoccupied with death and suicide, symptoms become obvious.

The disturbance may persist for weeks or months if untreated. Furthermore, it may be a warning of serious *physical* illness, such as metabolic disturbances or early cancers. That is why it's very important that anybody who experiences a progressive series of depressive symptoms like these should consult a physician.

Bipolar depressive illness is different in several ways. First, it tends to be equally common among men and women, affecting approximately 1 percent of the population in general. There is usually a strong family history of depression of one sort or another, and the illness begins earlier than the unipolar type, frequently in the late teens or early twenties. Associated with the depression are periods of excitement and euphoria in which the person has enormous energy, sleeps little, and early in the illness appears creative, later becoming grandiose and disorganized.

There are some interesting differences between the depressed phase of bipolar and unipolar illness. Most striking is that the bipolar victim tends to gain weight rather than lose it and to sleep excessively rather than very poorly. These conditions are, of course, reminiscent of the hibernation response and seasonal affective disorder. Indeed, those who have the severe form of hibernation withdrawal and SAD frequently have bipolar illness in their families. Some authorities suspect that SAD is a very mild form of manic-depressive illness, precipitated by the physical challenges of the changing seasons.

Major Depression and Hibernation: Knowing the Difference

It's essential that you understand the differences between seasonal and other, more serious mood disorders so that you obtain the right therapy for the problem and get relief as soon as possible. Here are some ways to tell the two apart:

MAJOR UNIPOLAR DEPRESSION	SEASONAL DEPRESSION
Hyperactivity	Decreased activity
Loss of appetite	Greatly increased appetite
Weight loss	Weight gain
Insomnia	Increase in sleeping time
Deep sense of despair	Sadness, irritability
Hopelessness, possible suicidal thoughts	Anxiety, inability to concentrate

Most important of all, of course, is the *timing*, the seasonal nature of the depression of hibernation. It returns each year with shortening days and falling temperatures.

If you're not absolutely certain that you're suffering from the seasonal affective disorder associated with the hibernation response or if you're so troubled that you've been considering ending your life, don't use the bright light therapy discussed in the next chapter until after you've first sought professional help. Bright light has caused some people to become highly irritable and disoriented, and if you're suffering a serious depression, even if it is compounded by seasonal factors, those responses could be precisely what you don't need. When in doubt, go to a psychiatrist or your general doctor and ask for a diagnosis.

Are You a Hibernator?

It is important to recognize that not all of those with a tendency to hibernate get seriously depressed. In fact, most do *not*. Most just slow down, get irritable, sleep a little more, and add a few pounds, preparing for the sleep that never comes. But even these symptoms need not be. There are ways of changing our environment and approach to winter that can be very helpful in keeping us at the level of springtime fitness. There are many common tools with which we can cope with the sometimes crippling winter depression of SAD and the hibernation slowdown in general. With some emergency care you can be a new person—perhaps as quickly as tomorrow and certainly within the next few days. You're now just a few pages from feeling a whole lot better.

Happy reading.

Let There Be Light:
Emergency Care for the Hibernator

I am always more religious on sunshiney days.
                    —LORD BYRON

In December 1980 Larry Pressman, the sixty-three-year-old Washington, D.C., hibernator with winter depression, sought help from Alfred Lewy, M.D., of the Clinical Psychobiology Branch of the National Institute of Mental Health in Bethesda, Maryland. Lewy studied Pressman's records with serious interest. Although seasonal depressions had been considered rare—supposedly not more than 4 to 5 percent of all depressions—Lewy knew about them.

Pressman's daily diaries confirmed his suspicions. His patient grew predictably more energetic, enthusiastic, and creative as spring approached each year and, like clockwork, became listless and comparatively unproductive as each summer passed. There could be no doubt: Something in the environment was triggering the man's seasonal depression.

Lewy and his colleagues at NIMH suspected that the increasingly shorter days—or decreased photoperiod—following June 21 each year was at least part of the problem. They played a hunch: They would treat Pressman not with drugs, psychotherapy, or hospitalization but with synthetic sunlight. They would again extend his daylight hours to those of spring.[4]

Pressman was instructed to arise every morning three hours before dawn and to sit in front of two banks of bright lights. With the rising sun he was to shut off the lights and go about his daily activities. At dusk he was to spend another three hours beneath the lights. His photoperiod would be artificially lengthened to that of a day in April. That was all there was to it.

Four days after he began therapy, Pressman's depression lifted completely. He found himself energetic, enthusiastic, and capable of enjoying life during the winter months for the first time in twenty-seven years.

That was a first for the Western medical community. Yet many individual sufferers of the hibernation response have discovered the healing properties of both natural and synthetic sunlight on their own. A forty-one-year-old computer systems analyst, Susan Nicholson, without understanding why, found herself attracted every winter to the bright lights she had installed for her indoor plants. She'd sit and work near them as often as possible and sometimes even slept under them. "This is strange," she reports thinking at the time, "but I feel happier somehow." Today, with a more sophisticated battery of lights in her recreation room, Nicholson says she blossoms under their illumination. Without them, "I just droop like a neglected plant, especially at this time of year [winter]."

Another woman recognizes what she calls light hunger when the days grow shorter. Her very first act upon entering her home during those dark months is to turn on all the lights. The habit has earned her a nickname among family and friends: Lights.

Millions of others living in the temperate zones—the part of the earth between either the Tropic of Capricorn or Cancer and the polar circle nearest it—feel a strong compulsion to flee their homes each year for vacations closer to the equator. Few are consciously aware that what they seek is not so much the sand and sea as the sun. What they do know for certain is that within a couple of days they feel like new people, with a sense of vitality and regained youth.

In November 1982 Dr. Lewy reported the Larry Pressman story in the *American Journal of Psychiatry,* and behavioral scientists around the world learned one reason that most of us prefer a winter vacation on a tropical island to one on an antarctic ice cap. Lewy's newly coined descriptive term, seasonal affective disorder, became an instant buzzword among professionals. Now therapists began looking for the symptoms distinguishing SAD from typical depression, and they found many of their patients, regardless of age, suffering from its symptoms.[3]

For example, Dr. Norman Rosenthal of NIMH recently reported treating six children, four boys and two girls, ages six to fourteen, some of whose symptoms of seasonal depression had begun at two years of age. During the final months of every year they developed difficulties with schoolwork. They suffered fatigue, sleeping longer and having great difficulty awakening in the morning. They became listless, sad, irritable, frequently breaking into tears without reason. January and February were their worst months.

Exposed to bright light morning and evening, five of the six children improved quickly and dramatically. They noticed the difference. So did their parents and teachers.[4]

Efforts to treat the hibernation response with synthetic sunlight are under way now in many countries around the world, including Switzerland, England, southern Australia, and the Soviet Union.[5] In the United States, from

Oregon to New York City, thousands of people of all ages and both sexes are now living dramatically improved lives through artificially prolonged sunlight.

In Alaska, writes Carla J. Hellekson, M.D., in the *American Journal of Psychiatry,* "Seasonal changes in mood and energy have long been accepted as part of the Alaskan life style." Until now this depression has been thought a symptom of cabin fever, the result of virtual imprisonment in a small space for months on end. But Hellekson suggests that cabin fever "may be synonymous with the recently described seasonal affective disorder, in which fall and winter depression, anergy [lack of responsiveness], weight gain and hypersomnia [oversleeping] alternate with euthymia of hypomania [elation, euphoria], weight loss and hyposomnia [reduced need for sleep] in spring and summer."

Hellekson has successfully used synthetic sunshine to treat a number of Alaskans suffering from SAD and cabin fever. Similarly, for those of you with a tendency to hibernate, synthetic sunshine can provide the ideal emergency care.

Making Your Own Sunshine

You can purchase a preassembled light box from any of the following companies; prices range from about $300 to $500.

1. The SunBox Company
   1132 Taft Street
   Rockville, MD 20850

   Phone: 301-762-1SUN

2. Philip C. Hughes, Ph.D., President
   MEDIC-LIGHT
   34 Yacht Club Drive
   Lake Hopatcong, N.J. 07849

   Phone: 201-663-1214

3. Henry C. Savage, Jr.
   APOLLO LIGHT SYSTEMS, INC
   352 West 1060 South
   Orem, Utah 84058

   Phone: 801-226-2370

Most of these units use Vita-Lite full-spectrum fluorescent bulbs, the same sort that the original researchers prescribed. There's some debate about whether bulbs

Light boxes like the above have transformed winter blues into cheerful days for thousands of people in many countries. (Courtesy the SunBox Co.)

producing the sun's full light spectrum are necessary for therapeutic results, but most professionals continue to use them.

The units are handsome and well made, but if you want to save some money, you can use ordinary fixtures and buy the bulbs separately. A fixture capable of holding four forty-eight-inch bulbs will cost about $90 new, and you'll probably need two. If the $180 threatens to be a new source of depression, call an electrical contractor and ask where you can pick up secondhand units. With luck, you'll find them for about $20 each.

Right now only three companies in the world make truly full-spectrum fluorescent bulbs. Duro-Test's are called Vita-Lites, North American Philips produces Indoor Sunlight, and General Electric makes the Chromaline. They're not inexpensive—about $15 each—and if you're tempted to buy the $2.50 variety and see how it works, some studies suggest it'll do fine. We recommend the bulbs that produce the full spectrum of the sun's radiation. Your local hardware store can order the bulbs. Specify −48″ (2180 lumens) if you're using eight bulbs, −48″ (2340 lumens) when using six. Depending on your choice of bulbs and whether you buy secondhand or new fixtures, your do-it-yourself costs will range from $64 to $300.

The easiest way to power your boxes is to have an electrician attach a six-foot cord and plug to each unit and plug them into any receptacle, just as you would a lamp. Actually it's a simple process to connect the wire and plug yourself if you've had some wiring experience. Use six feet of 18-3 gauge wire with a ground, and three No. 72-B wire nuts. Remove about one-half inch of insulation from both ends of all three wires in the six-foot cord and also from the wires in the light box. Twist the green (or copper) wire in the box with the matching wire in the cord until they're intertwined securely. Then insert them into the wire nut. Twist the nut clockwise until it's tight. Use electrical tape around the base of the wire nut and the wires to make sure they don't work loose.

Follow the same procedure with the black (or red) wires and then with the white.

You'll also need a three-eighth-inch connector clamp. Some fixtures have it built in, but if yours doesn't, you'll have to pick one up at the hardware store. Connect the clamp to a hole in the back of the fixture. Slip the cord through it, and tighten the clamp until it's reasonably firm. The clamp is essential for two reasons: It keeps the sharp metal of the unit from eventually cutting through the wire and causing a short circuit, and it reduces the likelihood that the connected wires will be torn accidentally from the fixture.

To attach the plug, wrap the copper (or green) wire clockwise tightly around the green screw in the plug and tighten it. Do the same with the two remaining wires and screws. Be sure that no wire is exposed beyond the screw heads.

If these instructions are confusing to you, have an electrician do the work or buy a preassembled unit.

In most cases, portable light boxes are preferable to permanently installed ones. They can be stored away in the spring and summer months when they're not needed and can be moved from room to room or from office to office should your schedule require it. And if you relocate, you can take them with you without getting an electrician—and perhaps a carpenter—involved.

As soon as your boxes are in operation, you're ready to undertake some exciting experiments. You'll see what we mean as we go along.

There is little argument that synthetic sunlight can reverse SAD, whether triggered by the shorter days of autumn and winter, the San Francisco fog, or a week of rain in April. But there is controversy indeed regarding the most basic questions: How bright must the lights be to work? How much daily exposure is needed? What time of day is exposure most effective? If we all were identical assembly-line products instead of individual human beings, the answers to those questions might be a snap. In fact, the results of most studies have been as varied as the humans participating in them.

Question 1: How Bright Is Sufficiently Bright?

Dr. Lewy and his colleagues made the first successful attempt to treat Larry Pressman's depression in 1980 using two ordinary fluorescent fixtures such as those you might see in your supermarket ceiling. Each was two by four feet in diameter and contained four bulbs of forty watts, each bulb four feet long. Every bulb produced the lumens (a measure of light) of about 230 candles at a distance of one foot. It was like sitting three feet from sixteen seventy-five-watt incandescent bulbs.

Eight fluorescent bulbs shining at you from a yard away is plenty of light—at least five times as much as you'd find in a typical home or office. Of course, it is no match for the sun, which on a summer day in the shade is ten times brighter and in an open field at noon is more than forty times as intense. Still, those eight bulbs were adequate to reverse Pressman's winter depression in just a couple of days.

Nowadays Dr. Rosenthal and his staff at NIMH are treating patients with a single fixture containing only six of the four-foot tubes. But these are brighter bulbs, producing the same lumens as the eight in earlier studies. For most people, six bulbs are probably the minimum needed to reverse the hibernation response. Numerous studies have shown that light less intense than this produces no significant improvement in typical hibernators with depression.

Yet *some* people show marked improvement even under dim light. That was true of two out of nine subjects in one study. Such people are thought to be extremely sensitive to light. Perhaps their pineal glands are trigger-happy. With the onset of darkness they produce melatonin profusely, quickly becoming depressed.[6] And when exposed to light of even weak intensity, they respond dramatically. In fact, these hyperresponders find bright light excessively stimulating and dim lights more comfortable. Some of them even develop headaches under bright light.

But it's altogether likely that you'll waste the whole winter if you try to work your way from dim light to that which proves therapeutic in combating seasonal depression. Instead, we advise that you start at the other end of the brightness scale, with eight forty-watt bulbs. Less than that seems to serve little purpose for real hibernators.

Of course, the distance between you and the bulbs crucially affects their therapeutic value. In the original studies the light boxes were placed three feet in front of the volunteers at eye level. They have been positioned both vertically and horizontally. Later the volunteers were as much as five feet from the lights. Since then individual sufferers, acting on their own, have even had positive results with light boxes suspended from ceilings, about six feet above their chairs.

If you suffer severely from the hibernation response, you'd be wise to begin with the boxes as close as three feet in front of you. Set them horizontally at angles about twenty-eight inches off the floor, so that they form a V. That will give you maximum exposure.

The important thing is to make sure that the light from

both boxes is in your direct line of sight at all times. It isn't necessary that you stare at the lights continuously; in fact, future studies may show that to be harmful. Researchers do recommend that you glance at the lights several times a minute. Unless the brightness steadily bathes the retina, it might not curtail the pineal's melatonin production. Overhead lights should be far enough in front of you to illuminate your eyes. And keep the fixtures close enough together so that when you face one, you're not turning your back on the other.

Question 2: How Much Daily Exposure?

The six hours of daily exposure used by the pioneering researchers are unnecessarily long for most people. And for some, prolonged exposure can produce headaches, a high-strung, jittery feeling, and irritability.

For most people suffering the hibernation response, two to four hours daily are sufficient. But keep in mind that you might well be different from "most" people and need a longer exposure period at first, or a shorter one. Start with a four-hour regimen daily, and if you notice no significant improvement within two days, increase the exposure period by fifteen minutes each day until you reach the "dosage" that does the job.

On the other hand, you may find yourself growing irritable and high-strung after four hours of synthetic sunlight, and after all, that is a lot of time to spend in one place each day if it's not necessary. Try reducing the daily period by half hour increments until you reach the point at which you sense that you're not getting quite enough light. Then add a half hour. That should be your ideal exposure time.

Question 3: What Is the Ideal Exposure Schedule—Morning, Evening, or Both?

Here again, the research findings are paradoxical, if not downright contradictory:

—Patients respond most effectively to light administered between 6:00 and 8:00 A.M. and should avoid using the lights during the evening.[7]

—Light exposure only during the evenings tends not to be as effective as morning exposure.

—Midday light may work as well as morning and better than evening exposure.

Our own informed findings indicate that the ideal time for phototherapy, like brightness and duration, is very subjective. However, in general, morning light does have an advantage over evening exposure.

In one study, Frederick Jacobsen, M.D., and colleagues at the National Institute of Mental Health found that seven of sixteen SAD patients improved when receiving phototherapy only in the morning or at midday. Four improved only with midday treatment, and three only with morning therapy.

Michael Terman, Ph.D., of the New York State Psychiatric Institute, reported, at the American Psychiatric Association Annual Convention in 1986, the responses on page 49.

Hence the one thing you can be rather certain about is that light exposure in the evening alone won't do you much good. Beyond that the great majority of hibernators respond best to two hours of light in the morning.

To summarize, because each of us is unique in the size, shape, and function of our brain, nervous system, endocrine glands—virtually every aspect of our body—we do not respond exactly alike to any stimulus, including artificial light. To have a positive response, some people re-

	OUTCOME (in percentages)		
	SATISFACTORY	PARTIAL	FAILURE
Two hours morning and evening	91	9	0
Two hours morning alone	67	16	16
Thirty minutes morning and evening	27	55	18
Two hours evening alone	0	0	100

quire very bright light for several hours a day, while others will suffer headaches and nausea when the illumination is that intense. There are those who respond best to light in the morning, while others do better in the afternoon—or rarely to morning *and* evening light. The same is true of the length of exposure. So with these guidelines for deciding what light prescription is best for you, experiment a little and make your own decisions.

There you have it, first aid for hibernators. If your problem is truly seasonal, the result of shorter days, your whole outlook will turn around as you sit beneath your synthetic sunlight. You'll eat less, feel more energetic, and crave less sleep—all starting within a few days.

But that's just the beginning, like any first aid or emergency care. There is another major cue, every bit as important as the photoperiod, to which your body responds profoundly: *the environmental temperature.* As the months grow cool, then cold, some people experience great discomfort. They become more susceptible to colds and suffer physical exhaustion (as compared with the general laziness associated with the shorter photoperiod).

But here's the crucial point: *Cold temperatures, like shorter days, can trigger the hibernation response.*

Next, what the cold does to us.

How Animals Survive the Cold: Learning from Our Fellow Creatures

But now a tomb-like coldness stills the air.
—JOHN W. THOMPSON

During the long antarctic winter winds howl with hurricane force at temperatures less than minus 77°F. The snow of blizzards accumulates in fused crystals by the billions, forming shifting mountain ranges of ice. It's a place "unfit for man or beast"—except that the emperor penguin seems perfectly happy there. It gives him the opportunity to establish arguably the greatest feat of endurance ever recorded. And he does it annually.

During the coldest months in the coldest place on earth emperor penguins get the urge to have sex. They leave the comfort of their seaside ice cap, where the squid, fish, and krill are plentiful, and lumber inland to rookeries and female penguins. It's not an easy trip for such awkward hikers, nor is it short. Some have traveled fifty miles to find the objects of their desire, frequently increasing their speed by belly-flopping and flaying the ice with feet and flippers like rotund toboggans.

In May the female lays her egg, gives it to her mate, and returns to the sea to feed. Now the emperor's stamina begins to be tested because in spite of his rigorous weeks-long sojourn, he hasn't eaten since leaving open water, his exclusive source of food.

For the next two months he continues to endure the darkest, severest period of the antarctic winter, still fasting, balancing the precious egg on his two feet and covering it with a fold of belly skin.

The chicks hatch in mid-July. If the female has been slow to return, the male can feed his offspring temporarily with a milky secretion from his esophagus. When his mate does arrive, the male finally begins his return trek to the ocean. When he arrives, he may have fasted 115 days and lost fully half his body weight. A harrowing ordeal, which he will eagerly undertake again the following year.

The mortal enemy in polar and temperate climates is the cold. Even the emperor penguin respects it; if the temperature should drop too deeply and remain there too long, causing the bird to utilize his entire store of body fat and begin breaking down muscle tissue to maintain core temperatures, he will do the unthinkable. He will abandon the egg or chick and return to the ocean to feed.

The cold threatens death. It is a truth etched into the primitive brains of all cold-climate creatures, even those most proficiently adapted to their environment. In innumerable ways their physiology is devoted to defeating the enemy. And here's a fascinating fact: Each species possesses its own specialized means of surviving the cold, and variations often exist within species. That's an important point since *adaptive variations exist within our own species as well.*

Depending upon the innumerable factors that make you who you are, both physiologically and psychologically, cold temperatures will probably affect you differently from the way they affect your neighbor, your boss, your spouse. You probably won't respond to the cold in the same way emotionally as they do, and you're not likely to have precisely the same physiological reactions.

Our purpose in this book is to help us learn more about our individual responses to winter conditions and the keys to controlling them by looking at how other animals that share the planet with us respond and adapt. We've found that shorter periods of daylight naturally trigger the hibernation response in both animals and humans. In fact, animals can be forced into hibernation even during the summer if they're kept in darkness. Some animals can also be starved into hibernation; a mechanism not yet understood triggers the hibernation response, conserving the animal's energy until the months of famine have passed. Cold, too, even on the brightest summer days, can induce certain animals to hibernate. During the millennia of ice ages a substantial drop in temperature, even when the days were yet long, proved deadly to those animals that continued to burn calories with the profligacy of warmer periods. Animals whose hibernation response was triggered by the cold as well as a shorter photoperiod had a much greater likelihood of survival.

Although we humans don't enter into hibernation when the temperatures plummet, there's ample evidence that the cold affects many of us in precisely the way that the shorter photoperiod does. In fact, Dr. Norman Rosenthal of the National Institute of Mental Health has reported that some patients believe that the cold is even more responsible for their seasonal affective disorder than the reduced photoperiod. Just as the shorter days trigger the behavioral aspects of the hibernation response, cold triggers much of its physiological reaction. We're not even consciously aware of some of those changes, yet they have dramatic effects on our health, our capacity to function, and, in some respects, even our moods.

It'll do us no good to study how hibernating animals react to the cold, for we are not among those animals currently capable of true hibernation. Instead, in this chapter we'll discover the various means whereby non-hibernating animals have adapted to the cold. Do read with attention, for you can be assured, as you'll see in the remaining chapters, that the arctic fox, deer—and penguin—have something intimate to offer in your own battle against the cold.

Response to Cold—and the Critical Temperature

Hamsters don't necessarily hibernate. They've developed a talent known as "permissive" hibernation. They respond to shorter photoperiods as we do—by overeating and gaining weight. They won't hibernate unless food supplies dwindle or temperatures plummet.

Birds vary even within species in their response to cold. Robins living in the northeastern United States during the spring, summer, and autumn fly a few hundred miles south to the milder Carolinas for the winter. Other robins migrate from New England only to Pennsylvania and New Jersey; they enjoy the territory temporarily abandoned by their brethren just fine.

Blue jays from the mid-Atlantic region stay at home; others, from farther north, migrate deep into the South and West. Chickadees neither flee nor hibernate but depend upon their high metabolism and capacity to forage for survival. The same is true of cardinals, mockingbirds, crows, pigeons, starlings, house finches, and house sparrows. They can endure all but the most brutal winters of heavy snowfall and continued low temperatures.

Other than the status of its food supply, a key factor in determining how an animal will respond to the cold is the critical temperature, the air temperature below which its normal resting, or basal, metabolic rate is not sufficient to maintain normal body temperatures. The critical temperature varies among species and even among animals of the same species. In tropical mammals the critical temperature is between 25° and 27°C (about 77° to 80°F), the same as in a naked person. On the other hand, the arctic fox and husky have critical temperatures less than minus 0°C (minus 30°F). Such animals can sleep comfortably on the snow of windswept plains in sub-zero weather.

The difference between birds, squirrels, and other creatures native to the tropics and their counterparts from temperate and polar climates is *not* their resting body temperatures, which are the same in all climates. Nor is it their basal metabolic rates; these, too, remain essentially the same. The major difference seems to be in their insulation. In general, the body insulation of tropical animals varies from almost complete nakedness to fuzz or feathers proficient at allowing heat to escape the body rather than to be contained by it. There are exceptions, of course. One is the tropical sloth, which has as much fur on its trunk as an arctic lemming, fur that indeed helps the notoriously lazy creature to maintain an adequate body temperature since its best efforts at basal metabolism are about half that of other creatures.

Nature Dresses for the Cold

When the outside temperature drops sufficiently, furry animals involuntarily raise their body hair, which produces the same results as the insulation in walls and ceiling. Tens of thousands of these hairs trap little pockets of air and, warmed by the animal's body, form a buffer against the frigid environment. Animals of sleek hide—the deer and elk and such—seem ill equipped for the sometimes long and brutal winters through which they continue to thrive. It's true that they lack the dense hair of the bison or alpine sheep, but they have a secret of their own: Each tiny hair is hollow, trapping air within itself. While the bison, in effect, insulates with four inches of fiberglass, the deer does the same job with an inch of Styrofoam.

Birds rely on their feathers to trap the insulating air. Those finches at the bird feeder last January weren't strutting with pride when they fluffed themselves into a huge ball. They were enlarging the air spaces between their feathers.

Physiology Versus Freezing

Another factor determining the critical temperature of a particular species is anatomy. There's a reason that the sand brown jackrabbit of Arizona is long and skinny, with great donkey ears, while his counterpart to the north has tiny ears and is short and plump. The first body is designed to allow heat to escape; the second, to conserve it.

The adaptation of other creatures has taken an apparently contradictory tack. At first they seem perfectly shaped for freezing to death. Their legs and faces are poorly insulated. For example, caribou, mountain sheep, and reindeer have three to five times less insulation on their legs than on their trunks.

Those spindly legs ought to freeze with the first sub-zero plunge of the thermometer or at least allow sufficient heat loss to cause the animal to perish. The same might be expected of penguins, seals, ducks, sea gulls, beavers, muskrats, otters, all those sub-zero-dwelling creatures with naked fins, flukes, flippers, and webbed feet.

Yet those appendages *don't* freeze. For one thing, the bird or animal protects them. In the early 1970's researchers from Duke University's Department of Zoology traveled to McMurdo Station on Ross Island, Antarctica, to study the emperor penguin's adaptive capacities under controlled conditions. They found that when the birds were subjected to a temperature of minus 74°F, they scrunched down, tucked in their necks, pulled in their flippers, lifted their toes under their belly feathers, and balanced themselves on heels and tail feathers. Nothing else touched the ice, and no appendages protruded.

These creatures possess an even more remarkable means of turning the seeming handicap of delicate appendages into an asset. They involuntarily regulate circulation to the extremities. In the cold they reduce the blood supply to legs and flukes or flippers, thereby substantially curtailing their loss of body heat. The temperature in these appendages falls far below that required of the body core for survival.

Sea gulls whose feet were kept in ice water for more than two hours had an increase of only 1.5 percent in their basal metabolic rate; even under those adverse circumstances they suffered virtually no heat and energy loss. Yet, their legs were still capable of conducting nerve impulses. Only when temperatures fall dangerously low does circulation increase for a time to prevent tissue destruction.

Specifically, in many arctic animals the temperature of the feet is often very close to freezing, while just above the feet the temperature might be fifteen degrees higher. And at the point where the leg joins the body the temperature approaches that of the body core.

That's a significant point to a husky or caribou. If even small amounts of very cold blood were to return steadily from four legs to the animal's heart and visceral organs, it would prove to be a most efficient—and deadly—refrigeration mechanism. A cunning adaptive mechanism prevents that, not merely in the caribou but a great number of arctic creatures, including the penguin. Those scrawny legs, flippers, fins, and such contain an interesting arteriovenous system; the veins carrying cold blood back to the heart are intimately intertwined with arteries carrying warm blood to the extremities. As a result of this close contact, the venous blood absorbs heat from the arterial. By the time it reaches the body, it's already as warm as the blood it joins.

Heating with Hormones

Many animals (and we humans are among them) respond immediately when the air temperature drops below their critical temperature.[8] The reaction is completely involuntary: The sympathetic nervous system triggers the reflex of shivering. Dogs and cats shiver. So do penguins and many other birds and animals, and all for the same purpose: Shivering is a muscular activity, and as such it generates heat. Since the heat lost to the atmosphere is generated near the skin's surface, the core temperature remains stable.

At the same time the sympathetic nervous system responds to the cold by stimulating the adrenal gland to secrete large quantities of catecholamines, particularly norepinephrine. These are the emergency "fight or flight" hormones, and they quickly boost the metabolism rate throughout the body. As each cell works faster, it produces more body heat.

While the acute cold emergency continues, the pituitary gland secretes TSH (thyroid-stimulating hormone), or thyrotropin. TSH prods the thyroid gland into releasing more thyroxine, which increases the rate at which the body burns the fuel to generate metabolic heat over the long haul. Such animals rely on increased thyroid function to maintain high metabolic rates throughout the winter—another form of adaptation.

Those are the means used by animals to survive the cold: heat-preserving fur or feathers, physiological adaptation, and the capacity to increase metabolism. You needn't envy the animal world these blessings; they are precisely the means we will learn in the following pages to use in our own victory over winter cold and the hibernation response. And if you believe you will have trouble growing feathers, we'll also discuss purchasing the proper garments.

The Intemperate "Temperate" Zones

In one very important respect you're going to achieve more than the arctic fox and husky in terms of adaptation. You're going to do so as a temperate zone dweller, a creature coping with the greatest adaptational demands on the planet. We have every right to bemoan the foolishness that drove our ancestors five hundred thousand years ago to drape themselves in the hides of beasts and plod north and south from the equator into territories hardly fit for human survival. However, we might give them the benefit of the doubt and offer three suppositions: first, that they were driven to such lengths in flight from enemies; secondly, that our mania to reproduce led to overpopulation then as it has today in many tropical areas, and thus we migrated to avoid starvation; finally, that the meteorological conditions of the day weren't such as they are now, that perhaps it was warmer in what are now the temperate zones.

However, these "temperate" conditions now, in terms of climate, are stressful. According to Jürgen Aschoff of the Max Planck Institute in West Germany, the "temperate" zone is the most demanding on earth in terms of adaption. The *swings* from hot to cold during the course of a year are nowhere so extreme. For example, in Browning, Montana, in 1916 the temperature changed from 44°F to minus 56°F, a 100-degree difference, within fourteen hours. Changes of 60 degrees or 70 degrees within twenty-four hours are not uncommon in the so-called temperate regions of the world, especially at higher elevations during the spring and fall.

Certainly polar climates are colder, although the northern plain states of America experience temperatures of minus 40° to minus 60°F. Nor do the temperate zones suffer the withering heat that parches equatorial latitudes of the planet: a world record of more than 136°F in Libya on September 13, 1922, and a mean average of 80°F in the Sahara.

However, virtually the entire central United States, so cold in winter, suffered highs above 100°F almost daily during the months of June and July in 1980. Although not as prolonged, such temperatures are reached every summer from California to the New England states.

In a stable climate human beings do adapt physiologically. The natives of arctic and tropical climates are designed for survival in the cold or heat, just as are the animals of those regions. According to anthropologist Albert T. Steegmann, cold-climate people typically weigh more than the rest of us. Their arms and legs are shorter, their chests larger, their torsos longer. They have shorter, stubbier hands. They have more evenly distributed body

59

fat and perhaps more blood vessels reaching the extremities. We of the temperate zone are usually not so well prepared physiologically for the cold, for we must also deal with 100°F summer heat. That's best done with long, lanky, hairless bodies, minimal fat for better heat dissipation, and heavily pigmented skin to prevent sunburn. What's required of temperate dwellers, pure and simple, is that every six months they undergo a phenomenal metamorphosis—both physical and psychological—from tropical to arctic-dwelling animals.

It is a downright stressful transition, but physiologically we have the capacity, just as do our fellow creatures, of making it, using the same mechanisms as they do. Human beings can adapt to almost unbelievably severe conditions. Here are two examples of how adaptable we really are.

The Human Potential

The Yahgan, a tribe of aborigines descended from American Indians, live at the very tip of South America, on the island of Tierra del Fuego. In the winter the climate is cold, damp, and stormy. Only fifteen hundred feet above sea level the fields are perpetually covered with snow and ice. Snow falls occasionally even during the summer, when the mean temperature is 50°F. On the windward side of the island, rain or snow falls almost continuously. Squalls and strong gales strike frequently.

The Yahgans are wanderers, living on mussels, crabs, and fish. They haven't invented hooks yet; they tie the bait to the end of a string, throw it in the water, lure the fish to the surface, and catch it bare-handed.

In fact, they do everything bare. Except for a small cape of fur which they occasionally drape over their shoulders and upper chest, they live entirely unclothed.

They don't even wear moccasins, except when undertaking long trips. On December 25, 1832, Darwin wrote this account of his introduction to the Yahgan life-style:

> The climate is certainly wretched: the summer solstice was now past, yet every day snow fell on the hills, and in the valleys it was rain accompanied by sleet. The thermometer generally stood about 45°F, but in the night fell to 38° or 40°. . . . While going one day on shore near Wollaston Island, we pulled alongside a canoe with six Fuegians. These were the most abject and miserable creatures I anywhere beheld. . . . The Fuegians in the canoe were quite naked, and even one full-grown woman was absolutely so. It was raining heavily, and the fresh water, together with the spray, trickled down her body. In another harbor not far distant, a woman, who was suckling a recently-born child, came one day alongside the vessel and remained there out of mere curiosity, whilst the sleet fell and thawed on her naked bosom, and on the skin of her naked baby! . . . At night, five or six human beings, naked and scarcely protected from the wind and rain of this tempestuous climate, sleep on the wet ground coiled up like animals.

On the arid steppes and deserts of central Australia another tribe of aborigines lives, hunts, and sleeps on the barren earth summer and winter in temperatures that are frequently below freezing. They do so without clothing or covering of any sort, although they often build windbreaks to protect them, and they also build small fires near which they sleep.

During the 1950's physiologists decided to study the Australian natives in order to discover how they were capable of enduring the prolonged cold. In fact, they went beyond the call of duty for the sake of research and actually attempted to duplicate the feat side by side with the aborigines themselves. Throughout the night the aborigines lay quietly, sometimes snoring, and aroused themselves from three to ten times to stoke the fire, depending on the temperature.

The researchers stoked their fires from eleven to fourteen times, slept poorly or not at all, and found themselves sweating on the part of their bodies facing the flames and shivering on the portions of their anatomies away from the heat! The scientists later discovered that the temperatures on the cold parts of both their bodies and those of the aborigines dropped to 53.6° to 59°F, while the side facing the fire reached as high as 113°F.

Both the natives of central Australia and those of Tierra del Fuego seem prime candidates for *Ripley's Believe It or Not,* but another aspect of their stories is even more amazing. Over countless millennia the Australians have evolved a method of cold adaptation entirely different from that of the Tierra del Fuego Indians, who rely on a high metabolic rate, as do most nonhibernating animals of the temperate zones. The Australians, on the other hand, according to Robert E. Smith of the Department of Physiology at the University of California, "have been found to exhibit no significant increase in metabolic rate while sleeping in the cold, but rather to solve the heat conservation problem by the insulative means of permitting the skin temperatures of the extremities to fall during sleep to as low as 12°C (53.6°F), well below the cold pain threshold of the modern white man." Rather like the caribou in fact.

Hence humans, like animals, have developed a variety of means for surviving the cold. Their adaptive capacity is for the most part genetic, just as it is among animals, and as is the case with fellow creatures, it has been shaped by the ancestral climate. The human response to the cold varies according to body build, endocrine capacity, cardiovascular condition, and a host of more subtle influences, not the least of them psychological. Just as a nonswimmer forced to leap into the ocean knows terror that an experienced swimmer can't quite understand, the individual whose genetic makeup is rooted in tropical prehistory confronts the cold with what to others seems irrational aversion.

But the truth is, all normally healthy people can learn to swim. We have the capability, whether or not we exercise it. We can also be comfortable in the cold. That's rooted firmly in our primitive capacity to adapt. In the next chapter you'll learn how to acclimatize to the cold. You need never fear it or feel uncomfortable in it again if you follow the guidelines.

But first, one last word about those emperor penguins, and it's a point worth taking quite seriously this winter. You might suppose that surviving as they do for the better part of four months without food in temperatures that plunge to minus 77°F, they have a few additional evolutionary tricks up their sleeves. They don't. They maintain body temperature of approximately 100°F throughout their ordeal, only fractionally lower than other birds. They are unable to hibernate or enter torpor or dormancy.

In fact, left on their own, they could not survive as a species. Duke University researchers have calculated that emperors have only fifteen to twenty milligrams of fat reserves when they set out from the sea to seek mates and that solitary emperors would require about twenty-five milligrams to achieve the three- or four-month undertaking without drawing upon muscle tissue to meet energy needs.

To conserve heat, say the researchers, the penguins huddle together. In that way they reduce their energy loss by almost 50 percent, giving warmth to others, gaining it from them. A social arrangement succeeds where pure evolutionary adaptation would lead to extinction. There's a birdbrained idea that deserves pondering.[9]

Conquering the Cold: Tapping Your Adaptive Potential

It is the coldness of the cold winters that
produces the biggest Americans.
                    —STEPHEN ROSEN

One way or another, like it or not, you're going to respond to the cold this winter.

You might relocate to the tropics, escaping it.

You might build a "den" and remain in seclusion, a
semihibernation response and another means of escape.

Or perhaps you'll confront it passively.

Few of us living in temperate areas can avoid exposure to
cold on a daily basis, if only while traveling to and from
work, shopping, cleaning the windshield of sleet and snow.
Yet being civilized, we respond uniquely in the animal kingdom: We make a conscious effort *not* to adapt our minds
and bodies to the cold. And we suffer. Do we ever suffer!

—Symptoms as wide-ranging as breathing difficulties, rhinitis, chest pains, constricted throat, and
allergies.
—Increased corticosteroid production in response to
chronic psychological stress. An excess of these
hormones has been associated with a decrease in
immune defenses. That might mean increased sus-
ceptibility to infection—colds and pneumonia.

—Symptoms of the hibernation response, including depression, craving for carbohydrates, weight gain, irritability, inability to concentrate, fatigue, and chronic laziness. That's because cold, like reduced photoperiods and starvation, can trigger the hibernation response.

—The normal response of an unprepared body attempting to adapt to cold:

Fluctuation in body temperature, leading to the continual discomfort of fever and chilling complained of by so many who find winters intolerable.

A rise in blood pressure after about fifteen minutes' exposure to cold, returning to normal after a few hours.

Increased heart and respiratory rate.

A dramatic increase in urine output—at least twice that ordinarily expected.

Acclimatize!

Make up your mind now to acclimatize to the cold. Just as synthetic sunshine is the secret to overcoming the behavioral and emotional aspects of the hibernation response, acclimatizing can be the key to victory over the physiological discomfort. For the most part, shivering will be a thing of the past, even when you are lightly clothed and temperatures hover in the forties. You'll find that the cold inspires you with exhilaration and alertness rather than depression and anxiety—and for a perfectly good reason. Those are normal behavioral consequences of increased circulation of the adrenal and thyroid hormones that the cold stimulates in quantity.

And there's the emotional satisfaction, too, the confidence that derives from knowing that you really *are* comfortable in the cold, that not only has your body, with its improved circulation and its muscular and hormonal efficiency, challenged the winter temperature and won, but your mind, too, has met the challenge.

Even your overall health can benefit. At least that was the conclusion of Lawrence A. Palinkas of the Naval Health Research Center in San Diego. Comparing a group of men who spent the winter in the Antarctic and another who left the area before winter set in, Palinkas reported, "One of the things I found is that the group that wintered over had a lower rate of all-cause first hospitalizations subsequent to Antarctic duty. In other words, those who went down there ended up being healthier than those who didn't."

Ironically, those who stayed in the cold had more health risks than the others; they smoked and drank more and were older. "Even when you control for all the different factors, such as personality, age, and education," said Palinkas, "people who winter over still end up being healthier than people who don't winter over. There's something about the experience itself that seems to have a beneficial effect."

It may be that, to quote Friedrich Nietzsche, "That which does not kill you will make you stronger." If your body's muscles aren't well developed, lifting a seventy-five-pound weight will prove hard work and probably leave you with a week's worth of aches and pains. But once you've built up those muscles through repeated stresses, hoisting seventy-five pounds will be child's play. The same process of strength through stress applies throughout the body, from bones to brain, from circulatory system to sex organs, as long as the stress isn't excessive.

Warning: Not Everyone Can Acclimatize

Unfortunately not all people can acclimatize. Hypothyroidism, for example, can make acclimatizing difficult or impossible. Low-thyroid symptoms include depression, severe intolerance of cold, dry hair, wrinkled skin, lethargy, muddled thinking, and weight gain. Certainly, if you have such symptoms, you should see a physician and have some thyroid tests done.

Other conditions making efforts at acclimatization dangerous are cardiovascular disease, circulatory problems, and significant underweight (we can't keep warm in the cold without some insulation between skin and bones). There are other ailments, too, which prevent adapting to the cold. So if you have the slightest question about your overall health or you're over forty and haven't had a recent physical, see a physician and have the proper tests made before risking discomfort and a potentially dangerous situation.

Phase I: Conditioning

If we were hairy beasts or birds, our fur or feathers would rise to trap air near the skin surface and utilize it as instant insulation. As humans we continue to make the effort. We develop gooseflesh, and the more hirsute of us will notice that many of those little "pimples" contain a single hair that suddenly stands upright. Although it doesn't do much good in keeping us warm, it does provide evidence that at one time in our past, before we began relying on clothing, we were capable of efficiently insulating ourselves from the cold.

Fortunately we retain all the essentials for acclimatizing. That is, those in good physical condition have them. People in poor physical shape often don't. That's because those who are inactive have less efficient circulatory systems. Their hearts are smaller and pump less blood while working harder. Their blood vessels are narrower and can't dilate as much. They carry smaller volumes of blood. And there are actually fewer of those tiny vessels—or capillaries—in the unfit. Even the hearts of physically well-conditioned men and women have more highly developed blood supplies, which may explain their greater likelihood of surviving a heart attack.

Those who are poorly conditioned, who can't climb three flights of stairs, jog a mile, or walk three miles without stopping, are never going to acclimatize fully no matter how efficiently they generate body heat simply because they can't get enough of that heat to the skin surface and extremities where it's needed. Lacking adequate vascularization, they must rely upon the less efficient and certainly less comfortable defense of shivering.

Here and now determine to make exercise part of your acclimatization process. And don't worry about breathing cold air. Inhaled through the nose, it'll be warmed and moistened before reaching the lungs; in freezing weather especially it's best not to breathe through your mouth.

The first steps in your acclimatization program should be taken long before frigid temperatures descend—in early autumn, when the days first begin to cool. Choose a sunny day; a gloomy sky will psychologically compound the negative aspects of low temperatures. Also, make sure there is no wind blowing since even a moderate breeze can turn a cool temperature into an apparently frigid one. Then go for a walk, wearing as little as the law and your courage permit. The pace should be as brisk as you're comfortable with, but not so rapid as to leave you breathless. The pace isn't as important as consistency, so exercise faithfully every other day.

These sessions should last from twenty minutes to

forty-five minutes or even longer, but use common sense. Prolonged or excessively violent shivering is a warning to add clothing or call it quits. If you feel pain or numbness in your toes or fingers, you've been out long enough.

Keep in mind, however, that you're *supposed* to shiver somewhat and feel discomfort at first. It's in response to this discomfort and the conditions causing it that your body becomes more efficient in heat production. That's why, even on the coldest days, you must continue your walking program.

Phase II: Enhancing Visceral Thermogenesis

We would not fare well in the cold if our only means of increasing heat generation were through shivering. Instead, the visceral organs increase metabolism and heat production, as they do in animals. And as in animals, adrenal hormones stimulate the onset of this visceral or chemical thermogenesis, as it's called.

Here, to a great degree, is what separates the acclimatized from the otherwise: Those who have adapted to the cold begin visceral thermogenesis even before shivering. The temperature of the liver in particular begins rising almost immediately in response to the adrenal gland's secretions; in the nonacclimatized, that response will not begin in less than ten or fifteen minutes. They'll spend the interim shivering and turning blue. The acclimatized respond more quickly to their adrenal hormones. And more dramatically. Their metabolic rate can increase as much as three or four times, raising the body temperature by a degree or two as the hormone speeds the breakdown of energy stores in the body to sugar (glucose) needed for heat generation.

As the thyroid gland increases its activity by up to 50 percent, the acclimatized also can produce thyroxine more quickly and efficiently than those who haven't adapted to the cold. That's essential because hardworking as the adrenal hormones are, they're not capable of maintaining the massive increase in metabolism needed for true acclimatization. They're like tinder, getting the fire started. Only triiodothyronine (T_3),[10] made from thyroxine, can keep it burning hot. Otherwise, long-term adaptation is virtually impossible.

Here's a summary of the heat-generating roles of the adrenal and thyroid hormones.

	ADRENAL HORMONES (especially norepinephrine)	THYROID HORMONES (especially T_3 from thyroxine)
Function	Immediate response to cold: Causes blood vessels to constrict; triggers shivering.	In acclimatized: Immediate response to cold, triggering dramatically increased metabolism of visceral organs.
Benefits	Conserves core body heat. Generates heat on body surface. Provides additional fuel for heat metabolism.	Increases temperature where most needed, in body core. Warms blood to surface areas and extremities, which decreases shivering, permits vasodilation, reduces or eliminates discomfort.
Side effects	Cold discomfort. Increased blood pressure. Raised heart rate—about 20 percent increase. Added heart stress.	Elevated temperature may persist for short while after leaving cold environment.

71

As you can see, the sooner T_3 starts to work, the less discomfort you'll feel in the cold. In fact, highly acclimatized people virtually never shiver; they begin visceral thermogenesis so quickly that shivering isn't necessary.

There's just one way to achieve that level of acclimatization: Expose yourself to the cold. Unfortunately there's no clever three-point program with a cute title. What is essential is the continuation of your outdoor walking program, wearing only enough to avoid frostbite, arrest, or commitment on grounds of insanity! (We'll have more to say about dressing for the cold in the next chapter.)

And although the matter hasn't been investigated scientifically as yet, there's anecdotal evidence that *thinking* visceral thermogenesis rather than allowing yourself to dwell on shivering helps ward off some discomfort and actually reduce the shivering process. It's certainly worth trying.

How long will it take to get fully acclimatized? A few years ago Dr. P. F. Scholander and eight more unacclimatized men lived in the high country of Norway for six weeks during September and October. During the day the temperature was decidedly that of winter, yet the men wore light summer clothing. At night, when the temperature fell to freezing, the men slept nude in individual sleeping bags made up of a single blanket and a thin wind cover.

The first few nights were less than delightful. The men shivered constantly, thrashed about simply to generate body heat, and hardly slept. But within one to two weeks, depending upon the individual, a remarkable thing happened. Shivering during the night decreased substantially. Instead, the volunteers' basal metabolism increased by some 75 to 90 percent. They began generating more heat more efficiently.

And instead of vasoconstriction's reducing circulation to the extremities, as it does among the unacclimatized—resulting in conserved heat at the expense of cold hands and feet—circulation improved in Scholander and his men. Throughout the night hands and feet remained comfortably warm. The men had no difficulty at all sleeping.

That's confronting the enemy head-on and knowing victory. That's triumphing over the hibernation response.

Dressing for the Cold:
Intelligent Accessories to Adaptation

The warmest clad sit nearest the fire.
—FRENCH PROVERB

The hibernator who wears flannel pajamas to bed and buries herself beneath three wool blankets while the thermostat is set at 75°F really can't be faulted. She can't be blamed for overdressing when ice is forming on the windows and the wind is howling across the roof. We hibernators are likely to be more in touch with our primitive instincts than those who don't respond to the seasons as dramatically as we do, and those instincts warn us unconsciously that we're facing death by freezing. That innate wisdom saved humankind from annihilation once, and who knows that it might not do so again. We needn't be ashamed of our fear of the cold.

In this particular era, however, it serves no purpose. Apart from truly extraordinary circumstances—getting buried in an avalanche, being stranded in the Alps, passing out drunk in a snowbank, and such—we're not going to freeze to death. In fact, we're quite capable of functioning with relative comfort in moderate cold with virtually no clothing at all, and we needn't be aborigines or Fuegians to do so. Here are a few examples:

—The Eskimo, who has neither a particularly high metabolic rate nor the ability to reduce circulation to the extremities, nonetheless generally sleeps nude under an insulated bedroll.

—A rural Ohio man in his mid-forties is representative of many who challenge the cold head-on, although his method is a bit unusual. Several times each winter, with temperatures invariably below freezing, while he is clad in boots, gloves, and an athletic supporter, he shovels a path through the snow from his house to the barn. He insists that the physical activity keeps his body warm and that he feels not in the least uncomfortable during the forty-five minutes the project usually takes.

—Even when volunteers for research studies sat motionless and unclothed in cold environments for more than an hour, they suffered no damage. That's been the case in numerous experiments, some of which we'll discuss.

Danger in Overdressing

Let's make this the first commandment: *Thou shalt not overdress.* If necessary, err in the opposite direction, and increase your body temperature, if necessary, through stepped-up activity. Mother, bless her, was wrong when she told us, "Bundle up or you'll catch your death of cold." In fact, burying us under tons of clothing before we were allowed to play on winter days probably caused us more harm than good. That's because we ended up sweating. That created two problems: First, the normal circulation of air in that textile sarcophagus we wore caused evaporation and the attendant *chilling* of skin and lowering of body temperature; the moisture that didn't evaporate became a highly efficient transmitter of body heat into the surrounding garments and, eventually, the atmosphere. In the end we returned home shivering—proof positive to mother that we hadn't been bundled sufficiently in the first place.

The same principle applies to the airtight nylon jackets and vests that have gained great popularity in recent years. Certainly they provide excellent protection from wind and rain, but even when we're inactive, even in the cold, we lose moisture through the skin through insensible perspiration. As it accumulates, perhaps along with ordinary sweat, our bodies grow damp and become chilled.

If you want to know exactly what that means in terms of discomfort, run lukewarm water over one of your hands, then hold both of them in your freezer for thirty seconds. The wet hand will feel significantly colder—even several minutes after being dried. Damp skin leads to loss of body heat. That's what it's intended to do, summer or winter.

Another possible side effect of overdressing in the winter may surprise you. Dr. G. Edgar Folk, Jr., tells the story of a young soldier stationed in the Arctic who spent much of the day pulling sleds and chopping timber in temperatures of minus 40°F. One day he collapsed without warning and was rushed to the hospital, where his condition was diagnosed as *heat stroke*. The young man, a newcomer to the climate, "had been so alarmed at the thought of working in the cold that he had piled on every item of insulation he could borrow," writes Folk. "Under these conditions some subjects will sweat three hundred and fifty grams per hour, others seven hundred and fifty grams per hour." That's equivalent to extremely strenuous exercise while lightly clothed on a hot summer day.

Protecting the Torso

The best jacket for the cold should be lightweight, have a high insulation value, yet allow moisture to be absorbed from the body and transferred to the environment. Eskimos have found the perfect garment in animal furs; but furs don't come cheap, and even those who can afford them might find it a bit showy to shovel the sidewalk or take out the trash in a mink.

Winter coats and jackets should, nonetheless, have the benefits of fur. The external material will be wind-resistant but not airtight since it must allow for the escape of body moisture. Porous synthetic fabrics can serve well. So can leather. And that outer layer should be dark in color—preferably black, although navy blue, deep green, or dark brown will do. Light colors *reflect* the sun's heat while dark ones *absorb* it and help keep you warm. (We'll have much more to say about color in the next chapter.)

The best inexpensive material for the insulating layer is probably cotton. It's a fabric so common that it's taken for granted. It deserves better treatment. A cotton quilt the same thickness as a polar bear's hide—two to three inches—will provide twice the insulation. While rabbit, reindeer, or caribou fur is a bit more effective, an equal density of cotton will keep you as warm as the hide of a wolf, grizzly bear, red fox, or beaver. For one thing, cotton fibers, when loosely spun, contain many air pockets, and that dead air provides the ideal insulation, just as it does in the hollow hairs of some animals. And cotton has another quality that even animal fur doesn't: It absorbs moisture from the body and carries it to the surface material.

Of course, goose down is an even finer insulator—and a great deal more expensive.

The inner lining should be of wool or cotton, or a

blend including these materials. It should definitely not be a synthetic, such as polyester, which, next to a perspiring body, is cold, clammy, and nonabsorbent.

Some superior types of jackets: lambskin, with the wool worn inside; 100 percent cotton with quilting, elastic at the cuffs and waist, zippered closure. Lighter jackets that will still keep you comfortable when you are active in temperatures in the low forties include cotton-lined corduroy and the typical wool plaid jackets worn by hunters over heavy shirts or sweaters. These jackets are just a single layer thick and fit so loosely that the wearers can practically carry their lunches up a sleeve. Although they button tightly around the neck, they're baggy enough at the waist to pass for a maternity top. That looseness works to its advantage, permitting an envelope of air between the garment and the body for both insulation and moisture evaporation. They're surprisingly effective heat conservers.

When the weather is particularly cold, or your exposure to it prolonged, the torso is one part of the body that requires more protection than others do. It encompasses virtually all the vital organs (the brains of most people being the exception) and generates most of the heat produced from metabolism. Much of that heat can be conducted to the body's surface and lost to the atmosphere if the torso isn't protected.

In fact, Paul Siple, in a report on Eskimos for the National Academy of Science—National Research Council, argues that warming the torso can prevent frostbite of the *feet:* "The average person who feels his feet getting cold first assumes that the simplest correction is thicker and warmer footgear. This is often not true. The addition of thicker footgear above the optimum will cause no appreciable improvement in insulation, whereas additional insulation placed on the trunk may warm the feet without further change of footgear. The excess accumulation of heat in the torso causes a cooling requirement which is achieved by shunting the excessively warm blood to the extremities and, as a consequence, the extremities act as radiators and are kept warm."

During the Second World War pilots flying at high altitudes in unheated planes often suffered frozen hands and feet, and that resulted in more than a few crashes. Engineers designed a special suit using electricity to heat the extremities, but it was found inefficient and dangerous. Later outfits heated the torso, arms, and legs, and the problem of cold hands and feet was eliminated.

Our great-grandfathers were no fools. They wore vests with their suits to keep warm, not fashionable, during the winter, and vestlike slip-on sweaters were perennially popular. An insulated vest, or windbreaker, can actually keep an active person warm when the temperature is below freezing, even when that person is otherwise scantily clad, as long as hands and feet are also protected.

The Head, Neck, and Face

In December 1812 Napoleon retreated from Russia, having lost some 469,000 of his 500,000 troops. Many had died of the cold, and according to Napoleon biographer Nigel Nicolson, "Baron Larrey, chief surgeon to the army, noticed that the bald died first."

Much of the blood circulating in the body flows directly to the head in order to keep the brain supplied with the nutrients and oxygen it needs. In cold weather the heat from that blood could be lost quickly. Nature has devised a method of preventing that loss, an excellent furry hide of our own in the one area still not routinely clothed—our scalps. Even infants quickly grow this protective fur coat. Some are born with it.

Allowed to grow naturally, scalp hair will reach to about shoulder-length before splitting, breaking, or falling out during brushing. And indeed, it should be precisely shoulder-length during the winter—full and flowing all over the place, protecting our foreheads, cheeks, throats, and necks from heat loss.

That's because when neck vessels serving the brain become cooled, lowering the temperature of the blood flowing through them, that blood, upon reaching the hypothalamus in the brain, sets in motion all adaptive responses to the cold by the adrenal and thyroid glands. Today many of us are extremely sensitive to a drop of even ten or fifteen degrees as our bodies undergo the continuing stresses of adapting to the autumnal roller coaster temperature fluctuations. It might well be that our distant ancestors had a much easier time of it, unconcerned as they presumably were with fashion and custom. Dense male beards, unrestrained female pulchritude, and shoulder-length hair in both sexes protected the face and neck from relatively minor temperature variation. Only significant decreases penetrated the natural insulation.

Today many men living in temperate zones begin growing beards in September. Their reasons vary from a desire for a new look to preparation for the hunting season, boredom with shaving, and such. In fact, the autumn beard may well be an instinctive effort to insulate the face and neck from heat loss.

Yet most men (and all women) confront the winter barefaced, often with neatly trimmed hair which exposes ears and neck to the cold. We're aware, however, of the need to protect these areas for the sake of comfort and so have invented such apparel as the hat, scarf, earmuff, and turtleneck sweater. Each has an important role to play in thermal adaptation.

To paraphrase the author of Ecclesiastes, "There is a

time to cover, and a time to bare." For example, except in severe cold or a time of high windchill factor, an ample head of hair is sufficient to prevent excess heat loss. On the other hand, men who are even partially bald should wear hats when out of doors in cold temperatures for prolonged periods. Buy a hat that's designed to keep your head warm rather than to look fashionable. You'll quickly notice the improvement in comfort as your body retains heat previously lost.

Although you won't need a hat in moderately cold temperatures if you still have your full head of hair, you will need ear protection on windy days. If your hair covers your ears, the problem is solved. Otherwise, earmuffs do the job nicely. Some coats have collars that can be lifted to protect the ears, and you can buy hats that fold down or can be pulled over the ears—the seaman's wool caps. They're mildly ugly, it's true; but they've served valiantly in the North Sea, and that's no mean challenge. Scarves, like turtleneck sweaters and high-buttoned collars, can give the same insulation that long hair and beards once did for the neck. But keep in mind that the blood flowing through the neck is *supposed* to be cooled when the surrounding temperatures are low in order to trigger an acclimatization response. When the neck is kept excessively warm, the body responds by releasing heat, not conserving it. A single layer of scarf loosely wrapped is sufficient, even on the coldest days, and except in the polar regions heavy coats buttoned around the neck are almost never warranted. The overriding goal is always to avoid keeping the body too warm rather than too cold.

To summarize, our bodies, even after being trapped for millennia in civilization, are perfectly capable of adapting as necessary to moderately cold temperatures if balding men prevent excessive heat loss from the scalp and those lacking long hair guard against frostbite of the ears. Only on severely cold days or those with a plummeting windchill factor need we take the additional steps discussed.

Hands and Feet

The governing principle regarding the ideal boots and gloves is the same as that for other winter garments: They should provide insulating air space between flesh and environment.

You can tell a lot about people, including their income bracket, by the gloves they wear. The stylish, ultrathin kid or deerskin, for example, starts at about thirty dollars and can reach dizzying heights.

Gloves also indicate common sense—or lack thereof. Outdoors on a cold morning, the hands inside those tight leather gloves are clenching and unclenching or are stuffed inside pockets. Designed to be tight-fitting and sexy, they provide little insulation and probably reduce circulation in the bargain. You rarely see them on children because mothers tend to be practical. They buy wool or leather gloves lined with cotton, and the most practical of all supply their youngsters with mittens so that the tiny fingers can exchange heat among themselves.

Practical women themselves also wear mittens. Men, however, almost unanimously avoid them, sacrificing utility to fashion. "Real" men don't wear mittens. Fortunately leather gloves with cotton linings serve the purpose unless they get wet or the temperature drops very low.

Winter boots, on the other hand, can be a real problem. That's because we often wear them while trekking through slush and snow. They should be waterproof, and the waterproofing drastically limits air circulation. While our feet remain protected from external moisture, they promptly become saturated with their own sweat. Rubber boots and others lacking ventilation should fit loosely, allowing air ventilation from the top. Felt liners are good insulators from the cold, and they're preferable to heavy wool socks because the socks cause the feet to perspire and the moisture in turn causes chilling. In fact, with felt-insulated boots, the feet seem to be most comfortable bare, if the tops are left open, permitting the moist air to escape.

As an overall guideline to dressing in the cold, we might adopt the Army Quartermaster Corps acronym COLD:

> *Clean* clothing that will not cling, mat down, or become greasy, destroying insulation
> *Open* to prevent overheating and the dissipation of body moisture
> *Loose* and *layered* garments that allow for insulating air spaces
> *Dry* garments that will not conduct heat from the body

In this and the previous chapter we've talked about dealing with the outside environment during the cold months. But most of us spend most of our time at home and the workplace, and the indoor environment more often than not produces many of the physical aches and pains and emotional distress that we associate with the hibernation response.

In the next chapter, how to create a springtime environment in your home.

Eternal Springtime in Your Home: Healthful Habitats for the Hibernators

For lo, the winter is past, the rain is over
and gone;
The flowers appear on the earth;
the time of the singing of birds is come. . . .
          —THE SONG OF SOLOMON

It takes all kinds to make a world. There are even folks—a great many, in fact—who *love* the winter. All summer they look forward to cuddling up before a blazing fireplace, listening to the wind howl around the corner of the house and the snow pelt the windows. They long to inhale the brewing coffee and burning applewood and imagine that's what heaven will be like.

So much for nightmares. While even hibernators can appreciate the romance involved, the prolonged reality of such an experience might just drive them to ripping their hair out by the roots.

Yet our own domiciles often prove even less satisfactory winter havens. Take the Manhattan apartment of a successful unmarried free-lance writer, John R., who is in his fifties and has lived there for more than three decades. Located in a good residential area, it has large windows and a good view to the east. But John hasn't seen the sun rise in years except in the summer; the heavy dark green drapes remain closed from mid-October until April.

The walls are dark brown, a surprisingly common color in New York City apartments. The furniture is large and bulky and upholstered in shades of vermilion, purple, and deep green. The room is cluttered with heavy tapestries and large paintings in black frames.

John says his color schemes and furnishings were selected instinctively. When he first moved into the apartment on a bleak November morning in 1956, he immediately set about following his inner compulsions. Although he had no idea where his instincts were leading him, he steadfastly shut out the world and created a dark and cluttered retreat.

John built himself a burrow.

That's a perfectly natural thing for hibernators to do. That's why so many of us do it. Insofar as we're able, we respond to the shorter, cooler days of autumn by retreating into our dens, the smallest, darkest, most cluttered rooms in the house. Some of us actually retreat underground—into basement rooms where sunlight can never find us. Like the chipmunk, who stocks its den with huge quantities of food on which it snacks during periodic arousals from hibernation, some of us equip our tiny hideaways with refrigerators and cabinets amply supplied with potato chips, pretzels, and other high carbohydrate goodies. While the whole thing might seem peculiar to those not genetically inclined to so extreme a response, the human hibernator is simply doing what comes naturally.

And there's nothing wrong with any of that. The problem arises when the would-be hibernator is forced to deal with the commitments and responsibilities of our complex life-styles. Most of us have employment responsibilities, family commitments. Our friends would panic if we simply dropped out of sight for three to five months. It's precisely because we can't allow ourselves the luxury of drifting off into a state or torpor every winter that we suffer the symptoms of the hibernation response. We can't have it both ways. We can't eat as though our lives depended on storing enough fat to last us for the winter, build our dark and secure dens, yield to a chronic zombielike state of walking sleep—in short, we can't yield to all the impulses of the hibernation response—and then *not* hibernate.

The only alternative short of relocating (and we'll talk about that later) is to change our own microenvironment. You've already done that in one respect if you've installed and used the artificial sunlight described in Chapter 3. The light is enormously effective in elevating moods for most people. But seasonal depression is but one symptom of the hibernation response. To experience all the benefits that springtime actually brings—the optimism, enthusiasm, increased interest in physical activity, reduced appetite, and improved capacity to lose weight, among others—you need to abandon the burrow and create springtime in your home.

That may not be easy from an emotional standpoint. Your intellect insists on the logic of transforming at least one room of your home to a Spring Room. Yet deep though your longing is to be released to such a fresh, breathy environment, there remains a visceral instinct, as deep as survival itself, which warns that to forsake the burrow is to perish. The ideal time to create a Spring Room is during the spring or summer. That's not to say that you can't do it at any time of the year. Just be prepared to confront a seemingly irrational reluctance to abandon the tiny, dark, and cluttered for the open and airy.

While we'll be talking in the following pages about converting a specific room in your home or even adding on room to create a springlike atmosphere, we recognize that many readers live in rented apartments owned by landlords who will frown upon their ripping gaping holes in the walls just to let in the sun. While you may not be able to apply all the suggestions we mention here, you'll be able to use a great many of them. In fact, if you have a small apartment, you might easily and inexpensively convert your entire living space into a spring home—a luxury that homeowners can rarely afford. Just allow your imagination to flow freely, and we'll drop a few hints for apartment dwellers as we go along.

For many of us, problems arise in the workplace, where we spend about one-third of our lives. Again, much of the information in this chapter—particularly on lighting, choice of colors, ideal temperature, and humidity—can be directly applied to office and factory environments, as you'll see. And productivity has been found to increase in direct correlation with the extent to which the hibernation response is held at bay. If you're in a position to effect changes in your work environment, simply adapt the following information as feasible. If that decision rests with others, you might consider giving them a copy of this book. After all, productivity is directly related to profits, in the business world at least, and that's what decision makers are supposed to be concerned about.

The Southern Exposure

The first step is to choose the right room for conversion or the ideal location to build an extra room. If you live in the Northern Hemisphere, that means knowing which side of your house faces south. The single most important criterion for a successful Spring Room is a southern exposure. Yes, it's possible to install bright artificial light, and you will; but that can't compare with the sun's brightness, warmth, and emotional balm.

Those of a less technological era often designed their dwellings specifically to benefit from the winter sun. The Native American Pueblo of New Mexico, for example, developed an ingenious means of exposing their houses to great quantities of sunlight in the winter while blocking that of summer so that the temperature in their dwellings remained relatively stable year-round. In what was certainly the first North American town house development project, they constructed semicircles of houses, each rising above the other, on a man-made terrace reaching to four levels. Each house received full exposure to the southern sun, while the thick rear walls blocked the northern wind. In the summer, when the sun passed overhead, thick roofs and carefully planned architecture prevented its rays from entering the dwelling.

New Englanders were equally environment-conscious. They situated their fireplaces and chimneys in the center of their houses, dispersing the heat democratically. And in building the saltbox, they made sure that the highest wall—with most of the windows—faced south, while the longest part of the roof, which sloped closest to the ground, confronted the bitter northeasterly winds.[11]

It wasn't until the early 1930's that the idea of inviting the sun indoors through elaborate use of glass really caught on. The Chicago world's fair of 1933 featured the House of Tomorrow and the Crystal House, and those who attended discovered firsthand the sun's capacity to heat indoors when walls are made of glass rather than wood. Frank Lloyd Wright and many other architects began to incorporate glass walls in their designs.

Yet the denning compulsion seems to be winning out, in both our homes and offices. J. Longmore of the School of Environmental Studies, University College, London, raises this point in regard to office buildings: "The designers of modern buildings tend to rely increasingly upon mechanical environmental services, and this inevitably leads to greater isolation of the building interior from its surroundings." Although modern technology can control temperature, humidity, and enough artificial light for working needs, such wizardry by no means replaces the sun. Writes Longmore: "There are indications that the penetration of sunlight into buildings can contribute a great deal towards the psychological well-being."

Longmore and E. Ne'eman of the Israel Institute of Technology in Haifa surveyed more than a thousand people, asking them to complete the sentence "Sunshine inside buildings is a ———" with either the word "nuisance" or "pleasure." About three in every four *office workers* voted for sunshine. So did a whopping 91 percent of *hospital patients*. An even greater percentage—93 percent—felt pleasure in seeing sunshine streaming into their *homes*. (Actually only 4 percent disliked the sun in their homes because of the heat it caused, the fading of color from fabric, and eye pain. The remaining 3 percent didn't know how they felt about the matter.)

Most of us do know. We *hunger* for sunshine. But if your house was built in the last fifteen years, finding a room that's easily adaptable to a Spring Room might be tough. Today's builders often sacrifice the practical in favor of the aesthetic, situating houses to look attractive and impressive rather than to provide maximum southern exposure.

One house recently built on a grassy hill overlooking Allentown, Pennsylvania, at a cost of $155,000, serves as an example. It was situated on the lot so that its impressive pillared front porch and oak doors would face the main road to the north. As a result, all winter the sun floods only the bathroom, kitchen, laundry room, a library with a small window—and the garage. The main rooms have no southern exposure and, incidentally, no view of the city skyline. It's a lovely place to see, but undoubtedly a depressing one in which to live.

Those small windows are another favorite of many architects since the oil embargoes of the 1970's. The argument is that they prevent heat loss, and in walls facing north that's true. But in south-facing walls that's not the case. According to Donald Watson of the Yale School of Architecture, who has been a designer or consultant for more than eighty solar houses, "Contrary to common opinion, energy conservation does permit the full use of windows, glass structures and skylights, provided that they are designed to receive the sun's rays in winter and have some means of controlling heat loss in sunless hours and excessive heat gain in summer."

The following table shows the average amount of heat, given in Btu—or British thermal units, the standard measure of heat—that's likely to penetrate a window on a southern wall in your house on a single day each month of the year, depending on your latitude. (These figures are at sea level and vary according to altitude and sky clearness. The higher your altitude, the greater your heat gain; atmospheric pollution, cloudiness, and humidity obviously reduce the amount of sunlight reaching the window. Additionally, triple-pane windows reduce the amount of solar radiation entering but prevent even more heat from escaping. In higher latitudes they actually increase heat gain.)

If you're committed to creating a Spring Room, determine now to have it face south if at all possible. If circumstances, including living in an apartment, make it impossible, you'll get by with windows facing east or west. If your only possible view is north—move.

Daily Heat Gain (BTU per Square Foot—South-Facing Glass)

LAT.	JAN.	FEB.	MAR.	APR.	MAY	JUNE	JULY	AUG.	SEPT.	OCT.	NOV.	DEC.
32°	1670	1560	1180	720	500	440	490	700	1150	1500	1640	1690
34°	1670	1580	1230	780	540	470	530	760	1200	1530	1640	1670
36°	1660	1610	1280	850	590	520	580	820	1250	1550	1630	1630
38°	1640	1620	1330	920	650	560	630	880	1300	1560	1620	1600
40°	1630	1630	1380	980	710	620	690	940	1340	1570	1600	1560
42°	1600	1640	1430	1040	770	670	750	1000	1380	1580	1570	1510
44°	1570	1640	1470	1100	830	730	810	1060	1420	1570	1530	1450
46°	1510	1680	1510	1160	900	800	880	1120	1440	1560	1480	1370
48°	1410	1610	1580	1210	970	870	940	1170	1470	1540	1380	1250

From Hill and Harrigan, Consulting Engineers

Designing the Structure

Once you've identified your southern exposure, you should make that southern wall of glass. The more the better. An eighteen-foot room, for example, could easily include two six-foot patio doors with solid two-by-six support studding between them and on each end.

And if you're building a sun-room onto an existing structure or as part of a new house, don't limit glass to the southern wall only. During the winter months the sun rises in the Northern Hemisphere from the south*east*, and its sunlight each morning has a velvety, soothing quality. Windows on the east wall will give you the earliest possible exposure to the sun while it's still so low that its rays stream across the entire floor of the room.

A glass west-facing wall is even more important. By midafternoon the sun is at its hottest. That may not seem like much of a consolation during midwinter, when the outside temperature is below freezing, but if the sky is clear and your sun-room is well insulated, the solar radiation beaming through the floor-to-ceiling windows of your west wall can keep the indoor temperature at a perfectly comfortable level without any assistance from your heating system.

There are two areas of your room where we don't recommend glass. One, of course, is the north wall. In the winter the sun's rays never strike it. Instead, it receives the onslaught of vicious northern winds, and even when the windows fit well, there's likely to be some exchange of warm air for cold at each window. What's more, windows simply can't provide the insulation qualities of ordinary walls with fiberglass or other recommended insulating materials. At night, unless you take extraordinary precautions, heat will escape through your windows—all your windows, not just the northern ones. The difference is that it can be regained the next day from those windows on the south and west walls. The major legitimate function of north-facing windows is to allow you to keep an eye on your neighbor.

The second disadvantageous use of glass is in the ceiling. Although several companies now produce "solar rooms" entirely of glass, including a roof/ceiling that slopes into the front wall, the only practical value of a glass ceiling, unless you're building a greenhouse, is to permit gazing at the moon and stars at night. Depending on your latitude, you'll lose more heat than you gain through the ceiling in the winter. And if you don't go to the added expense of installing reflective insulation during the summer, you'll gain enough heat to roast a pig by noon each day. After a few years one or two of the many tracks supporting the roof glass will probably start leaking. The insulating sliders will stop sliding. What once seemed like a charming and romantic idea will turn out to be a genuine pain in the something or other. Better just to go outside and look at the moon and stars if you get the urge.

That's not to say that these prefabricated solar rooms are not a good idea. They are. Depending upon local building costs, they may even prove economical. What's more, most of them can be adapted to your personal preferences and space limitations. Just make sure that the roof is sufficiently insulated to keep the heat in during the winter and out during the summer.

The goal is to allow the sun to shine directly into the room all day during the shortest days of winter, when its path is closest to the southern horizon. When the days grow longer and the sun grows hotter, a decreasing portion of the sun-room floor should be bathed in direct sunlight as the sun moves higher across the sky. By the end of June none of the sky's blistering radiation should reach the room directly.

The way to accomplish that is to build the roof overhang at least twelve inches out from the south wall. The overhang serves as a sort of thermostat, keeping the temperature in the room reasonably stable.

The minimum size of your Spring Room shouldn't be much less than twelve by fifteen feet since a major goal is to create an open, airy atmosphere. One somewhat smaller room we've seen near Buffalo, New York, has the entire north wall paneled in full-length mirrors. It not only increases the room's apparent size but reflects the outdoor light, significantly increasing brightness.

Choosing the Right Colors

Choosing the right colors for your sun-room is very important. An imbalance of color or an inappropriate one can jar you emotionally, yet so subtly that you'll have a hard time identifying the cause of your discomfort.

We can distinguish, believe it or not, more than two million shades, and there are probably other colors that we cannot see for the simple reason that the waves are too small. That is to say that some of the electromagnetic waves given off by the sun (and artificial light) are so tiny—less than a thousandth of a millimeter in length— that we cannot see them as they are reflected from objects. Actually we don't see any electromagnetic waves, even those responsible for the colors we know, unless they strike an object capable of reflecting them.

Take a typical summer day and a typical town, where all things bathe in the sun's rays. In the town square the white marble monument receives the same rays as do the green lawn surrounding it and the black asphalt street.

Should you perchance touch the statue's base, you will note, in spite of the blazing sun, that the gleaming marble is not a great deal warmer than your own body temperature. Should you then proceed to the street and place your hand upon the black asphalt, you will experience a tendency to develop blisters. While the white marble has reflected the solar radiation with its heat and full spectrum of colors, the black asphalt has absorbed all the waves.

We see no color when we look at the asphalt. It has absorbed them all. We see only reflected waves, not those which are absorbed.

Some materials absorb all wavelengths of radiation except red. We see that color reflected and call the object red. So it is with all colors.

If you are a stickler for details, you will appreciate knowing the length of waves that are reflected as specific colors. Wavelengths are measured in angstrom units (AU), each equaling one one hundred-millionth of a centimeter. The measurements are as follows:

Violet	4,300–4,600 AU
Blue	4,700–5,000 AU
Green	5,000–5,500 AU
Yellow	5,800–5,900 AU
Orange	5,900–6,000 AU
Red	6,000–6,700 AU

The purpose of this information goes beyond helping you win at Trivial Pursuit. The fact is that *color is radiant energy.* Every color has its unique physical properties, each of which has an effect on our bodies. Some researchers believe that it is not the entire spectrum of sunlight (and full-spectrum artificial light) but only one or two wavelengths of light/color that reverse the hibernation response during light therapy. Although there has been virtually no research in the field, it is altogether likely that our response to colors, our sometimes emotional love for some and hate for others, the energy and cheerfulness we feel when surrounded by some colors, the fatigue and depression that others produce, may well be a physical as well an a psychological response.

Whatever the pathway, colors affect us profoundly.

—Researchers at PPG Industries painted some heavy boxes white and some lighter ones black and asked factory laborers to move them. The workers consistently had more difficulty moving the black boxes, convinced that they were heavier than the white ones, although the reverse was true.

—It was no accident that the houses of pleasure in the old West were famous for their gaudy red boudoirs. We now know that those blood-red rooms with their crystal chandeliers were as effective an aphrodisiac as any before or since. (We'll have more to say about the color red and passion later.)

—The next time you're in a fast-food restaurant, note the lavish use of yellow, orange, beige, and red tints. Such colors have been found to stimulate appetites and speed behavior. In this case that means ordering plenty, finishing it quickly, and making space for the next customer.

Another example of our response to color is a classic in the professional literature. It comes from Roland T. Hunt's book *Complete Color Prescription:* "In a factory cafeteria, which was air-conditioned and had light blue walls, employees complained of the cold although the temperature was 72°. Some employees even wore their coats to meals. Later, when the temperature was raised to 75°, the employees still shivered and complained. Finally, a color consultant advised repainting the walls orange. The employees then complained that the 75° temperature was too warm. Finally it was reduced to 72° and everyone was happy again."

The wrong colors, whether in your Spring Room, your entire house, or your wardrobe, can leave you cold, lonely, and depressed regardless of how loudly your lights scream, "Cheer up!" Colors can make you edgy, irritable, and unable to concentrate. You may even suffer headaches. Colors, even your favorite colors or the ones you think most attractive or sophisticated, can do that.

Selecting the proper therapeutic colors can't be done by a simple thumbing through some paint charts at the hardware store. Nor should such choices be left to an interior decorator, regardless of the individual's reputation. Colors are too personal and important a matter to be left up to another person.

One of the world's great color experts, Faber Birren, puts it this way: "It is poor wisdom to let the individuality of others impose on your own taste for color." He adds that while there might be a "scientific" way to select ideal colors for each room of a house, the approach would fail dismally because "logic does not usually prevail where color and human personality are involved." Birren condemns the tendency among some interior decorators to ignore the individuality of people by, for example, choosing the same colors for introverts that would appeal to extroverts. Although we'll give recommendations for choosing and using colors that will bring you out of your winter shell and into a fresh, new, vibrant spring, keep in mind that your own feelings should be the ultimate criteria governing your choices. Do you need stimulation, relaxation, open space, coziness, excitement, peace? Allow those subjective needs to dictate your decisions.

Some colors stimulate. Think in terms of the kindergarten paints you used for those youthful masterpieces—blue and yellow, red, green, orange, the pure colors unadulterated by tints (added white), shades (added black), or tones (added gray). They're the brilliant colors that snap us to alertness. But in excess, or if we're highly sensitive to them, they can do more than make us alert. They can irritate, create tension, anxiety, headaches.

One recently married young man explains the dilemma bright colors can create. "We read somewhere that bright colors can increase passion, you know, so we papered the new bedroom red with a little black and gold. It worked great—our lovemaking was great—but there was no way I could sleep there. I always felt hot and restless. Lucky for us we had an extra room."

Some colors are restful. When colors are tinted with white, losing their brilliance, they become soft and relaxing. These are the colors most frequently used in hospitals, where a restful, peaceful atmosphere is needed. They encourage introspection and concentration since they don't intrude and demand attention. But an entire room of pastels can become boring and encourage drowsiness— definitely not a positive quality for those confronting the hibernation response.

Some colors are warm. Shades of red, orange, and yellow actually make us feel warm, and whether or not the reaction is psychological, our heart rates quicken and our blood pressures and body temperatures rise in rooms painted in these colors. The brighter or purer the color, the greater our reaction. A room painted in brilliant red or orange can be stifling to some people. In lighter tints they suggest friendliness, security, and comfort.

Some colors are cold. They include blue-violet, blue, blue-green, green, and greenish yellow. Like the warm colors, they retain their coolness even when tinted with white, shaded with black, or toned with gray.

Some colors are depressing. Large areas in any deeply shaded color both look heavy and make us feel weighted down and sad. That's particularly true of the cool colors—particularly purple, deep blue-black, dark brown, and black itself.

Some colors retreat. They can be used in small rooms—sparingly—to increase its apparent size. We say sparingly because these are the dark colors that can also lead to depression. They include dark blue, dark green, and any of the shaded cool colors.

Some colors attack. They can make a large room feel cozy and more friendly, but they can also cause irritability. They're the warm, bright colors—brilliant red, orange, and yellow. They should be used discreetly.

Although the colors named are the most blatant retreating and attacking ones, you can produce similar effects more subtly by keeping this point in mind: We respond to a given color not in a vacuum but as it relates to surrounding color. That means that even a medium turquoise wall can add a sense of space if the surrounding walls are a light ivory; a soft peach wall can reduce the apparent largeness of an otherwise pale yellow room.

Here's how most of us respond to specific colors:

Red: From its pure hue into darker shades, red stimulates excitation, aggression, increased brain activity, and muscle tension along with a feeling of warmth. Chronically tense people find the color obtrusive and anxiety-producing, and one study has shown that, while the color speeds up reaction time, it decreases efficiency.

Nature splashes red across the landscape every spring, on tulips and roses and geraniums and wild strawberries and wineberries and even a cardinal here and there. But in the scheme of nature's artistry red is a highlight color, never dominant. If you choose it to stimulate alertness in your sun-room, keep that in mind.

Orange: According to Bonnie Bender, the former manager of color marketing for Pittsburgh Paints, "Orange has the same properties as red, but to a lesser degree." She adds, "Objective impressions of orange are jovial, lively, energetic, forceful; subjective impressions are hilarity, exuberance and gratification."

Orange, too, is a springtime color, from the black-eyed Susans to the tiger lilies, butterflies, and golden carp. The sun itself is a brilliant orange just before it sets. In its lighter tints orange seems the color of day itself, at once relaxing and stimulating.

Yellow: The great German poet, dramatist, and novelist Johann von Goethe felt a particular affection for yellow, especially when a day was cold and gloomy. He wrote, "We find from experience, again, that yellow excites a warm and agreeable impression . . . this impression of warmth may be experienced in a very lively manner if we look at the landscape through a yellow glass, particularly on a gray winter's day. The eye is gladdened, the heart expanded and cheered, a glow seems at once to breathe toward us."

If orange is the sun, yellow is the sunlight, and because we make that association, says Bonnie Bender, the color "exudes cheerfulness, gaiety, and liveliness. With the proper use of yellow, people are stimulated to greater production and efficiency." While bright yellow, like all the stimulating colors, can produce headaches and even nausea, lighter tints can help us concentrate and work more efficiently. Yellow, in various tones and tints, might be the perfect compromise color. Since it has the same qualities of warmth and stimulation as red and orange, but to a less intrusive degree, it can be used on large areas without risking the negatives.

Green: Pale to medium green is the second most common color of spring. Faber Birren suggests that the color "corresponds to the [individual's] withdrawal from the outer world and retreat to his own quietness, his center." Bonnie Bender finds it the "ideal environment for sedentary tasks, concentration and meditation. . . . It is a quiet, peaceful, and refreshing color in most tints, particularly the blue-greens." Depending upon the use to which you intend to put your Spring Room, green might be an ideal dominant color choice.

At least some green is a must in your sun-room, if for no other reason than that you'll want to have plants there. Beyond that you might want to use bright green as an accent color or even a light green or blue-green as a basic color. The critical question is whether you mind having your Spring Room on the emotionally cool side. As we've said, green is a cool color. That's not particularly a problem since spring itself at least starts out being a cool season. Some people find those mornings when the earth is greening the most pleasant time of year. Others hate the coolness. If you're among the latter, use green only for accent.

Blue: The sky is blue—or so it appears. (Actually the sky has no color. The blue energy waves from the sun are so tiny that they bounce off atmospheric molecules rather than penetrate them, and what we see in the sky is the reflection of these blue waves.) The ocean is blue. The blood of the aristocracy is blue. It is the most common color we know.

A cloudless sky, a placid lagoon, a light blue wall—all make us feel at peace. Blue is a tranquilizer. A college football coach with a knowledge of color psychology is reported to have painted the opposing team's locker room in pastel blue and his own team's in bright red. His rather mediocre team enjoyed an undefeated season that year.

Blue produces physiological responses as well. Doreen Hamann, the color expert who recently completed the interior renovation of Pacifica Community Hospital in Huntington Beach, California, says that a blue environment can lower a person's vital statistics—heartbeat, blood pressure, respiratory rate, and such—by about 20 percent. That can be extremely beneficial in high-pressure offices and in mental hospitals, where people are being treated for extreme stress, tension, and anxiety. But, Hamann adds, "I'd never use blue in an intensive care unit because it depresses the responses you're trying to encourage, like blood pressure, heart rate, respiration, and eye blinks."

Typical hibernators need *more* pep and energy, not less, and should generally avoid large, uninterrupted fields of blue, especially medium and dark shades. However, medium blue trim and accents can work well against soft, warm colors like pale yellow, peach, or ivory, suggesting a breezy, spacious atmosphere.

Pink: The findings on this color are conflicting, probably because of the subjectivity we each bring to it. According to Dr. Alexander Schauss, when an admission cell at the Naval Correctional Center in Seattle was painted bubble gum pink, inmates held there were found to begin to grow calmer, within about two and a half seconds after entering the facility. The effect "is noticeable in about 10 to 15 minutes. In 45 minutes, it is fully realized." The detainees remained calm for thirty minutes after leaving the cell. However, other studies have shown that after forty-five minutes in such cells, the effect begins to reverse, triggering anxiety.

Pink, of course, is a tint of red, and as such it probably

stimulates alertness and activity as well as sedates some people. If you like the color in the first place, it will prove the ideal compromise between the overstimulation of red and the lackluster warm colors. But weigh carefully so bright a hue as bubble gum pink. In the words of Faber Birren, "Colors will seem more intense in large areas than in small . . . be particularly careful of pale luminous colors like yellow. They are most deceptive in a chip. On the walls of a room, and because of high reflectives, the light colors will 'bounce' back and forth and hence increase in purity. For example, if a cheerful yellow (or chartreuse, peach or pink) is wanted, choose the chip and then dilute the paint with as much as 50 percent white—the color on the chip and that on the wall will then probably look the same."

White: Most people find pure white emotionally negative unless its bland, stark nature is balanced with bright paintings, wall hangings, and trim. Pure white can be demanding and distracting. Far better is an off-white, cream, or ivory. These shades are not intrusive, provide some warmth, and still work well with any other color you might use.

Select trim and highlight colors that not only are different from the primary one but also have different values—more white, black, or gray added—so that they dispel boredom. Highlight colors usually are darker or brighter.

Colors of the same values seem to fight each other. Bonnie Bender tells of a Packard Electric plant that was painted blue, with columns in yellow, green, and orange, "all the same value as the blue. It is a traumatic experience just to walk through the area."

Another important matter to consider is *psychological* balance. Subtle though our responses might be, we can't help being uncomfortable when there is a heavy, dark color on a ceiling supported by light-colored walls. On an unconscious level we expect the ceiling to come crashing down at any moment. That's not so much a problem with a light carpet and darker walls, but those walls will trouble us if the upper half is a heavy color and the lower is light.

Finally, keep your color scheme uncomplicated, uncluttered. The safest approach is to use solids throughout— for the drapes, carpet, walls, and ceiling. If you really love floral patterns, use one in the drapes *or* the carpet, and nowhere else. Use wall hangings only on walls that are distant from patterned drapes. Thoreau's advice to simplify should be the guiding light not only in Spring Room decorating but throughout your house or apartment.

In the rooms she decorated at Pacifica Community Hospital, Doreen Hamann used Wedgwood blue, lavender, pinks, peach, and teal green and says, "The overall effect is quite uplifting." Those are wonderful spring colors and balanced—the lavender and blue by the warm pinks and peach.

For a warmer, more stimulating environment, you might also consider ivory, with orange, brown, green, and white highlights.

Or design an arrangement around your own favorite colors, based on what you've just learned. When all is said and done, the colors that make you happy are the right ones.

Furnishings

In planning your Spring Room or adapting your apartment or office to a springlike environment, keep these criteria in mind:

- *The theme:* You're creating the environment of a pleasant midspring day under a friendly sun. You're not likely to have an overstuffed sofa on your patio; it would be equally inappropriate in your sun-room. Wicker furniture or even genuine lawn furniture might do. Whatever you decide upon, make it light and outdoorsy.
- *The function:* Wicker furniture probably won't work if you spend hours each day in your Spring Room— for example, if it also serves as your office, TV room, or family room. You'll want to put a premium on comfort. Consider high-quality rattan with a soft, unobtrusive pattern in the fabric or some modern Danish furnishings. Leather and chrome pieces also work nicely and wear well. Unfortunately the leather is usually dyed a dark brown, the primary color of the burrow. Unless the room is large, the furniture is widely spaced, and all the coordinating colors are light—white, ivory, pale yellow, and so on—avoid dark brown furniture.

Pampering the Senses

After you've done all the painting, carpeting, and furnishing and hung your drapes, you'll have created a really fine stage setting. But that, of course, is not the production. What must be added now are the *physical sensations* associated with the season of light, growth, and renewal, the sights, sounds, fragrance, and feel of spring. The sensations you include depend on your own preferences; there's no right or wrong. Try, however, to work toward a harmony. For example, if the colors you've selected are shades of blue and tan, you're probably unconsciously creating a beach environment. If that seems true, select sensations that reinforce that theme. A preponderance of greens suggests woodlands, while we often associate yellow, light brown, and orange with open fields and hills. Each has its own sensuous characteristics.

Sounds

We respond quite emotionally to some sounds: screeching tires; sirens; crying babies; explosions; breaking glass; crashing vehicles. Sounds like these increase the heart rate and respiration, raise blood pressure, trigger heightened releases of adrenaline and other hormones.

Other sounds go in one ear and out the other—figuratively. Unless you suffer a hearing loss, you are probably hearing sounds right now and ignoring them. Yet your brain is processing them, interpreting them. It does so for many people even while they sleep. A young woman living in Queens, New York, beside elevated train tracks says, "I've been here for years next to those tracks. They go by all night long. The whole house shakes. I sleep like a log, no problem. But let my baby so much as whimper three rooms away, I'm awake in a flash."

Other sounds catch our attention by their absence.

Says Lucy Freeman, author of the best-selling *Betrayal* and more than sixty additional books on psychotherapy, "I hate to be away from the city overnight. I just can't sleep. It's too quiet without all the horns and traffic."

During the winter we miss sounds of spring and summer. Remember the birds chirping? The leaves rustling? Waves breaking on the beach? A summer shower has its own soothing sound. Perhaps you live in an area where the warmer weather is greeted with open-air markets and outdoor cafés and laughing children. Perhaps your springs include the cries of sea gulls and the gentle lapping of water against barnacle-encrusted pilings.

If you plan to use your Spring Room for quiet activities—relaxing, reading, meditating—go ahead and treat yourself to springtime sounds if only as an experiment. It won't even cost you money if your local public library has tapes and records of environmental sounds; they were popular some years ago as adjuncts to transcendental meditation and relaxation exercises. You can also purchase them. Known as ambient nature recordings, they're available in a truly remarkable—and occasionally ridiculous—assortment of subjects. Here's a list of some of them. If you can't find them at your local record store, write directly to the company.

Meadow (birdsongs and babbling brook), Cassette No. 9513

Sailing (sea, gulls, and creaking mast), Cassette No. 9514

The Sea (gentle ocean waves), Cassette No. 9511

Thunderstorm (soothing rainfall), Cassette No. 9512

 From: The Art of Relaxation
    Peter Pan Industries
    88 South Francis Street
    Newark, New Jersey 07105

A Day on Cape Cod, vol. 1: Early Cape Morning, Compact Disk No. 30014

A Day on Cape Cod, vol. 2: Babbling Brook, Compact Disk No. 30015

A Day on Cape Cod, vol. 3: Sunset Surf, Compact Disk No. 30016

A Day on Cape Cod, vol. 4: Summer Rain, Compact Disk No. 30017

 From: Rykodisc—The Atmosphere Collection
    40 Essex Street
    Salem, Massachusetts 01970

Ultimate Seashore/Optimum Aviary, Record No. 66001

Tintinnabulation (bell sounds)/Dawn at New Hope, Pa. (sound of the breeze), Record No. 66002 (also available on cassette)

> From: Atlantic
> 75 Rockefeller Plaza
> New York, New York 10019

Ultimate Heartbeat/Wind in the Trees, Record No. 66005

Dawn & Dusk in Okefenokee Swamp, Record No. 66006

Intonation/Summer Cornfield, Record No. 66007

Wood-masted Sailboat, Record No. 66008

Pacific Ocean, Record No. 66009

English Meadow, Record No. 66010

(also available on cassette)

> From: Syntonic Research
> 2007 Mathews Lane
> Austin, Texas 78745

By Canoe to Loon Lake/Dawn by a Gentle Stream, Record No. DG-81001

Heavy Surf on Rocky Point/Ocean Surf in a Hidden Cove, Record No. DG-81002

Among Giant Trees of Wild Pacific Coast/Spring Morning on the Prairies, Record No. DG-81003

Niagara Falls, the Gorge & Glen/Among the Ponds & Streams of Niagara, Record No. DG-82005

Night in a Southern Swamp, Record No. DG-83007

Sailing to a Hidden Cove/Hiking over the Highlands, Record No. DG-83008 (also available on cassette)

> From: Moss Music Group
> 48 West Thirty-eighth Street
> New York, New York 10018

Waldkonzert: Winter, Spring, Summer & Fall (ambient nature recordings by Walter Tilgner: sounds of the forest), Compact Disk No. SM9001-50

From: Wergo Harmonia Mundi
3364 South Robertson Boulevard
Los Angeles, California 90034

Source: Schwann Catalog, Spring 1987

A single recording will do fine as audio atmosphere. After you have discovered how satisfying these sounds can be, you might like to wax creative and record the very ones you hear around your home or vacation place each spring. All it takes is a cassette recorder; if you don't own one you might borrow one from your son, your daughter, or any teenager in the neighborhood. Simply wait until the warm weather and the sounds of spring surround you, record on both forward and reverse tracks, and you'll have what amounts to a continuous recording.

Fragrance

The relatively new field of aroma science suggests that the fragrance of spring may trigger even more profound psychobiological responses than do the sounds of that season. That's because the nose is directly connected to the brain's limbic system, which plays a significant role in regulating emotions. In fact, the olfactory nerves seem to be the first to develop in humans. A three-month-old infant can identify a well-worn garment of its mother in a pile of clothes belonging to many people, even after it's been washed.

In a study using forty Yale students, Gary Schwartz, professor of psychology and psychiatry at Yale University, tested emotional response to four fragrances: lemongrass, lavender, eucalyptus, and peppermint. "We predicted," writes Schwartz, "that if subjects enjoyed a fragrance, they would inhale deeply, taking in more oxygen, and would thereby feel more alert." But that wasn't the case. Students reported that lavender consistently made them feel more alert, even if they disliked the scent. Apparently the response was physiological rather than emotional.

Another fragrance with which Schwartz has experimented is apple-spice, associated by many of us with childhood holidays and baking apple pies. In preliminary studies the apple-spice fragrance seems to have a calming effect and to reduce blood pressure. It has even stopped panic attacks in some people.

A fragrance needn't be overpowering to be effective. Perhaps it won't even be consciously noticeable. Scientists at the Tenth International Congress of Essential Oils, Fragrances and Flavors, (IF&F), held in November 1986, even discussed research to create a chemical copy of fresh air. Eugene P. Grisanti, chairman of IF&F, urged those attending the meeting to give research emphasis to developing "environmental fragrancing." He was talking not about the sprays that overpower undesirable odors with theoretically less offensive odors of their own but about aromatic chemicals that trigger an "up experience," a natural high, possibly so subtle that we won't even realize that we're smelling it.

Even now you can buy a number of fine air fresheners, both liquid and solid-based, at your local supermarket. They cost from under a dollar to two dollars and function for two weeks to two months. In addition to flower fragrances, you'll find such descriptive names as April Showers (Stick-ups), Gentle Rain and Cool Breeze (RoomMate), Lemon Whisper (Airwick Magic Mushroom), and Gentle Breeze (Renuzit). Other fragrances include wild herb, spice, wildflowers—a wide enough assortment to please just about every nose.

Be sure to select a subtle fragrance. Most of these manufacturers also make products designed to overpower strong odors just as the aerosol sprays do. Although such overkill might be useful in the bathroom, you won't want to get punch-drunk on perfume in your sun-room. Also, some air fresheners come in adjustable plastic containers which allow you to control the amount of fragrance released. Spring is a soft, muted season when even the fragrances are subtle.

You might prefer to get your spring fragrances the natural way, by growing fragrant plants and flowers. Of course, plants—hanging plants, potted, climbing the wall—are a must in any self-respecting Spring Room, apartment, and office. But most common indoor plants don't perfume the air.

One approach is to cultivate an indoor herb garden. An advantage of herbs: They'll survive in spite of you. As one longtime herb raiser, Barbara Eastland of Lynnville, Pennsylvania, puts it, "They're as close to weeds as you can get, and as hardy." Some grow better indoors than out. Depending on your selection, you can raise herbs that produce beautiful flowers, lovely leaves, or fragrances so refreshing that they're used in perfumes.

And you can always eat what you raise.

"Herbs don't release their fragrances spontaneously as flowers do," says Eastland. "To get their essence, you must trim them—a quarter of an inch will do—and crush the clippings." Those who heat with wood or coal stoves often put herb clippings in a pot of water on the heater. As the moisture evaporates, it fills the room with a lovely scent.

Among the more popular and fragrant herbs are lavender, lemon mint, chervil, fennel, coriander, tarragon, thyme, oregano, basil, and dwarf dill.

If you choose to raise just two herbs, make one of them lavender. It produces lovely purple flowers and exudes one of the most popular fragrances ever known. You'll recall that lavender is the scent which Dr. Schwartz of Yale found to be most effective in stimulating alertness.

Your second choice might well be chervil, a sturdy plant with beautiful leaves and licoricy fragrance. It tastes the same.

You can raise herbs from seeds, and you can buy them as plants. Make sure they're hardy and healthy before you begin clipping. Rotate the clipping schedule so that each plant has a chance to grow back before the next trim.

If you can't imagine spring without the sweet smell of flowers, you can choose from several that grow well indoors in the winter. Separated from windows or patio doors by an insulated drape, they'll endure overnight indoor temperatures of 55°F—some lower—and actually prefer an evening temperature below 65°F.

The heliotrope, for example, blooms all year, reaches a height of three feet, and has a fragrance reminiscent of vanilla pudding.

French perfume, which smells the way you'd expect it to, is a vine, perfect for an indoor trellis as long as it's able to get plenty of sun. It, too, blooms all year.

Both the star and tea jasmine are very fragrant—some people might say overpowering. They produce flowers continuously and have the virtue of thriving in the reduced sunlight from east- and west-facing windows.

So does the Australian laurel, which is also very fragrant. The laurel blooms only in the winter, but that's when you need it most. Even without its flowers, it's a lovely plant, reaching a height of three to five feet.

These are just a few of the most popular varieties. Your local gardening supply center can recommend many others that do well in the winter in your particular area.

More Benefits from Plants

Plants will do more for a Spring Room, apartment, or office than add beauty and fragrance. They're natural humidifiers, helping combat the tendency of virtually all heating systems to dry out the air. The recommended relative humidity level for health and comfort is 45 to 55 percent at 68° to 72°F. When the air is significantly less humid, mucous membranes dry up and make us more susceptible to infections. Dry air also wreaks havoc on most plants. What they—and we—need is a springtime moisture environment. Remember the damp, rich smell of the earth in April? That, too, needs to be a part of the Spring Room environment.

One solution is to place shallow pans of water near the heating ducts or on the wood or coal stove if you're heating the room with one. (We don't recommend this, however, since it's difficult, if not impossible, to stabilize temperatures within a narrow range when heating that way.)

Another approach: Sprinkle marble chips or tiny pebbles on the bottom of shallow pans, add water, and place the potted plants on the chips. Be sure that the bottoms of the flower pots are high and dry. Otherwise, the soil in them will absorb the water and the plants will face the lingering death of root rot. You might lay a whole row of pans in front of the south-facing patio doors and create something of a hedgerow of plants. The evaporating water will provide more than enough humidity for the plants and you. You'll be surprised how quickly the water will evaporate, though, so check the pans daily.

If you really enjoy tinkering with plants, consider gathering some cuttings and placing them in water-filled jars around your sun-room. They will add moisture to the air, and a few of the cuttings will probably develop roots, giving you new plants to play with.

On mornings that follow nights of freezing temperatures, you might pull back the drapes of your Spring Room to discover the morning light gleaming through intricate patterns of frost on the windows. In fact, that's what you *want* to find, although as the sun melts the ice, it'll trickle down the glass to form sizable puddles on the floor. If that won't cause damage, don't worry about it. The water will evaporate again as the room grows warmer. Otherwise, simply place towels at the base of the windows or patio doors. What the frost patterns mean is that the air's moisture content is adequate. Unless the furniture is noticeably damp in the morning, you needn't worry about excess humidity.

The moisture pans work well, and they're inexpensive; but they do have to be cleaned regularly to prevent the growth of microorganisms, and of course, they have to be filled every day or two. One obvious alternative is a humidifier. The one drawback is that even the most quiet "whisper-soft" models can be intrusive. Before buying one, listen to it run in a quiet location, and decide if you can harmonize the sound with the sounds of spring.

Probably the ideal humidifier, if you want to spend the money, is an indoor fountain or waterfall. It recirculates the same water, so it needn't be constantly refilled, it produces a sound that's conducive to relaxation—the pumps on some models can hardly be heard—and ones that weren't bought at a bargain-basement sale are rather attractive.

The important thing is to match the size of the unit to that of the room. A large waterfall in a small space will turn the sun-room into a rain forest overnight. Your plants might like it, but you won't. A little water does a lot in these contraptions.

Lighting

None of the sensory effects in your Spring Room is more significant than the lighting. Even the shorter photoperiod of winter days can't be depended upon; there are fewer sunny days during the winter in most northern cities than at any other time of year.

CITY	JUNE	JANUARY
Chicago	18	11
Boston	15	12
Wilmington, Del.	17	12
Buffalo	24	12
New York City	14	10
Cleveland	23	12
Pittsburgh	22	13
Washington, D.C.	16	11

Source: National Oceanic and Atmospheric Administration

Your plants won't like those overcast days either. The solution is the high-intensity lights discussed in Chapter 3, and the object is to make the room dazzlingly bright compared with typical indoor lighting. In a room fifteen by eighteen feet, for example, you could use twelve four-foot bulbs to approximate the intensity reached in light therapy. Depending on the layout of the room, you might use three four-bulb units: one each on the east and west walls and one in the center of the south wall or on the ceiling above the south wall. Another alternative is to install two four-bulb units above the south wall and two-bulb units on both the east and west walls.

Since you'll probably want to use your Spring Room at night occasionally without the bright lights that will chase away sleep for several hours, be sure to plan for lamps or other ordinary lighting.

If you find that you're not responding as well to the lighting in your Spring Room as you did when you sat in front of the two units, rearrange the units so that you sit within three to five feet of them.

Lighting is even more critical in apartments and office buildings without sufficient exposure to sunlight. You simply can't have spring without brightness, and if you decide to make only one change in your work or home environment, *let there be light.* As a last resort you can always brighten your office by placing a portable four-bulb unit against the wall to the back of your desk. In your apartment you can follow the lighting recommendations we gave for the Spring Room. With a little imagination you can blend them in with the decor. Dollar for dollar, it's the best investment you can make to banish the hibernation response.

The Ion Question

Unless you have a miniature waterfall in your Spring Room—and there are a few who do—you should know a little about ions and how they affect moods. Ions are oxygen molecules that have been knocked around in the environment to the point where the typically equal (or neutral) balance of positively charged protons and negatively charged electrons breaks down. Lightning, sun-

light, water falling or crashing over the beach, rain—
these and many other natural processes can start relatively unstable electrons spinning off on their own. When
they do, the remaining molecule, minus one electron, is
no longer neutral but has a preponderance of positively
charged protons. The electron, on the other hand, at-
taches itself to another molecule, thereby giving it a negative charge. These electrically charged molecules are
called ions.

There are about twenty-seven billion oxygen molecules
per cubic centimeter of air, about two thousand to three
thousand of which are ions. Typically there are more
positive than negative ones, a ratio of about six to five.

Most people are apparently unaffected by the number
or ratio of ions in their immediate environments, but just
as 25 percent of the population is estimated to suffer significantly from the hibernation response, so the same
number is believed to be ion-sensitive. When the ratio of
positive ions grows particularly high, these people develop headaches, nasal obstructions, fatigue, and the dry-
ing of mucous membranes. They also become depressed
and lethargic.

One phenomenon associated with the natural accumulation of positive ions is a hot, dry wind, such as the foehn
in Germany, the Santa Ana in California, and the
chinook that howls through the Rocky Mountains. In Israel the wind is called the *sharav*. Historically these winds
have been infamous for the symptoms which accompany
them: tension, irritability, sleeplessness, nausea, migraine,
dizziness, depression, apathy, and fatigue. Suicides have
been linked to the hot, dry winds. Felix Gad Sulman,
M.D., of the Bioclimatology Unit at Hadassah Hospital,
Hebrew University Medical School, in Jerusalem, has la-
beled these complaints the "serotonin hyperfunction syn-

drome." Masses of people begin to experience them about twelve hours before the sharav reaches Jerusalem, when the normal ion ratio of 5 positive to 4 negative ions soars to 132 to 4. Dr. Sulman reports excellent results in treating victims of the serotonin hyperfunction syndrome with drugs which interfere with the production of serotonin, but truly scientific studies of the phenomena are lacking.

In the 1950's some enterprising individuals began building and selling negative ionizers, gadgets which send a small electrical current through a clump of copper fuzz resembling steel wool. The resulting release of electrons increased the ratio of negative ions in the rooms where the generators operated.

Not content to stick with the facts, a few hucksters began claiming fantastic healing powers for their negative ion generators. As a result, the FDA investigated, found no health benefits at all, and prohibited their sale for any medical purpose. You can still buy them today, but only as air cleaners.

There's no question that the negatively ionized air of the seashore, a mountain waterfall, or even a thunderstorm is associated with a brightened mood and perhaps even produces exhilaration in some sensitive individuals. We know, too, that positively charged ions have been associated with both physical and emotional complaints and that most heating systems produce a disproportionately large number of positive ions. Whether negative ion generators are truly beneficial is still an open question in our opinion. The devices operate silently, and their impact is anything but dramatic, so it's impossible to know just how useful they really are. Some who claim they have benefited from using them may actually have experienced a placebo effect; but negative ion generators do not cause harm, and for some people a preponderance of negative ions in the sun-room may be beneficial. Cost is probably the major consideration. They range in price from $79.95 to $249, the more expensive ones generally being more effective in terms of removing smoke and other pollutants from the air. For the full story on ions, read *The Ion Effect: How Air Electricity Rules Your Life and Health,* by Fred Soyka and Alan Edmonds (New York: Bantam, 1977).

An Ideal Temperature

We haven't yet discussed an ideal sun-room temperature, and that can be very important.

Europeans seem comfortable doing light work when the air temperature is between 60 and 68°F, but Americans usually insist on higher temperatures, even in winter. The difference is probably due in part to the warmer indoor clothing worn by Europeans. But it is also the result of acclimatization on the Continent, for people there are habituated to the lower temperatures that prevail indoors.

The best temperature for your sun-room is one at which you're comfortable, but not warm. For most Americans, that's about 72°F. If you're raising winter-flowering plants, they won't like temperatures much higher than that; most of them can handle the low fifties more easily than the high seventies. Guard strenuously against overcompensating for the cold outside by baking yourself indoors. In addition to the hazards of overheating discussed in Chapter 6, you'll find yourself getting drowsy all the time and probably develop sinus problems and a sore throat.

Finally, there's the matter of outdoor landscaping to

119

control summer temperature. Unless you intend to keep the drapes drawn during the hot days, consider planting some fast-growing deciduous trees. Under ideal conditions, hybrid poplars will grow four feet a year until they reach about twenty-five feet. In the winter, when the leaves have fallen, their skinny trunks and sticklike branches are insignificant obstacles to the sunshine. Their life-span is comparatively short, however. Maples and willows are also fast growers, and both have dense foliage.

Try to keep trees twenty feet or more from the house so that their leaves don't clog your drain gutter every autumn. The twenty-foot rule is arbitrary. Everyone knows there is *no* absolute distance at which to plant a tree and keep the leaves out of the drain gutters.

Tips for the House or Apartment

While it's probably impractical to make every room of your house or apartment a Spring Room, you can make a few very effective changes without spending a great deal of money. Here are some recommendations; some can be implemented at work as well:

—Eliminate narrow-band energy-saving lights such as sodium bulbs. Rather than give you a sense of spring, these bulbs have been related to nausea, dizziness, headache, and eyestrain. Yellow light is particularly depressing. While it may be neither feasible nor desirable to illuminate your entire house or apartment with bright full-spectrum lighting, consider installing a combination of bright incandescent and fluorescent lighting in the rooms most frequently used. The incandescent will provide the warm colors of the light spectrum while the fluorescent supplies the cool, providing much of sunlight's own full spectrum.

—Paint or paper your walls light, pastel colors; off-white; beige; yellow; pale green; blue. If you can't redecorate right now, break up any depressing darkness by hanging light, bright paintings or carpets over large areas of your walls. One woman hung a huge yellow drape along an entire wall and highlighted it with a spotlight, increasing the sense of space in the room dramatically.

—Remove unnecessary furniture, and if the walls are cluttered with knickknacks or pictures, take some of them down. A spring day is simple, spacious, natural. Make your home or apartment reflect that.

—In winter months especially, except when you watch TV, keep the room you're in brightly lit without glare.

—Spring means plants. Hang them lavishly without cluttering.

—Spring also means the fresh moisture of thawing snow or an afternoon shower. Buy an inexpensive humidistat, and keep the humidity throughout the house in the range of 45 to 55 percent. Purchase a humidifier if necessary.

Is a Spring Room really worth the time, trouble, and expense? As one man puts it, "I'm almost fifty years old. I put eight thousand dollars into an addition—that's about a third of my annual income. My wife thought I was crazy. Now she's in there all day long. Her sewing machine's in there. Her TV's in there. I still get to use it nights and weekends. She's easier to live with now. And we don't have to take so many winter vacations. I figure we've got it almost paid for in money saved on those winter vacations."

Whether you build a Spring Room, adapt a room, apartment, or office, bringing springtime into your environment offers a cost-to-benefit ratio you can't beat. Go ahead and do it, and you'll be celebrating your own brilliance every winter hereafter.

Charting the Ebb and Flow: Recognizing Normal Body Rhythms

Individuals may need a sense of the oscillations within, the rising and falling of energy, undulations of attention, mood, weight, activity, sexuality and productiveness. Because the clocks and calendars of social activity are designed for economic efficiency or convenience, an individual may have to learn to detect his own cycles, and become aware of scheduling to protect his health.
— GAY GAER LUCE

Life is a paradox. Living systems maintain their consistent adaptation to a changing world by constantly changing themselves. We have already recognized some of these normal oscillations in the responses we all have to our changing planet.

So in the spring those normal body rhythms which virtually force you to gain weight in the fall will help you to lose it.

- Some people, especially those who don't have recognizable seasonal affective disorder, have ninety-day depression cycles in the spring and fall.
- If you suffer high blood pressure, your condition will probably improve in June and July.
- You will do better as an athlete during the summer months, and you'll be more generous and friendly then as well.

123

- If you're typical, your sex drive will be greatest from July through September. (Perhaps that's why you'll be friendlier then.)
- Your energy levels will peak in August and September.

Those are just a few of the normal circannual ("circa" = approximately; "annual" = a year) rhythms we all experience. As it is true of the hibernation response—one of the most obvious and profound circannual rhythms—so it holds for all such seasonal and daily influences governing our existence. Knowing what to expect helps us plan ahead, avoid undesirable situations, and improve substantially the quality of our lives. That's what we'll accomplish in this chapter.

The Universal Rhythms of Everyday Life

We must begin with some humility. We are, after all, part and parcel of our environment. We are separate organs in the body of the universe, functioning according to our unique natures, yet totally dependent upon the whole, profoundly affected by its state of well-being.

Yet we as a species have long believed too literally that we are created in the image of God, "a little lower than the angels," therefore embracing the absurd and dangerous notion that we are somehow set apart from the laws governing the survival of other living organisms. We tempt Providence by building our homes on the slopes of volcanoes, the shores of flood-prone rivers, at the feet of snow-burdened mountains, and across the earth's shifting faults. We pour deadly pollutants into our air and water. We fill our blood, stomachs, and lungs with poisons that we know would soon make a corpse of the family pet.

There is this to be said for sufferers of the hibernation response: We understand our status. We are not merely influenced by the environment but recognize that we are one with it. Its verities dominate us. Its tides flow through us.

Planetary forces have generated and in many instances still synchronize the major rhythms and cycles that constitute our existence. Some are so familiar that we are not consciously aware of them: the predictable circadian (about a day) sleep-wake cycle with which are linked the rise and fall of adrenal and thyroid hormones, sugar, and amino acids in the blood; the associated, subtle, and equally predictable rise and fall of normal body temperature, by as much as two degrees in each twenty-four-hour period. Others are obvious: the menstrual cycle frequently tied in regularly menstruating women to the lunar cycle; the circannual sexual activity/breeding cycle, demonstrable even in humans, in spite of our spirited efforts to overcome it.

Chronobiologists (those studying the biology of life in the context of time) have also found that biochemicals in the brain and spinal cord follow a twenty-four-hour production rhythm. So do liver enzymes, cell division, and most of the body's vital functions. In the afternoon you are quite literally not physiologically the person that you were in the morning. Your heart rate, your blood pressure, your urinary output all are at a different phase in their daily cycles. The burst of energy or concentration that is needed to complete a task is much more difficult to muster at four in the morning than at four in the afternoon. That's why there are more single-vehicle highway accidents involving long-distance trucks in the early morning than at any other time of the day.

Many of these rhythms are basically endogenous—that

is, they appear to exist within us apart from environmental cues. In fact, this oscillation, this ebb and flow of functions, actually exists in the cells themselves. But it is the environment that synchronizes or "entrains" them, as the chronobiologists say, on a daily basis. And depending on the phase of the cycle, our vulnerability may change.

So we seem to be more susceptible to infectious diseases at certain times of the day. According to Czechoslovakian researchers, of 1,649 cases of influenza studied over a ten-year period, 96 percent showed symptoms in the afternoon or early evening. About 85 percent of tonsillitis attacks started in the morning, most of them around 9:00. Appendicitis developed between 1:00 A.M. and noon in 87 percent of the cases, most of them at 6:00 A.M.

In short, bacterial infections apparently develop most frequently in the early morning, viral ailments in the late afternoon.

Pain, too, has its rhythm. Perhaps we all recall feeling greater distress at night than during the day when we're suffering a cold, and hospital workers confirm that their patients are much more likely to demand painkillers during the evening than they are earlier in the day. Possibly the body's natural analgesics reach their lowest levels as the night draws on, as do other hormones.

Even aspirin is less effective during the night, apparently, than at other times; it remains in the blood five hours longer during the day.

And mental depression, of course, is usually worse in the morning.

The major challenges that living creatures face, as we have seen, derive from the motions of the earth relative to the sun. Right from its origin, some billions of years ago, life has been coping with the daily and annual change in light and temperature. Since these environmental cycles were basically stable, many creatures evolved a biological program adaptable to the circadian and circannual changes of the external world. One example: Some animals—like the rat—are most likely to survive if they feed during darkness, when they're less likely to be preyed upon. So with the coming of night the rat experiences an increasing secretion of the enzymes necessary for digestion by the intestine and metabolism of the food.

It all runs like clockwork. In fact, the cells that command these programs are called just that, internal clocks. We now suspect that there are one or two master clocks and lots of other clocklike rhythms generated by individual cells that are "slaves," or entrained, to the master clocks.

We've recently discovered that in mammals like ourselves, one of the most important master clocks is in the brain—specifically in the front part of the hypothalamus—just above where the nerves bringing information from the eyes cross each other. Because of its location, it is called the suprachiasmatic ("chiasma" meaning "crosspiece") nucleus, or SCN. We've already discussed how this area controls body temperatures. Either directly or indirectly it also regulates virtually every endocrine function in the body—and continues functioning even when isolated from the rest of the brain.

But even the SCN is influenced by the most important clock of all—both for circadian and circannual rhythms. The ebb and flow of sunlight, the same cue involved in the hibernation response. Another example: We ordinarily excrete bursts of adrenal hormones, the body's natural stimulant to activity, just before awakening. But when volunteers were kept in darkness for four hours after awakening, blood samples showed that adrenal hormone release was also delayed four hours—until the onset of light. And when volunteers were subjected to twenty-three hours of darkness, hormone levels remained lower than those of volunteers living under normal lighting conditions. In some way sunlight regulates function of the adrenal.

The same is true of other endogenous rhythms.

Dr. F. Hollwich, of the Universität Augklinik in Münster, Germany, has found that fifty people blind with cataracts had abnormally functioning hypothalamus, pituitary, and adrenal cortex regulating systems. In other studies Hollwich linked these abnormalities to metabolic breakdowns in water balance, blood sugar levels, electrolyte levels, and processing of carbohydrates, fats, and proteins. After successful cataract surgery all these processes became normal. In Dr. Hollwich's opinion, light is essential in synchronizing the hypothalamic-pituitary-adrenal mechanism that regulates the hormone secretion rhythms controlling metabolism.

If all that seems rather esoteric, let's put it this way: A good part of the way you feel, behave, and perform—both physically and mentally—is predictable. It follows a daily clock and an annual calendar.

But here's an important point, and although we'll return to it later, keep it in mind as you read the following pages: Your clock and calendar are unique to you, perhaps only subtly different from those of Mr. and Mrs. Statistical Average, perhaps profoundly so. That's why we recommend that you keep daily and annual charts. They'll make it possible for you to recognize your cycles and make the best use of that self-knowledge in the chapters that follow.

Circannual Rhythms: Checking the Annual Calendar

Take the time now to prepare a blank chart as illustrated. Don't add the plotted lines (they indicate typical cycles, but not necessarily yours). Instead, use those lines as a general predictor of your responses for the next twelve months (or if you keep a diary, try reconstructing it for last year) while plotting your actual physical and emotional rhythms. In general, think of the center line as you would a C grade, the top as an A+, and the bottom line an F. Grade your responses accordingly. Begin your chart with the current month; we're beginning arbitrarily with June/July in discussing typical circannual rhythms.

JUNE/JULY

Depression: Clinical depression—requiring treatment or hospitalization—is generally least common in the summer months across the United States. In fact, most people maintain high spirits during the summer months. Bouts of minor, short-term depression, particularly among hibernators, can be triggered by a series of cloudy days. On your chart, record your overall mood level for the month, not the daily fluctuations.

Appetite/Weight: Most of us eat less during the summer months. You're probably still finding it rather easy to lose weight in June and July.

Energy/Enthusiasm: Most of us are at our annual peaks of enthusiasm, working out of doors and exercising, perhaps playing sports. Our relationships with others are at a high point. Psychic energy is increasing.

129

Circannual Rhythms Chart

	JULY	AUG.	SEPT.	OCT.	NOV.	DEC.	JAN.	FEB.	MAR.	APR.	MAY	JUNE
	1 2 3 4	1 2 3 4	1 2 3 4	1 2 3 4	1 2 3 4	1 2 3 4	1 2 3 4	1 2 3 4	1 2 3 4	1 2 3 4	1 2 3 4	1 2 3 4

DEPRESSION
Decreasing
Average
Increasing

APPETITE/
WEIGHT
Decreasing
Average
Increasing

ENERGY/
ENTHUSIASM
Increasing
Average
Decreasing

SLEEP (Hours)
Decreasing
Average
Increasing

130

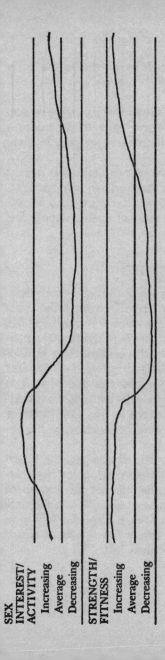

SEX
INTEREST/
ACTIVITY

Increasing
Average
Decreasing

STRENGTH/
FITNESS

Increasing
Average
Decreasing

131

Sleep: We don't need as much as we did in the early spring. Yet we feel refreshed.

Sex Interest/Activity: Neither satyrs nor duds, we're sexually active and satisfied. Younger men might notice a heightened libido, especially if the temperature is high.

Strength/Fitness: You'll reach your peak of fitness during these months, work and play harder, recover from activity faster and enjoy the active life more than at any other time of year. Make the most of it now—you'll feel differently in a few months.

AUGUST/SEPTEMBER/OCTOBER

Depression: Early hibernators will find their moods deteriorating in late summer, particularly during the early days of September, as the air grows cooler and the leaves begin changing color. While others laud the beauty of autumn, the hibernator deplores the season. Also in September severe (major) depression, not to be confused with seasonal affective disorder, reaches one of its two peaks. So if severe depression (usually associated with difficulty in sleeping and rapid weight loss) is a problem for you in the fall, you should consult a psychiatrist.

Appetite/Weight: As autumn officially begins, the hibernator develops an almost insatiable craving for high-carbohydrate foods. These months will set the course of weight control for the rest of the season. Now is the time to begin the Antihibernation Diet (Chapter 10), for as your body adjusts to storing fat, a few weeks of casual excess nibbling can put on pounds fast.

Energy/Enthusiasm: Although moods are deteriorating, mental energy levels actually peak for most of us during August and September. Perhaps this extra capacity is related to an unconscious frenzy of preparation for hibernation before we begin vegetating in November. This is the time to complete major projects that need a final surge of intensity. It's one of the best times of the year for decision making.

During October, while our psychic energy may still remain high, many of us grow somewhat sluggish physically. Our bodies are slowing down. Even our metabolism apparently decreases.

Sleep: By October we're probably sleeping longer but feeling less rested.

Sex Interest/Activity: The good news: Sex activity among most adult males reaches its peak in September. That was the conclusion of studies involving five young Parisian men who showed a measurable increase in sexual activity—both intercourse and masturbation—from July to December, with a peak during the first month of autumn. There's also an increase in the number of spermatozoa in the ejaculate and in the level of the male hormone testosterone in the blood during this season.

Let's digress here just a little.

A great deal of evidence suggests that we humans, like other mammals, birds, reptiles, and fish, have a primary breeding season. In our case it's during the summer and early fall, a clever arrangement, since it permits our fragile young to enter the world not in the winter but in April, May, or June. Birth records tend to support nature's plan, but not firmly, for human young are born every day of the year. It may be that, as our struggle for

133

survival has come to consume less time and energy, we have devoted more of both to sexual pleasure year-round.[12]

Yet those rhythms still exist as predictable as clockwork, and researchers are now beginning to understand why. They're saying, in effect, that the sun is our most erotic natural resource. In warm weather we expose more of our bodies to public view. We stroll hand in hand through all those romantic fields and forests. What's more, sunshine makes us feel good about life, relaxing us and allowing our libidos to take over. The sun does all that, but that's not all.

Sunshine is a *physiological* aphrodisiac. It performs this wonderful achievement in the same way that it rescues us from the hibernation response.

Says Dr. John Hartung of the Harvard University Medical School, the length of dark phase—the scotoperiod— "has a demonstrable effect on the gonadal activity of all mammalian, avian and high-altitude reptilian species thus far tested. . . . In each of these cases, the hypothalamus-pituitary-gonadal axis is moderated by photoperiodic effects of the pineal."

In simpler terms, the gonads of virtually all living animals—male and female—are affected by the reduced sunlight. In some animals the testicles actually decrease significantly in size during the winter months. Sperm production falls. Testosterone levels decrease, sometimes dramatically.

The females of many species simply don't come into heat during the shorter days of fall and winter.

Once again, the culprit seems to be the pineal gland hormone melatonin, which is known to have clear-cut antigonadal effects; it reduces the size and function of the reproductive organs. Medical researchers have even used pineal extracts to shrivel the testicles of men with

Peak Sex Activity According to Various Criteria

June	July	August	September	October to December
1 2 3 4	1 2 3 4	1 2 3 4	1 2 3 4	

Most frequent rate of intercourse reported by American couples.[1]

Peak frequency of intercourse and masturbation among five French young men.[2]

Greatest number of gonorrhea cases reported, city of Houston, Texas.[3]

Greatest number of rapes in Paris, France.[3]

Greatest number of rapes in Houston, Texas.[3]

Highest sales of over-the-counter contraceptives, London, England.[4]

135

prostate cancer in order to prevent the disease from spreading. What's more, Franz Waldhauser and his colleagues found much higher nighttime melatonin levels in sexually undeveloped youngsters than in mature adolescents. They write in the February 18, 1984, issue of the *Lancet*, "Nighttime melatonin levels apparently decline progressively from the early years of life throughout prepuberty and puberty, thereafter remaining relatively constant during adolescence and young adulthood."

Among blind people complaining of low sex drive, successful cataract surgery has led to a prompt increase in testosterone levels—and sex activity. The obvious explanation: The additional sunlight reaching the retina triggered a curtailing of melatonin production by the pineal, which allowed the gonads to function normally.

So far there have been no studies specifically devoted to discovering the effects of artificially extended photoperiods on improving one's sex life, although Dr. Rosenthal of NIMH has reported anecdotally that at least one patient became hypersexual following light therapy for SAD. But in the absence of studies involving humans, anyone whose sex life is for the birds might take a lesson from observations involving those creatures.

Neuroendocrinologist Joel R. L. Ehrenkranz points out that "the Chinese had noticed the influence of light on reproductive functions in birds more than 600 years ago. By exposing the male song bird in winter to additional light after sunset, they kept the bird singing throughout the year. Simultaneously, sizeable testicular growth would occur in birds so treated. The centuries-old Japanese practice of *yogai* consisted of exposing pet birds to artificial light after sunset during November and December. This brought them into song in January instead of the normal time in the spring."

Farmers have known about the aphrodisiac effects of the sun for almost two hundred years and surround their chickens with artificial sunlight throughout the night to increase egg production. Even dairy farmers have found that lengthening the duration of light increases milk production.

Now back to the seasonal cycle.

Strength/Fitness: Most of us will still feel strong well into September—perhaps even October. Only as depression settles in do we respond with a sense of exhaustion. We're every bit as strong and fit as we were a month earlier—we simply don't *feel* it. If you can press through this barrier of lethargy, it will make a world of difference both physically and psychologically.

NOVEMBER/DECEMBER/JANUARY/FEBRUARY

These are the months when the hibernation response is in full swing. As we've discussed in previous chapters, most people react to the shorter days of winter with negative shifts in mood, energy, enthusiasm, and sex drive. They sleep longer but feel less rested, and they gain weight.

For some people the hibernation response is accompanied by a winter depression, although usually not so debilitating that they seek professional help. Yet depression, along with related chronic fatigue, is often the most troubling aspect of the hibernation response. Since it's impossible to predict when an individual will begin to develop symptoms, it's particularly important to maintain your annual chart during these months. As you'll see in Chapter 11, it'll show you precisely when to take a southern vacation in order to disrupt—and perhaps to short-circuit for the entire winter—the debilitating aspects of the season. You'll learn when to anticipate elevated mood and energy levels in order to plan your life in harmony with your capacity to function. Some people begin improving as early as late January, while others don't notice a change until spring has actually arrived. Your chart will help you avoid guesswork.

MARCH/APRIL/MAY

Depression: While seasonal depression is decreasing or vanishing completely, serious depression reaches its annual peak during these months. No consensus among professionals exists regarding the reason for this, although most authorities believe it's related in some way to the environment. Zick Rubin, professor of social psychology at Brandeis University, offers another possibility in the December 1979 issue of *Psychology Today:*

> My own hunch is that the interplay of meteorological influences and self-perception is responsible for the springtime upturn of the emotional distress. In the spring, as the weather warms, people spend more time outdoors and a general mood of optimism prevails; people who feel alone, unloved, and unsuccessful are likely to feel more acutely distressed by comparison. And there is more. In the bitterness of winter, people in northern climates can blame their troubles on the cold, the ice, frostbite, stalled cars, frozen pipes, the perpetually to-be-shoveled snow. In the mildness of spring, people can blame their troubles only on themselves, their fears, their ruined relationships, and unfulfilled dreams. In spring, we must account to ourselves most honestly for our failings,

which may push some troubled people over the edge of despair. For them, April is, as T. S. Eliot insisted, the cruelest month.

Another possibility: Springtime weather is chaotic. One day the sun is shining and the temperature hits eighty degrees; the next, a cold wave tumbles from the north, bringing snow. (The Great Blizzard of 1888 arrived on March 11.) Then it's rain, followed by heat, cold. Not only does the thermoregulatory mechanism take a beating, but the levels of hormones regulating it—those from the thyroid and adrenals, among others—soar and plummet. These rapid changes in hormone levels, some of which dramatically influence our emotions, reflect just how important the challenge to a smooth regulation can be. And when these regulatory mechanisms get pushed too far, depression can be the result.

Appetite/Weight: This is the best time of year for the hibernator to go on a diet. Polish researchers Barbara Zahorska-Markiewicz and Andrzej Markiewicz recently studied the weight loss efforts of 146 women over a period of three years. The women reported to a special clinic for one week every three months. During their stay the environmental temperature, activity level, and diet of each participant were carefully recorded and found to be stable throughout the year. Yet the women lost an average of half a pound more per week during the spring than at any other time.

That baffled the researchers. Why were the women losing more weight in spring, while their food intake, exercise output, and all other factors remained unchanged? Another study provided the answer. The investigators monitored nine men and nine women each month for a year as they pedaled a stationary bicycle at constant speed and work load. They made two discoveries that show why early spring is the best time to start a diet:

—The subjects used 10 percent more energy in March and April than in midsummer through late autumn to do the same work. Apparently nature has provided a means for speeding up the shedding of fat not utilized for warmth and energy during winter hibernation.

—Although the body typically burns both protein and fats for energy when we diet, it "prefers" to burn fats in the spring, utilizing a higher proportion of them during those months than at other times of the year.

The best approach is not to gain weight in the first place during the autumn and winter months (see the Antihibernation Diet in Chapter 10), but if your best intentions amount to naught, the time to get serious about weight loss is March 1 for most of us. (Your chart will show the best time for you personally.)

Energy/Enthusiasm: The energy that surges through us in the spring is peculiar. We don't feel like building a house or chopping wood or starting a major research project. Our endocrine glands are a bit sluggish; our brains a little fuzzy. There are days when we're still lazy and passive, but we also feel hope and optimism.

What stirs us to action is the out-of-doors. We find ourselves planting flowers and seeds, moving dirt from one place to another, painting the fence and doing this and that to make our places look pretty, in harmony with the fresh new beauty that nature itself is beginning to display. This is a good time for physical rather than intellectual activity. If you haven't been exercising during the winter, begin a fitness program now, but don't push too hard. Let your body shake off the lingering sloth of winter at its own rate.

Sleep: You'll notice that you're sleeping less during these months and awakening more refreshed. At first there's no consistency to the pattern. Some mornings getting out of bed is as difficult as it was in the dead of winter. That will change as the season progresses.

Sex Interest/Activity: In spring a young man's fancy turns . . . Not necessarily. As we've seen, sex drive apparently reaches its peak during late summer. What *does* take place in the spring is that many of us have a renewed *awareness* of our sexuality. That isn't to say that we haven't been enjoying sex all winter but that during those months it was usually more mechanical and cerebral, unless we were lengthening the photoperiod through bright light exposure. Now, in the spring, we feel the stirrings of libido. We not only experience sex as we have during the winter but really *want* it now.

Strength/Fitness: Sluggishly—oh, so ploddingly—you are beginning to stir. The joints are stiff and the muscles weak and inflexible. But now the spirit is at last rising to the challenge.

Circadian Rhythms: The Daily Clock

We've been talking about charting *circannual* rhythms. In some respects it's even more important to recognize the rhythms that ebb and flow within us on a twenty-four-hour basis. We'll prepare a daily sleep/wake/alertness chart to track those cycles. It will help you recognize the least safe time to take toxic drugs or to do strenuous physical labor, especially if your fitness level isn't great. You'll learn the times of day when you're most likely (and least likely) to do accurate work requiring concentration. And if you find your sleep pattern out of harmony with the rest of the world and your own physiology—if you're not getting enough sleep because you go to bed too late or awaken too early—the daily chart will help you pinpoint when the phase breakdown occurs. You'll need that information to reprogram your sleeping schedule (we'll discuss that in detail in the next chapter).

Prepare a chart like the one illustrated, omitting, of course, the line indicating the statistically average daily sleep/wake/alertness rhythm. Remember to think of the middle line as a C grade, the top as an A+, and the bottom an F.

Daily Sleep/Wake/Alertness Chart

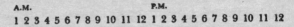

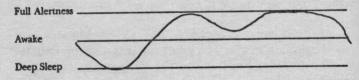

To discover your individual alertness cycle, you'll need a deck of cards, a sheet of paper, a pencil, and thirty seconds each hour until the time you go to bed. The time invested will be eight or nine minutes, well worth the effort.

Immediately upon awakening, shuffle the cards and place the deck facedown. Now, for exactly thirty seconds, turn over as many cards as you can, one at a time, and write its value. Use just two symbols for each card—AH for ace of hearts, 10D for ten of diamonds, and so forth. Be sure to write as fast as you can. When the thirty seconds are up, record the number of cards counted next to the hour.

If you have a wristwatch with an alarm, set it immediately so that you don't miss the following hour's test. Take the test until your usual bedtime. And don't worry about the hours you sleep and are unable to take the test. Consider yourself not very alert then.

The card-counting test is a psychological one, similar to those given by professional researchers. They also use physiological tests, including that of body temperature. In normal, healthy people, a rise in body temperature correlates with maximum alertness, and a drop to its lowest twenty-four-hour level occurs during sleep. If you want to use this method to confirm your sleep/wake/alertness cycle, you'll need a sensitive thermometer because the variation is no more than two degrees maximum. Record your temperature hourly from rising till bedtime. If you awaken during the night, take your temperature then, too. Unless you suffer a severe sleep disturbance, it isn't necessary to take your temperature every hour during the night.

If your results are typical, you'll discover two alertness peaks during the day, hours when you are able to record more cards than at any other time. One will probably be at around noon and the other—greater—one between 9:00 and 10:00 P.M., although individuals may vary an hour or more in either direction. You'll also notice a period when you are not alert, in the early-morning hours when you awaken. Many people also have a slump during the late afternoon. Office workers have long recognized that fact and have stated it pointedly: "Nothing good is ever accomplished after four P.M."

Let's assume that your personal chart turns out to be the same as the one illustrated. Here's some of the practical information it gives you: Don't plan to cram for a test, complete a homework assignment, prepare a report for your boss, or balance your checkbook by awakening early, downing six cups of coffee, and going to it. Maybe your body will be mobile at 5:00 A.M., but your brain won't be fully awake until 8:30 A.M. Until then try to do routine chores. That's the time when successful businessmen usually read their mail, skim the newspaper, and block out the day's schedule.

Even your body may be functioning under duress in the early-morning hours. Last night around midnight your adrenal hormone secretions probably reached a twenty-four-hour low. That helped bring about decreased body temperature and metabolism during the early-morning hours, both essential to sound sleep. Then, about 6:00 A.M., nature provided its own wake-up call, a hefty jolt of adrenal hormones. If you think it was tough getting up this morning, try it without the help of your adrenal gland.

It works, and we get moving. But it's something like starting our automobiles on a cold winter morning: Some of us race our engines too soon. Excessive physical stress during those early hours can be dangerous if we're not in good physical condition. That might well be the explanation behind the finding of Harvard cardiologist James E. Muller that most acute miocardial infarctions occur between 6:00 A.M. and noon.

Many fitness buffs arise early in the morning to jog, bicycle, or swim before going to work, and if they've achieved a substantial fitness level, they may well continue with such a schedule year after year without incident. As we mentioned earlier, we are adaptable creatures, enormously so, and our muscles and cardiorespiratory systems and capacity to metabolize energy can certainly become accustomed to early-morning stress, and when that happens, it's likely that our alertness levels, too, will increase earlier. In fact, your entire sleep/wake/alertness cycle may shift to meet the early-morning physical stress needs; you may go to bed earlier and awaken earlier.

But for the physically untrained, running to catch the train when you're not used to it, shoveling snow from the driveway so that you can get to work early in the morning, or any other unusual physical demands during your "down" period can have disastrous consequences.

The best time, according to the chart, to start the day's serious mental work is from about 10:00 A.M. to 2:00 P.M. Most of us will accomplish more in those four hours than we will in the five hours from 1:00 P.M. to 6:00 P.M.

There's also a best time to study for exams—and a worst time. A good many of us recall with some nostalgia those nightlong marathon exam-cramming sessions and the next day's tests. We took them with eyes bleary and brains befuddled and celebrated our passing grades as though we had won Olympic golds. In fact, the only credit we're due is for endurance. We could have retained a great deal more information with less effort had we simply been aware of our circadian alertness cycle. We'd have been refreshed and alert and made fewer silly errors.

But what fun would that have been?

As the class intellects already seemed to know instinctively, most of us learn best from midmorning through 10:00 P.M. or midnight. Those who suffer an afternoon slump (and those who want to use a slump as an excuse) have every right to relax and party from 4:00 to 7:00 P.M and hit the books from then till midnight.

Again it must be stressed that we're talking about those whose personal daily charts resemble the one illustrated.

Millions of people bound out of bed at 6:00 A.M., charging full speed ahead, and they don't do it just to humiliate the rest of us. They may go full speed throughout the day without the slightest slump, and by 10:00 P.M., while the rest of us are wondering what to watch on television, they're sound asleep again. You can see why it's important to keep your own chart if you're to make the best use of your daily potential.

The evening hours are often the best time for *creative* as well as intellectual undertakings, and it seems that the later the hour, the more imaginative we become. There is no consensus to explain that observation, but one theory is that as we grow more sleepy, the cerebral cortex loses some of its influence, and the unconscious drifts closer to the conscious. This might be a presleep stage, similar to the rapid eye movement (REM) stage of sleep, which is very shallow, in which we do most of our dreaming.

Now here are some ways to combine the daily and annual charts to your maximum advantage. Suppose you're planning a major building project—a garage, a boat, perhaps a Spring Room. Your daily chart gives you the hours when your mind and body are most alert and energetic. But your annual chart shows that there will be months when even your "most" isn't going to be very much. Major physical projects, the annual chart shows, are best undertaken when your body is functioning at its peak—during the late-spring and summer months.

If the project is an intellectual one—let's say you plan to write your memoirs—your intellectual and creative energy probably will reach its peak in the late summer and early fall. And your daily chart shows the hours at which you're likely to accomplish your best work.

Incidentally it's a good idea to prepare one alertness chart for Daylight Savings time, which begins in April, and another following the third week in October, after you've adjusted to Standard time. The time switch and reduced photoperiod might well cause a change in your sleep/wake rhythm and some reduction in the alertness phase.

In similar fashion, we'll use both the daily and annual charts in the next few chapters. Until you've plotted your entire annual chart, use the ones on pages 130 and 131 and page 142. You're not likely to vary from them dramatically.

Of all the ebbing, flowing rhythms going on within us each day, none is more important to our health—in fact, to our survival—than the sleep/wake cycle. Given the restrictions of our work and social schedules, few of us actually have the opportunity to allow our sleep/wake cycles to run free according to the dictates of our bodies and the environment. Yet we get by, and many of us aren't even aware that we are getting too little or too much sleep or that our alertness levels don't synchronize with our sleep/wake phases.

Millions of others are entirely aware of those problems. They sleep too much—or too little. They work swing shifts, which play more havoc on their systems than they or their employers realize. Many spend their days as walking zombies, never quite aware, never coming anywhere near fulfilling their potential. In the following chapter we'll learn how to get the sleep/wake cycle back on track.

The Harmony of Sleep: Maximizing Its Benefits

Sleep mildest of the gods, balm of the soul
Who puttest care to flight, soothest our bodies,
worn with hard ministries, and preparest them
for toil again.

—METAMORPHOSES

A deservedly anonymous British proverb maker once said, "Six hours' sleep for a man, seven for a woman, and eight for a fool." On the basis of that insight, we now may assume that its originator got plenty of sleep. No one can tell you how much sleep you really need. Babies sleep all but a few hours a day. During the teenage growth phase, youngsters need more sleep than they did a few years earlier. We all tend to get less sleep as we age; whether we *need* less or not hasn't been determined. Sleep requirements vary dramatically from one person to another. Albert Einstein slept almost twelve hours a night. Thomas Edison slept four. Both were brilliant, well-adjusted, and exceptionally productive men who lived long lives.

You're the only one who knows how much sleep you need: enough so that you awaken rested and refreshed. By that criterion, many of us don't get enough sleep. A survey reported by the Sleep Science Information Center has found that one-third of the population has problems sleeping, and half of those say the problem is serious.

One of the few positives about being a hibernator is that at least for a few months in late autumn and winter, you sleep soundly. While others are awakened by trivial sounds such as the wailing fire engines surrounding the house, you continue in peaceful repose. Those months are easily identified on your annual rhythms chart.

But what about the rest of the year? If you're among those with sleeping difficulties, this chapter will show you how to adjust your sleep phase to:

— Bring it in close alignment with your alertness phases
— Realign it with your working schedule
— Harmonize it with your family's sleep/wake cycle

Insomnia: Types and Causes

There are three types of insomnia, and most of us have suffered at least two: transient and short-term. These bouts last from a few days to three weeks. They're triggered by all sorts of emotional experiences: wonderful things like falling in love or buying a new home; troublesome ones such as additional responsibilities at work without compensating pay; you-be-the-judge experiences like getting married.

The more serious sleep disorders are long-term. These cases might start out the same as the short-term ones, especially those triggered by grief, sorrow, disappointment, and depression. After a few weeks the original problem may cease to be so troublesome as to disturb sleep, but by then the pattern of insomnia has become established. It seems more and more likely that the long-held theory that most sleeping problems are psychological is in error. There is good reason to believe that many, if not most, long-term insomnia victims have a biological condition.

Let's begin with these facts: From the hippo to the hummingbird, from the groundhog to the gazelle, all earth creatures and many in the sea cease activity and take a lengthy rest at least once in every twenty-four-hour period. That's more than a curious piece of trivia. It's a first clue that the sleep/wake/alertness cycle is somehow related to the photoperiod/scotoperiod (or light/dark) rhythm. The same phenomenon that controls the hibernation response also dominates our sleep and waking. Not so long ago scientists and the public alike believed we could go to sleep at any time of the day or night, awaken six to eight hours later refreshed, and function perfectly well. Now researchers know that isn't so. That's because certain endogenous rhythms important to inducing sound sleep are kept on time, or entrained, by the circadian light/dark cycle. When we get out of synchronization in our personal sleep/wake schedules, the result can be long-term insomnia.

In the last chapter we found that our body temperatures normally decline markedly at about the time most of us go to bed and continue dropping until shortly before we awaken. In contrast, poor sleepers maintain higher temperatures both before and during sleep, and although their temperatures decline, the drop is neither as steep nor as predictable as is found in the sound sleeper. In some cases the temperature doesn't begin to drop until well into the morning hours, and then, instead of rising an hour or so before awakening, it continues to drop for several hours after arousal. These people are typical night owls; they can party until three or four in the morning and sleep till noon unless social responsibility dictates otherwise. The real night owl will insist, truthfully, that he simply can't fall asleep much earlier than he does; he would just lie in bed wide-awake or would doze off to awaken immediately. That's because the night owl's body reaches its peak temperature, which we've seen in the last chapter corresponds to his or her alertness peak, hours later than is true of most people. While the clock says, "Sleep," the body says, "Party!"

A second rhythm that is synchronized with our sleep/wake/alertness cycle is that of the adrenal cortex hormone cortisol. This hormone has many functions in the body. Normally it reaches its maximum levels in the blood at around 7:00 P.M. and its minimum at about midnight, paralleling the temperature rhythm. But among poor sleepers, the cortisol cycle, like that of temperature, may be delayed by several hours.

At least part of the reason that those rhythms get out of step with the twenty-four-hour day is that, left to run free rather than be reset each day by light and darkness, they slow down. In various studies volunteers have lived in caves, underground shelters, windowless rooms, and laboratories for days, weeks, and months—conditions under which they received no time cues whatever. They had no idea whether the rest of the world was basking in the noonday sun or snoring in the dead of night. They simply followed their own "free-running" sleep/wake cycles, as dictated by their endogenous temperature and cortisol rhythms.

The result was that they soon began living approximately twenty-five-hour days.

Apparently these rhythms, like old-time windup clocks, tend to run slow and must be reset to the correct time each day. Otherwise, what started out as a rhythm—or phase—delay of only a few minutes on Monday can end up a real mess by Friday. Those clocks are supposed to be reset each day by an external cue, or *Zeitgeber*, the German word for time giver. The cue: the twenty-four-hour light/dark cycle.

Consider typical victims of transient or short-term insomnia. Whatever the reason, during the week they're unable to get much sleep, and comes the weekend, they do their best to catch up. They sleep until noon and arise feeling refreshed for the first time in days. It feels good, but like a great many things that feel good, it's unwise. That's because the pineal hormone melatonin, triggered by darkness and functioning as a sleep inducer, remained rather high in their blood until they opened their eyes and saw the light of day (even the light of an overcast day seems to be sufficient to curtail melatonin secretion for most people).

It appears that when sunlight stops the pineal's melatonin release, it remains stopped for at least twelve hours. Even sitting in a closet without the tiniest speck of light to keep you company won't trigger renewed melatonin production until approximately twelve hours after initial exposure to sunlight. What that means is that our insomniacs, planning to rise late and get to bed early in order to catch up on their sleep, won't begin to feel weary until a new batch of melatonin, secreted around midnight, begins to take effect a few hours later.[13]

If these insomniacs are being supported by spouses, parents, lovers, or the government, or are independently wealthy, they have no real problem. They simply go to bed later and awaken later each day until suddenly one morning they have circumnavigated the clock and awaken with the rest of us. In fact, many sleep clinics use precisely this approach in helping chronic insomniacs who can spare the two weeks or more involved.

That explains how emotional pressure or a temporary disturbance can lead to long-term insomnia, but many people insist that their prolonged sleeping difficulties developed without any recognizable reason. Thomas J. Savides and his colleagues at the Department of Psychiatry,

University of California, San Diego, and at San Diego's Veterans Administration Medical Center have an answer. They measured the amount of sunlight ten volunteers received during a typical day by having them attach illumination transducers to their foreheads (an interesting conversation starter). They found that medical students spent only twenty-six minutes a day getting sunshine. Fitness buffs spent four hours in sunlight. The average exposure was an hour and a half, most of it while the subjects commuted to and from work or school. And this is in sunny San Diego.

These people worked indoors under artificial light that was too weak to synchronize daily rhythms. Artificial light has been found to be effective only when brighter than 2,000 to 4,000 lux, the level reached by the sunlight boxes described in Chapter 3. Even then, exposure must last three to eight hours to be effective. The researchers concluded: "Thus, natural and artificial light exposure for many Americans may be insufficient for optimal circadian synchronization."

They add, "[T]he timing and total duration of daylight exposure for modern industrial man differs [*sic*] markedly from the natural conditions to which our species has evolved. It is of concern that dim artificial lighting may alter contemporary people's adaptation to our natural environment."

Synchronizing the Phases

One medical treatment for insomnia, known as phase delay, places patients on twenty-seven-hour days, until their actual bedtimes correlate with their bodies' temperature and hormone cycles. The regimen apparently has helped some people, as has another common treatment: partial sleep deprivation (PSD). This involves awakening patients for several hours during the night, usually in the latter half of it, such as from 1:30 A.M. to 6:00 A.M. Those treated with PSD fall asleep more quickly and easily than do insomniacs not receiving the therapy, and attest to having slept more soundly. They also say they feel better during the day.

But the problem with these approaches is that while they temporarily seem to unify circadian rhythms with the sleep schedule, they can't stop those rhythms from continuing to march to the beat of their own drummer—the twenty-five-hour day. As a result, they're often only temporarily beneficial.

Many sleep therapists are using a quicker, less expensive, and often more effective treatment: the same bright light originally employed to treat the hibernation response. It's now known that temperature and cortisol rhythms can be manipulated through properly timed exposure to artificial sunlight. As Alfred Lewy and Robert Sack Explain, "Phase delays [shifts to a later time] occur in response to light exposure during the first part of the subjective night and phase advances [shifts to an earlier time] occur in response to light exposure during the second part of the subjective night." Light exposure during the day seems to have no significant effect, according to the researchers, since, as we've said, melatonin production "has well-defined 'on' and 'off' periods that alternate like an hourglass at approximately 12-hour intervals." (Note that other researchers have recently reported that midday exposure to bright light is effective in some cases. Refer to Chapter 3 for details.)

Lewy and Sack tested their theory on eight depressed patients with poor sleep histories. For one week they permitted the subjects to sleep only between 10:00 P.M. and 6:00 A.M. and prevented them from being near bright light after 5:00 P.M. That should have led to high melatonin levels by 7:00 P.M. It didn't. The investigators found that "the time of the onset in melatonin production occurred significantly later in the patients than in the healthy control subjects."

The following week each of the patients sat in front of bright light from 6:00 A.M. to 8:00 A.M. daily. They experienced two changes, neither of which will come as a surprise to the hibernator using bright lights. They ceased to be depressed. And they began to produce melatonin at the normal time each evening so that their biological and social sleeping rhythms became synchronized.

In another study, this one at the Psychiatric University Clinic in Vienna, Austria, patients received two light treatments, one from 5:00 to 9:00 P.M. and the second from 6:00 to 9:00 A.M. the next day. By that night, they slept significantly longer and more soundly, with fewer awakenings. Upon arising the next morning, they reported increased senses of well-being and demonstrated objectively measured improvements in attention and concentration.

Here's the bright light exposure schedule that seems most effective in treating sleeping problems:

If you find yourself *getting sleepy too soon,* use bright light in the evening, between 6:00 or 7:00 P.M. and 10:00 P.M., and keep away from bright light in the morning (until 8:00 or 9:00 A.M.), although you should awaken by 6:00 A.M.

If you want to be able to *sleep and awaken earlier* than you do, you need bright artificial light between arising at 6:00 A.M. and 8:00 or 9:00 A.M. Keep away from bright light after 4:00 P.M.

Here's a typical treatment approach to the night owl syndrome. First, determine how long you tend to sleep when not awakened by outside disturbances of any kind—the amount of sleep you really need. Let's assume it's seven hours. What time must you awaken to get to work on time? If the answer is 7:00 A.M., and you want to start with a half hour of light therapy, you must awaken at 6:30 A.M. and be in bed by 11:00 P.M. (We're providing thirty minutes to fall asleep.)

Regardless of the time you actually go to bed the first night, set your "alarm clock" for 6:30 A.M. This will be an unusual alarm clock. Chances are you'll have the only one in the neighborhood. It will consist of eight fluorescent light bulbs, each four feet long and forty watts, in fixtures as described in Chapter 3. They will be set up on each side of your bed, approximately three feet from it, so that whether you're facing to the left or the right, you're going to be blasted with brilliant synthetic sunshine at precisely 6:30 A.M., and even burying your head under pillows won't help much. A simple electric timer, available at any hardware store at a cost ranging upwards from ten dollars, along with a multioutlet adapter, is all you need.

If you're married, you're facing a major negotiating problem. Does your spouse wish to be awakened at 6:30 A.M. to the visual equivalent of blaring trumpets? Does said spouse prefer that you sleep in the guest room? Might this lead to divorce?

After these obstacles have been overcome, set the light units up safely on chairs or tables so that they are at eye level while you are reclining. Be sure not to use them after 5:00 P.M., even to test their positioning. Now go to sleep.

As soon as you awaken, sit up and open yourself to the cheerful, sunny brightness pouring over you. Don't move away from the lights until you actually feel your body temperature increasing and your energy expanding, compelling you to get up and start the day on its way. In any case, stay under the lights, glancing at them occasionally while reading, planning your day, or whatever for at least half an hour.

If after two days you don't notice clear-cut improvement in both the quality of your sleep and your desire to sleep earlier, set the timer to 6:00 A.M. and spend an hour under the lights.

Remember, don't extend the photoperiod in the evening. Instead, tack extra hours onto the morning, and wake up earlier. The longer the period of darkness at the end of the day, the more melatonin is released into your bloodstream. That natural sleep potion, along with your own efforts to relax your body physically through stretch exercises,[14] will help you fall asleep hours earlier than usual. Continue the process as long as necessary and until sleeping and rising on the new schedule become automatic.

To stay up longer in the evening and sleep longer in the morning, simply reverse the cycle. Use synthetic sunlight for an hour or more each evening as daylight wanes and before melatonin production begins.

If you find yourself craving more sleep than you need, you may be getting insufficient sunlight. The preferable approach is to spend more time out of doors, both morning and evening. Or increase artificial light exposure in increments of one additional hour every two days until you find the amount that's effective: half in the morning; half at night.

If you continue to crave sleep in spite of the light regimen, or if your sleep is fragmented and too short, with arousal before the lights go on, chances are good that you're suffering depression, although you may not even be aware of it. Since "hidden" depression can affect many aspects of your life, including job performance and sexuality, it's a good idea to seek professional help.

Sleep problems grow more common as we age. In fact, researchers report that the most obvious change in bodily function among those forty to seventy years old is in sleep patterns. About 40 percent of those over sixty-five complain of inability to fall asleep quickly or stay asleep.

The culprit could be a decrease in melatonin production by the pineal, which commonly calcifies as we grow older. In the absence of research in the field, it can't do any harm to rely on anecdotal testimony from those elderly who (1) make it a point to get plenty of sunlight, especially early in the morning, and (2) sleep in total darkness. Many of them report that although their age makes them prime candidates for sleeping difficulties, they experience none. Others who have moved from the North to retirement communities in the Sun Belt also have noticed dramatic improvements in their ability to sleep.

Hazards of the Swing Shift

Of all the many areas in which we humans live out our lives in intentional disharmony with our own nature, none is more blatant and dangerous than the rotating or swing shift in the workplace. Yet 26 percent of adult men and 16 percent of adult women in the United States hold jobs which require that they shift their working schedules from days to evenings to nights, sometimes on a weekly basis.

Physically that internal chaos leads to 20 percent more heart attacks than are suffered by nonshift workers. Swing shift employees also suffer ulcers and other stomach problems and insomnia.

Large corporations have become concerned about the problem because obviously poor health leads to absenteeism and a decrease in productivity, and that means lost profits. In fact, the productivity level of about 56 percent of all night shift workers is zero during at least some portion of the night, according to clinical psychologist Richard M. Coleman, former codirector of the Sleep Disorders Clinic at the Stanford University Medical Center. That's because the workers routinely fall asleep on the job.

Changing workers' shifts regularly can cost more than profits, though. As David Dinges, sleep researcher at the University of Pennsylvania, notes, the chemical disaster at Bhopal, India, occurred at midnight, during the late-night shift. The nuclear accident at Three Mile Island occurred at 4:00 A.M. The Chernobyl disaster began at 2:00 A.M. All three catastrophes were traced to worker error.

Harvard physiologist Martin C. Moore-Ede has the right idea when he says, "Humans should not be placed on rotating shift schedules that strain physiological capacity—or, just like machines pushed beyond their design specifications, they'll break down."

Moore-Ede, researcher Richard Coleman, and Harvard chronobiologist Charles A. Czeisler began enlightening big industry about the dangers of ignoring Mother Nature in 1980, when Great Salt Lake Minerals & Chemicals in Utah requested their help. The company's hundred swing shift employees reported being wide-awake during the day at home and often asleep on the job.

The night shift itself wasn't the culprit, for only 8 percent of those at other companies who permanently worked night shifts reported overwhelming sleepiness at work. The difficulty occurred when schedules were switched every week or two. Let's say it again: We humans are very adaptable. But we simply can't handle sleeping from 11:00 P.M. to 6:00 A.M. one week, 9:00 A.M.

to 4:00 P.M. the next, and 2:00 A.M. to 9:00 A.M. the third week. That's the schedule the Utah plant had, and it's by no means unusual.

The researchers changed a few things. First, they limited rotations to once every three weeks, and the workers were given several days off between shifts during which they could adapt to the new schedule. Secondly, they changed the rotation schedule from the original—from days to late nights to early evenings—to one in line with the circadian twenty-five-hour day: days; early evenings; late nights. Thus the schedule actually moved in the same direction as the normal phase delay. If workers on such a schedule sleep in totally dark rooms, their exposure to sunlight upon awakening, even at 4:00 P.M., will suppress melatonin for at least twelve hours. According to Charles A. Czeisler and his colleagues at the Harvard Medical School, an entraining effect—bringing the temperature and cortisol rhythms into synchronization with the required sleep schedule—could occur in as few as one or two days.

Greatly preferable, of course, is elimination of the swing shift altogether. Even under the best of circumstances, continually switching sleep/wake cycles puts the body under chronic stress. At the least workers on such schedules should be eligible for hazardous duty pay.

A better alternative being practiced by a number of companies is the establishment of permanent evening and late-night shifts. Employees receive more pay for accepting these schedules. The major complaint is that working nights interferes with the employees' social lives. But many people don't mind that inconvenience, especially if the pay increment is substantial.

Where permanent shifts aren't feasible, Dr. Czeisler, director of the Neuroendocrine Laboratory at Brigham and Women's Hospital, Boston, suggests that employers "install bright lights at factories. Then, workers on rotating shifts could get therapeutic doses of bright light on the evening shift to reset their internal clocks in preparation for the next week's rotation to the night shift."

While it will certainly increase the utility bills, it's a step that all industry will take sooner or later—if not through pity, then for profit.

The sleep/wake cycle isn't the only one to go haywire on occasion. Every autumn millions of people—even those who don't recognize a hibernation response—lose control of their appetites. They have three solid meals a day—plus a couple. And they gain frightful amounts of weight.

Perhaps you'll be surprised to know that according to your natural circadian rhythms, those five meals you may be having each day may be too few. And they're probably not in the right order.

And they're almost certainly not the right food.

Read on.

The Antihibernation Diet:
Eating for Energy and Health

*By eating what is sufficient, man is enabled
to work; he is hindered from working and
becomes heavy, idle and stupid if he eats too much.*
                                    —SOCRATES

Let's start with a simple fact: There's no sense trying to lose weight during the late fall and early winter if you live where it gets cold during that time of year. You're not *supposed* to lose weight then. In the grand scheme of things, you're not even supposed to *want* to. And unless you're put together with a very peculiar set of genes, you won't be able to.

We've already seen that your body, bless it, anticipates a life-threatening food shortage as the days grow shorter. It becomes much more efficient in its use of calories. You'll use 10 percent fewer calories to bicycle a mile in November than you will in April.

So you maintain your usual activity level and reduce your calorie intake by, say, 20 percent. That would certainly result in lost weight regardless of season. True. Except that try as you might, you'd not maintain your activity level. Your body would interpret the calorie shortage as starvation, one of the three phenomena capable of triggering a hibernation response. As Charles P. Lyman

162

of the Department of Anatomy at the Harvard Medical School has written, "even in normally nonhibernating species, it is possible to induce daily torpor by food deprivation." Your activity level would plummet. You would sleep. Even your synthetic sunshine and your Spring Room could not counter the effects of calorie deprivation.

What's more, the only way you'll manage to cut your calorie consumption by 20 percent is to staple your lips together. At no time of the year does your appetite compare with that of the cold months. If you lacked the willpower to diet successfully in the spring and summer, don't even think about it now.

Besides, when the bitter chill of winter descends and you continue with the outdoor acclimatization program, that ravenous appetite will be justifiable; you'll be needing more fuel for the furnace in order to cope with the cold.

In research with volunteers lightly clothed in extreme cold (minus 20°F), scientists have found that heat production increased by 300 to 400 percent to keep the core temperature stable. Creating all that heat requires a lot of food. In fact, as nutrition expert Marjorie Edman points out, the overriding need to maintain the body's core temperature, even when food supply is adequate, may explain "the slower rate of growth observed among the young in colder climates compared with that in the temperate zones." Although you're not likely to lounge on the patio in loincloth or bikini in sub-zero temperatures, the fact is that if you spend as much time out of doors in the winter as you should, you're going to have a healthy appetite and increased nutritional demands.

To repeat, you'll have a frightfully difficult time of it losing weight in the winter, and it's an unhealthy proposition in the bargain. As we'll see, you'll need more, not fewer, nutrients during the cold months—vitamins, minerals, protein, as well as high-calorie carbohydrates. That doesn't mean that you should give up the ship, throw in the towel, abandon all hope, and eat anything remotely digestable for three months. You still need a diet, a weight *control* diet, balanced according to the particular nutritional demands imposed by cold weather.

Specifically, we need to control the amount of *potential energy* we eat.

All the cells of our bodies have their special jobs to do. Some produce hormones or enzymes; others help build additional bone and muscle cells. The number of cell functions is almost beyond comprehension. Yet every one of those cells derives its energy from one simple carbohydrate. It's the sugar that makes grapes sweet. It's found in abundance in plants, fruits, and milk. Some people call it dextrose or corn sugar, but it's most commonly known as glucose. Glucose is the fuel that keeps the body running.

But it would be virtually impossible to meet all our glucose needs through glucose-containing foods. Yet short of starvation, we're not likely to suffer a glucose shortage since any number of nutrients can be converted to the simple sugar. One of these is fats, both in our diets and in our own adipose tissue.

Fats

If you should ever find yourself stranded at the North Pole, you'll thank heaven and your weak will for every ounce of fat between you and the cold. That lard, which you've always despised so bitterly, is about twice as good a thermal insulator as muscle. What's more, one gram of fat (about one twenty-eighth of an ounce), when burned to keep you from freezing, will release about nine calories of heat—more than twice that of any other fuel source.

(Protein and carbohydrates release four calories per gram.) Fat is a major part of the diets of Eskimos and others who spend a great deal of time outdoors in severe cold.

But there's a basic difference between winter in Chicago, for example, and at the North Pole. While diets of five thousand calories and more daily might be essential under arctic conditions, much of it as fat, such a regimen would leave most of us rotund in short order. We just can't use up the calories. We'd store them in the liver as glycogen and all over the place as rolls, bulges, and wrinkles of fat.

We don't need any more fats in our diets, especially saturated fats—those solid at room temperature and usually from animal sources. You already know that high-fat diets have been repeatedly linked to cardiovascular disease—heart attacks and strokes. Unless you average a couple of hours daily out of doors in strenuous activity during the winter, only 30 percent or less of your daily calorie intake should come from fats. Don't misunderstand. Some fats are essential to our health. But there are fats in almost everything we eat, from watermelon and raisins to rye bread and sunflower seeds. Unless you live and work in the frigid cold, you'll get all the fats you need without trying. It's probably easier than you think to avoid them, if you follow the Antihibernation Diet, which stresses eating the right foods rather than avoiding the wrong ones.

While avoiding saturated fats, use *un*saturated ones, like corn oil and olive oil, when possible. Foods containing saturated fats and cholesterol should play only a minor, if any, part in your diet. Specifically steer clear of hydrogenated vegetable shortening, butter, lard, coconut oil, and cottonseed oil. Many nuts, especially peanuts, almonds, and Brazil nuts, are also high in fats.

Carbohydrates

There are three types of carbohydrate: simple, complex, and more complex. Glucose is one of the simple ones (also called monosaccharides). The two other monosaccharides, galactose (from milk) and fructose (primarily from fruits), are converted into glucose during digestion.

Structurally more complex are the disaccharides. Lactose, which comes from milk, can be broken down into one molecule of galactose and one of glucose. Another disaccharide is sucrose, ordinary table sugar, composed of one molecule of glucose and one of fructose.

There are still more carbohydrates, the polysaccharides, the most important of which is starch. Ultimately starch breaks down into two molecules of glucose.

The primary source of calories in the Antihibernation Diet is complex carbohydrates. For one thing, that's what our appetites will crave, and the instincts of hibernators all over the world can't be wrong.

There is another very good reason to get energy from complex carbohydrates. The process of reducing them to glucose itself requires extra energy. The net result is fewer calories from complex than from simple carbohydrates and from protein.

That was the finding in a study in which soldiers wearing light clothing were exposed to an extremely cold minus 28°F for up to eight hours. In order to maintain normal weight and body temperature, they needed a 91 percent increase in calories when those calories came from a high-carbohydrate diet, but only a 62 percent increase when the calories came from a low-carbohydrate, high-protein diet.

The increased metabolism of the high-complex-carbohydrate diets also produced an unexpected side effect: It delayed the decrease in the soldiers' core and surface temperatures; they stayed warm longer.

Still, we won't abandon all restraint when it comes to complex carbohydrates in the Antihibernation Diet. That's because if they're not utilized for energy, they can be converted to fat and stored for emergency needs. You already know that. You saw it last winter in your mirror. And you're perhaps still waiting for the emergency that will make use of it.

About 50 percent of the calories in the Antihibernation Diet come from carbohydrates.

Protein

People can survive on diets deficient in either fats or carbohydrates. When one is absent, the other can be broken down into glucose and used for energy. What may come as a surprise is that when the diet lacks both fats and carbohydrates, the body has still another source of glucose. In an emergency even protein can be converted to energy fuel. It's another of the body's awesome capacities for adaptation and survival.

But protein itself has no stand-ins, no understudies. We can't get along without it for even a few minutes. As nutritionist Marjorie Edman says, "In the complex we call metabolism protein contributes not only to the production of energy but also to hormone and enzyme synthesis." The very catalysts that trigger energy release, thereby keeping every cell and organ in the body alive and functioning, are made from protein.

That doesn't mean that if we miss our quota of protein for a day, we'll promptly drop dead. What *will* happen is that our bodies will quietly begin breaking down muscle tissue and using the protein therein for more immediate needs—perhaps the fuel to keep us warm if there are no

167

carbohydrates or fats available; perhaps the enzymes and hormones that are also required for the process. We can go on like that for a maximum of about sixty days, tearing down the house to keep the wood stove burning. After that there's not enough muscle tissue left to sustain life. At that point the body has lost up to 50 percent of its muscle mass, some of it from such vital organs as the heart and liver. We needn't waste away to skin and bones to die of protein loss. A deteriorated heart will do the trick.

Of course, apart from being stranded in some remote zone of the world, you'd have to make a truly dedicated effort to die of protein starvation. It's not difficult at all, however, to develop a protein *deficiency*. That's because your metabolism speeds up in cold temperatures, and metabolism exhausts protein stores. Symptoms of subclinical (not serious enough to require medical treatment) protein deficiency include chronic fatigue, a lack of energy, chilliness even in temperatures that others find comfortable, lethargy, and depression.

These latter symptoms are particularly important to us because they mimic—and may be related to—the hibernation response. To understand how they are caused by a protein deficiency, we must learn something about neurotransmitters. They're chemicals found in neurons, or nerve cells, and they're released when the cell fires, instantly stimulating an adjacent neuron. Without neurotransmitters the brain couldn't communicate with the rest of the body. The telephone lines would be down.

Three of these neurotransmitters are important in regulating our moods. One is serotonin. It's produced from tryptophan, one of the amino acids in protein. The neurotransmitter serotonin tells the brain cells to relax the body, to feel drowsy, even to sleep. (Some researchers believe there's a special relationship between melatonin and the serotonin from which it originates and that it is actually serotonin which is directly responsible for some aspects of both the hibernation response and the sleep/wake cycle.)

The other two neurotransmitters that affect our moods are dopamine and norepinephrine. They're manufactured from another amino acid, tyrosine. While serotonin tells the brain to calm down, these two chemicals give opposite orders: Fight. Run. Get the energy flowing. Come to attention!

Although the body manufactures some amino acids, the only way to get the essential tryptophan and tyrosine is through diet. Deficiencies in either or both of these amino acids can affect moods. As Dr. Richard Wurtman of the Massachusetts Institute of Technology explains in the April 1982 issue of *Scientific American*, "Most psychiatrists who seek biochemical explanations of mental illness think that in many patients depression reflects inadequate neurotransmission mediated by either norepinephrine or serotonin. If norepinephrine release is inadequate in certain regions of the brain of some depressed patients, the administration of tyrosine could conceivably be helpful to them."

The Antihibernation Diet is designed to keep depression at bay as well as to provide energy and enthusiasm throughout the day. That's why we stress protein, and particularly tyrosine-rich foods such as those listed below, until dinner. That's also why we avoid traditional breakfast foods like the stack of pancakes, bowl of cereal, muffins, toast, and other baked products until the evening. Those complex carbohydrate foods stimulate insulin secretion, and insulin drives most amino acids from the blood and into the muscle tissue. Tryptophan is an exception. It's bound to the plasma protein albumin, so it stays in the blood and is used to increase serotonin production.

That's why an all-carbohydrate diet has been found to decrease intellectual performance and coordination and to make some people very sleepy. We crave carbohydrates, we need them for energy, and we shall have our fill of them—at dinner and thereafter, when drowsiness will be a virtue. But not during the day, when we need to be intellectually sharp and energetic.

The Antihibernation Diet stresses protein throughout the day, including tyrosine-rich foods. Although you'll want to avoid foods which are good sources of tryptophan, that amino acid is far less common in most foods than are other proteins. That's good news because tryptophan has to compete with the protein molecules that greatly outnumber it in order to bind with the relatively few carrier molecules that transport them across the blood-brain barrier where the neurotransmitters are produced. The result is that as long as dietary carbohydrates are low, so are tryptophan and serotonin.

Incidentally, alcohol, like carbohydrates, should be avoided during the day. If you have trouble sleeping at night, however, a midevening cocktail, a glass of wine, or beer will possibly work as well as an over-the-counter sleeping pill, and it might even taste better. Recently researchers have suggested that late-night heavy drinkers might actually be self-medicators, seeking the calming and sleep-inducing effects of alcohol as an antidote to insomnia.

The Mood Foods

Use these foods to fine-tune your moods. If you find yourself becoming irritable and tense during the day on the high-protein diet, reduce your consumption of foods rich in tyrosine. For an even more calming effect, include some tryptophan-rich foods. Reverse the process if the problem is low energy levels or mild depression. That's how the Antihibernation Diet works. Armed with all the information you need, you custom design it to meet your unique needs.

TYROSINE FOODS (DURING THE DAY)

Eggs
Green beans
Lean meat
Natural aged cheese
Peas
Seafood
Seaweed
Skim milk
Tofu (bean curd)
Whole wheat bread
Yogurt

TRYPTOPHAN FOODS (DURING THE EVENING)

Bananas
Beef
Cookies
Dates
Figs
Pastas
Peanuts
Pineapples
Processed cheese
Sweets
Turkey

We mentioned earlier that we have a greater demand for all nutrients, not merely those providing calories, when we confront the prolonged cold. Without them, temperatures low enough to make most people merely uncomfortable will seem intolerable to you. For the most part that's because glucose alone isn't sufficient to carry out the metabolism that keeps you warm in the cold. Here are some of the other essential nutrients.

Iron

John L. Beard, Ph.D., assistant professor of nutrition at Penn State University, is subjecting some young women volunteers to memorable experiences these days. They are not pleasant experiences. After sitting for forty-five minutes up to their shoulders in small tanks of delightfully warm water, they maintain a quiet stoicism while buckets of ice are dumped around them. Soon the water temperature falls to 82°F, 16 degrees below normal body temperature. Each volunteer remains in the icy water for an hour.

During that time her body temperature drops. That's unavoidable. It's the amount of the decrease that fascinates Beard. If she has adequate blood iron levels, her temperature will fall about three-fourths of a degree. Those with minor tissue-iron deficiencies will lose a full degree. But the temperatures of iron-deficiency anemics will drop 1.5 degrees or more. Among homoiotherms, creatures whose survival requires a relatively stable core temperature, a decrease of a couple of degrees can be serious business.

Why is iron necessary to maintaining body temperature? Let's review some facts we learned in Chapters 4 and 5. The increased metabolism necessary to maintain body temperature is triggered by the neuroendocrine system. First, the sympathetic nervous system responds instantly to the cold, producing norepinephrine—yes, the very same that's manufactured from the amino acid tyrosine. Norepinephrine not only snaps the mind to alertness but causes an instant speedup of metabolism. That's why even hibernators respond to the brisk, cool air of a sunny winter day by feeling more awake and energetic.

But norepinephrine can keep the fires burning, so to speak, only so long. Within a few minutes the thyroid glands of people with adequate iron stores mobilize the hormone thyroxine and convert it to a more active compound called T_3 (triiodothyronine). Apparently norepinephrine is the tinder that gets the fire going, and T_3 is the log that generates heat over the long haul.

In studies with rats, Beard has found that "iron-deficient rats had depressed levels of T_3, and when you cold-stressed them, their T_3 levels didn't rise as much as a normal animal's would. So they couldn't increase their metabolic rate, even though their norepinephrine levels were higher. They got cold, they got hypothermic, and if they were anemic enough, they died."

In humans the response is almost the same. The one difference: The sympathetic nervous system tries to compensate for the lack of T_3 by pumping out enormous amounts of norepinephrine, and in humans the metabolic rate continues to shoot up, consuming great quantities of calories. But somehow the fire doesn't burn hot enough, and body temperature continues to fall.

If you've just decided that an iron deficiency (perhaps combined with an ice water bath) sounds like the perfect diet, the quacks have beaten you to it. Says Beard: "At the turn of the century hucksters from Europe made a killing selling hookworms to American women who wanted to lose weight. The worms caused a serious blood and iron loss, which led to a higher metabolic rate to maintain body temperatures." No doubt the worms did the job. So would slitting an artery.

In addition to its crucial role in the production of oxygen-carrying blood cells, iron appears to be essential in forming thyroid hormones. As Beard, who is to complete his study shortly, explains, "I think we're going to find that iron-deficient people are functionally hypothyroid. That limitation on the activity of the thyroid hormone system may be the key defect in iron deficiency."

We can't keep warm in the cold without adequate supplies of iron, and many of us—particularly women—may well suffer cold intolerance each winter because of a deficiency. Women need 18 milligrams of iron a day—the equivalent of 4.5 ounces of calf's liver—to stay ahead of what they lose each month through menstruation. More than 11 percent of U.S. women under forty-five years of age and *half* of those in third world countries suffer from iron deficiency. Pregnant women, young children, and adolescents are also vulnerable. Iron deficiency is the single most common nutritional problem worldwide.

The Antihibernation Diet stresses an adequate iron intake.

Calcium

The rhythmic beating of a heart, contracting of muscles, integrity of cells, firmness of bone—these are just a few bodily functions requiring calcium. It's also vital to the activity of the nervous system. All this is true throughout the year, as much so in January as in July.

But a study by Dr. Joseph Bohlen of the University of Wisconsin has shown that a great deal of ingested calcium is wasted during the winter. He and his wife studied ten Eskimos around the clock for ten days in each of the four seasons, visiting each subject's house every two hours to gather urine samples, to record oral temperature, blood pressure, and pulse, and to make tests. Among their findings: The excretion of calcium in the urine was eight to ten times higher in the winter than in the summer.

It's been suggested that an arctic mental ailment known as winter madness may be related to this enormous increase in calcium loss. If the calcium leaves the body in urine, it can't be utilized by the nervous system.

The problem is no doubt related at least as much to lack of sunlight as to diet, and we'll discuss that in detail in the next chapter. For now let's simply stress that we need a great deal more calcium in our diets during the winter than throughout the rest of the year if we're to keep our minds and bodies functioning at their best. The Antihibernation Diet well surpasses the minimum daily requirement of calcium.

Magnesium

This mineral regulates more than three hundred enzyme systems in our bodies. Except for zinc, no element approaches the scope of magnesium's importance. Yet until very recently few researchers have seriously studied it.

Magnesium plays a role in the normal functioning of the heart and other muscles and in building bones. It's essential to production of the electrolytes which keep the nervous system functioning properly. It plays a crucial role in protein synthesis—remember those amino acids tyrosine and tryptophan? And of particular significance to the hibernator, it activates the enzymes responsible for fat and carbohydrate metabolism, the process that produces body heat.

Magnesium is relatively plentiful in most diets, from cocoa and nuts to unprocessed cereals, beans, green leafy vegetables, and seafood, even in drinking water in some areas. For that reason a clear-cut magnesium deficiency is rare.

Borderline deficiencies may be much more common, especially among diabetics, those on severe diets, people with kidney disorders, and those with diarrhea-causing diseases. The Antihibernation Diet is high in magnesium, well above the recommended daily allowance (RDA). In fact, the diet contains at least the recommended daily allowance of all essential vitamins and minerals.

Use the following list in preparing your daily menu. Be sure to include *more* than the RDA of magnesium in your winter diet: 350 to 400 milligrams (mg) for men; 300 mg for women; 50 to 250 mg for children.

Foods Rich in Magnesium

FOOD	MAGNESIUM (mg per 100 g)
Egg yolk	1,500
Instant coffee	456
Powdered cocoa	420
Wheat bran breakfast cereal	420
Cashew nuts	267
Dry soybeans	265
Peanut butter	173
White beans	170
Dry oatmeal	144
Skim milk	143

NOTE: Deep green leafy vegetables are also a fine source of magnesium. Keep in mind that a hundred grams is more than three ounces. While that's not much milk to drink, it's quite a lot of dried instant coffee.

Vitamin C

The Black Plague notwithstanding, rats have undoubtedly done more good than harm for humankind. Many scientific discoveries have been made at their expense. Consider the lowly rodents that were condemned to a frigid environment for months at a stretch, only to have their organs analyzed for weight and ascorbic acid, or vitamin C, content. Through such experiments we have learned, in the words of Alan C. Burton, Ph.D., professor of biophysics at the University of Western Ontario, that "the survival rate is increased, and the degree of cold the rats can withstand is directly related to, the dose of ascorbic acid."

Typically the adrenal glands of animals exposed to cold increase in size in order to produce the greater quantities of hormones needed to generate more body heat. But when vitamin C is added to the diet, it's been found that (1) greater quantities of the hormones are produced, and (2) the adrenals *don't* grow larger, but the vitamin seems to increase their capacity to produce.

That's the case in experiments with guinea pigs, rabbits, monkeys, and humans. In all studies, vitamin C increased the resistance to cold and diminished its damaging effects. But these processes increase the amount of vitamin C needed in your diet. That is why the Antihibernation Diet is high in vitamin C, well above the recommended daily allowance.

Here's an important point: If you're one of those people who must wear a sweater when others are comfortable in light shirts or blouses, if you always find yourself shivering even when the temperature is in the high sixties or low seventies, if in the winter you can never be com-

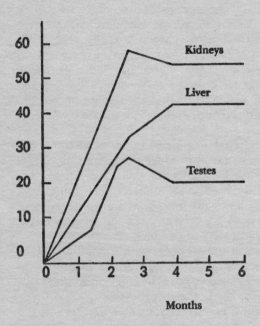

Cold temperatures increase the body's demand for vitamin C, or ascorbic acid. Here is the percentage of increase in ascorbic acid content of kidneys, liver, and testes of rats kept in the cold as compared to those living in normal temperatures.
(From Dugal and Therien, *Canadian Journal of Research*, Sect. E., 25, 1, 113, 1947.)

fortable out of doors unless you're interred under a mound of clothing, your problem may very well be a nutritional one. *Among the six nutrients found to be low in the diets of American women according to a recent survey, four were iron, calcium, magnesium, and vitamin C.* (The other two, in case you're curious, were vitamin A and vitamin B.) Most women were getting less than 70 percent of the recommended daily allowance of those nutrients—and keep in mind that we need even more of them in winter if we spend much time out of doors. You simply must follow a diet high in these nutrients if you feel chronically cold and you know the condition isn't related to a circulatory problem.

Here they are again—essential "winter warrior" nutrients and the National Research Council's recommended daily allowances of each. You'll need these figures to plan your daily meals.

Recommended Daily Dietary Allowances for Calcium, Magnesium, Iron, and Vitamin C

Revised 1980 Food and Nutrition Board, National Academy of Sciences—National Research Council

	AGE (years)	CALCIUM (mg)	MAGNESIUM (mg)	IRON (mg)	VITAMIN C (mg)
Children	0.0–0.5	360	50	10	35
	0.5–1.0	540	70	15	35
	1–3	800	150	15	45
	4–6	800	200	10	45
	7–10	800	250	10	45
Male	11–14	1,200	350	18	50
	15–18	1,200	400	18	60
	19–22	800	350	10	60

	AGE (years)	CALCIUM (mg)	MAGNESIUM (mg)	IRON (mg)	VITAMIN C (mg)
	23–50	800	350	10	60
	51+	800	350	10	60
Female	11–14	1,200	300	18	50
	15–18	1,200	300	18	60
	19–22	800	300	18	60
	23–50	800	300	18	60
	51+	800	300	10	60
	Pregnant	+400	+150	18	+20
	Lactating	+400	+150	18	+40

Scheduling Meals

Having discussed *what* we need to eat, we come to the matter of when. Considering the mountain of typewriter ribbons sacrificed to creating weight-loss diets over the years, it's troublesome that so little has been said about just *when* throughout the day those nutrients should be ingested. Our digestive processes, like so many other aspects of our physiology, operate according to their own circadian rhythms. And the timing of our meals in relation to these cycles will determine to a large degree whether the food we eat is quickly utilized in metabolism, is stored as fat, or spends the night slopping around in our stomachs.

Here is what we know: The heartiest meal of the day shouldn't be the dinner we have each evening. It should be breakfast. That's when we're most likely to use calories rather than to store them as fat. In an experiment at the University of Minnesota Dr. Franz Halberg allowed seven healthy volunteers to eat only one meal a day, consisting of two thousand calories. He also strictly regulated their exercise levels. Halberg found that when his subjects ate the meal in the evening, their weight either increased or remained the same. When they ate the same food an hour after awakening in the morning, they lost weight.

The explanation is simple. You'll recall that body temperature and cortisol rhythms reach a low at around midnight. Both are associated with metabolism, and when metabolism is low, so is the demand for calories. Instead of being utilized, late-night calorie sources are stored as glycogen or fat. The next morning's breakfast provides the energy requirements for much of the day, so the calories of the night before never get utilized.

Breakfast should not only be the main meal of the day but be a far cry in content from the breakfasts we're accustomed to. Although the Antihibernation Diet will have you formulating your own menus from recommended foods, the sample menu (pages 201–202) will undoubtedly make you blink twice. High-protein chicken for *breakfast?* Yes. There's simply no justification for the rut most of us have fallen into in terms of breakfast foods. We've somehow become thoroughly brainwashed into believing that if it's not pancakes, French toast, waffles, bagels, eggs, toast, or pastry, it's not edible before noon. So boring and unimaginative are those selections every day of our lives that it's no wonder most adult Americans simply avoid breakfast completely. More to the point: With the exception of eggs, the typical breakfast is top-heavy with sleep-inducing carbohydrates.

The Antihibernation Diet *will* stand your meal planning on its head, providing protein and carbohydrates when you need them, not when tradition says you should have them.

Here's one of the best—and most revolutionary—aspects of the Antihibernation Diet: We urge you to have as many as six meals between waking and 9:00 P.M. Humans are instinctive nibblers—grazers, if you wish. Under circumstances that permit it, many of us nibble from six to twelve times a day, some of us stopping only long enough to eat our main meals. The Antihibernation Diet takes that natural tendency into consideration. Theoretically we need never stop eating. We can have a meal every two and a half hours, six meals a day—and still keep our weight under control.

The key, of course, is that the calorie content of the six meals must be the same as three ordinary meals. In our sample menus we show how easily and successfully this can be done.

If you have doubts that more frequent meals are worth the trouble, consider this: Researchers have found that both performance and body temperature maintenance were higher when volunteers ate three meals within eight hours than when they had only one meal containing the same calories. (Two meals were also found to be better than none during a six-hour period, but that shouldn't surprise anyone.)

After a meal is digested, whether large or small, excess carbohydrates and fats are converted to glycogen for storage in the liver and to fat (we can see where that gets stored). The body has only ten or fifteen minutes' worth of glucose, its ultimate energy fuel, circulating in the blood. As that is utilized, the body replenishes it by converting glycogen to glucose. But fat stores are a different story. They're the body's savings account, and the body is stingy about making withdrawals. Instead, it responds to low sugar levels with the minor stomach spasms that we interpret as hunger.

More than sixty years ago researchers began to suspect that those hunger contractions followed a roughly ninety-minute cycle. In 1965 Dr. Stanley Friedman and colleagues at Mount Sinai Hospital in New York City virtually proved it. They created a cozy room in which each volunteer spent nine hours alone reading, writing, listening to music—whatever activities he wished, as long as they didn't involve time cues. The best thing about being a volunteer for this study was that each had access to a stocked refrigerator, a pot of fresh coffee, soft drinks, and cigarettes. From behind a mirror, an observer, invisible from the room, recorded everything the volunteer put into his mouth, along with the time.

The findings were clear-cut. Left to our natural inclination, we don't eat nonstop. Nor do we eat just three meals a day. The subjects nibbled at intervals of from 85 to 110 minutes, with a mean periodicity of about 96 minutes.

The Antihibernation Diet concedes to the practical requirements of modern life in that meals are spaced two and half hours apart rather than one and a half. Between times, if you find your stomach grumbling or having the urge to nibble, try these low-calorie appetite appeasers:

Apples
Breadsticks
Broccoli spears
Carrot sticks
Celery sticks
Dried fruit
Gelatin desserts
Green pepper sticks
Pears
Plain low-fat yogurt
Popcorn
Radishes
Rice cakes
Sunflower seeds

One more word about getting the most out of the Antihibernation Diet. If you've been following the advice in this book step by step—if you've installed and are using synthetic sunlight and have set aside an area as a Spring Room—you should have no problem at all in maintaining the Antihibernation Diet until spring, when you can switch to any sensible weight-loss diet you choose. But if you find yourself still a victim of insatiable carbohydrate craving, in spite of daily use of artificial lights, the problem is almost certainly that you're still not acclimatized to the cold.

Our natural reaction to a shorter photoperiod and falling temperatures is to gorge ourselves on carbohydrates in preparation for hibernation. Our bodies do not reason that in fact we are not going to hibernate or even be exposed to a winter of freezing and starvation. The response is automatic and involuntary, and it can't be reasoned away or ignored. The increased calorie intake among one group of nonacclimatized men averaged 25 percent daily—much of it not needed for increased metabolism. That can amount to a weight increase of a pound or more a week if there's no change in exercise habits. Acclimatized men working in the cold for several hours a day have an increased calorie intake of about half that—apparently the amount needed for the increased metabolism to maintain body temperature. While they gained no weight, the unacclimatized uniformly did. If you have real difficulty sticking to the diet, go back to Chapters 4 and 5 and get yourself acclimatized.

Your Calorie Requirements

The first thing you have to know before you undertake any diet is your own personal calorie requirements—the number of calories you need each day just to maintain the status quo, neither losing nor gaining weight. If anyone has ever offered you a quick and easy answer to that question—say, 2,000 calories or 2,500—you can bet the figure was either inaccurate or a mighty lucky guess. That's because our individual calorie requirements are . . . individual. Yet you can easily calculate with sufficient accuracy the number of calories you burn.

To calculate your basal (resting) metabolic rate (BMR)—the number of calories you use each hour to keep your body functioning while you sit quietly or sleep—simply multiply your weight by 11. (Most of us burn eleven calories per pound per day maintaining our BMR.)

But most of us do more than sit or sleep all day. Even those confined to hospital beds and wheelchairs use additional calories. If you're in that category, add 20 percent of your BMR. If, for example, you weigh 120 pounds, 120 × 11 = 1,320. We'd multiply 1,320 by .20 and get 264. We'd add 264 to the 1,320 to discover that a woman or man weighing 120 pounds recuperating in a hospital would require 1,584 calories daily to maintain weight.

If you're not incapacitated, decide which of the following describes you, and add the indicated percentage to your basal metabolic rate:

If you are inactive but ambulatory, add 30 percent.

Those who are healthy and active, doing nothing physically exerting—such as housewives who leave the cleaning and most of the cooking to others, physically inactive students and secretaries, desk-bound executives—should add 40 percent.

If you're on your feet or use upper body muscles—not just typing fingers—as do heavy equipment operators for at least two hours daily, add 50 percent. Obviously this category includes housewives who do their own housework and anyone who cares for young children all day.

Those who get those two hours of exercise and *also* work as manual laborers—farmers, truck drivers, waitresses, nurses, and such—along with those involved in physical education classes, sports, or a regular fitness program, should add 60 percent.

Men and women who do heavy work daily in construction, mines, loading and unloading, and students who take physical education classes and also participate in moderately taxing sports, like baseball, add 70 percent.

Finally, professional and amateur athletes who train for and play such physically demanding sports as football, wrestling, track and field, and cross-country running and people in basic training for the armed services—those whose days for the most part are constant physical challenges—should add 80 to 100 percent.

There's just one more figure to add, a very simple one. For every hour that you spend outdoors during the winter, dressed lightly enough that you'd shiver if not moderately active, add the calories burned in half an hour at your basal metabolic rate.

Here are two examples that'll make for an interesting comparison. A 170-pound man (1,870 BMR) is a sedentary computer operator ($\times 40$ percent = 748 + 1870 = 2,618 calories). He *never* shivers during the winter because he hates the cold and avoids it with a passion. If the fellow consumes any more than 2,618 calories a day or thereabouts, he'll put on weight.

Meet, on the other hand, a typical woman of 135 pounds (1,485 BMR) a dynamic kindergarten teacher, on her feet all day, who enjoys aerobic dancing for an hour each night (60 percent $\times$ 1485 = 891). Maintaining that level of activity, she needs 2,376 calories daily to maintain her weight. She's only 300 calories short of the man's calorie equilibrium—the equivalent of a slice of chocolate cake. And if she really wants that cake and it's winter, she can spend the night on the back porch, where six hours of shivering will consume another 320 calories or so. (We *don't* recommend that.)

Now you know the total number of calories that you should permit yourself on the Antihibernation Diet. Enter that at "Total Calories" on your Menu Planner. (See sample, page 202.)

How many should come from protein? Multiply the total figure by 20 percent (.20).

To find out how many calories should be in carbohydrate form, multiply your total calorie needs by 50 percent. Write both these figures under the proper headings on your Menu Planner.

The rest will come from fats. Don't worry about them.

On the next pages, you'll find a list of some high-protein foods. Select any three you like, and write them under "Food" on your Menu Planner, for meals 1–3.

Now write down the number of calories (the figures in parentheses) in the foods you selected. Be sure to make entries in all three columns—protein, fat, and carbohydrates. Otherwise, your total calorie count for the day won't be accurate.

Add the calcium, iron, and vitamin C contents of your choices.

Turn to the vitamin and mineral selections list on pages 192–195 and make selections for all six meals.

For the last three meals of the day, turn to the carbohydrate selections list, pages 196–199. Your menu for the day is complete.

Some reassurances:

—Don't drive yourself nuts trying to make the first three meals carbohydrate-free and the last three protein-free. It can't be done, and if it could, it wouldn't be healthy. Take the positive approach, stressing protein for the first three meals (or four, if you find yourself getting drowsy too soon), carbohydrates later in the day and evening.

—If, after totaling the columns, you find that you've come within fifty calories of your goal for protein and a hundred for carbohydrates, consider yourself a success. If the variance is beyond that, or more important, if the total number of calories from all sources is higher than your daily limit, change your food selections as necessary. With a few days' practice you'll learn to plan meals quickly and accurately.

On pages 201–202 you'll see what a completed Menu Planner looks like. Note the great variety of foods that can be enjoyed in a single day. In this era of freezers and microwave ovens it's a rather simple matter to prepare ten or twelve 3-ounce portions of tasty foods at once and freeze them for quick reheating. And setting aside a few hours for the week's meal planning and preparation has this advantage: You're more likely to be painstaking about portion sizes. And that's important. For example, if you choose to have a slice of ham the size of a quarter-pound hamburger, you'll be getting almost twice as many calories as those listed on the Protein Selections list for a 1.7-ounce slice.

Start this diet either a week or two before, according to your charts, you normally begin to feel the effects of the hibernation response or at the first craving for carbohydrates. Within a few days you'll be in for a few pleasant surprises. First, you'll notice that, after eating consistently small meals, you'll be hard put to finish large ones. That's because your stomach will shrink back to its normal size, a phenomenon unknown to many of us since our adolescence. When that occurs, you won't be comfortable stuff-

Protein Selections: Emphasize in Meals 1-3

Number in parentheses is the number of calories from that source per serving.

FOOD	SERVING SIZE	PROTEIN (g)	FAT (g)	CARBOHYDRATE (g)	CALCIUM (mg)	IRON (mg)	VITAMIN E (mg)
Dairy Products							
Blue or Roquefort cheese	1 oz	6 (24)	9 (81)	0.6 (2)	89	0.1	—
Camembert cheese	1⅓ oz	7 (28)	9 (81)	0.5 (2)	40	0.2	—
Cheddar cheese	1 oz	7 (28)	9 (81)	0.6 (2)	213	0.3	198
Cottage cheese (uncreamed)	1 cup	34 (136)	1 (9)	5.4 (22)	23	0.3	—
Eggs	1	6 (24)	6 (54)	0.5 (2)	27	1.1	—
Skim milk	1 cup	9 (36)	—	12.5 (52)	879	0.4	5
Yogurt (partially skim)	1 cup	8 (32)	4 (36)	12.7 (51)	294	0.1	1
Meat, Poultry, Related Products							
Beef, vegetable stew	1 cup	15 (60)	10 (90)	16.5 (66)	28	2.8	15
Corned beef (canned)	3 oz	22 (88)	10 (90)	—	17	3.7	—
Chicken (broiled, no skin)	3 oz	20 (80)	3 (27)	2 (8)	8	1.4	—
Heart, beef (lean, braised)	3 oz	27 (108)	5 (45)	0.6 (2)	5	5.0	1
Lamb (lean only)	2.6 oz	21 (84)	6 (54)	0.5 (2)	9	1.5	—
Lamb leg (roasted; leg only)	2.5 oz	20 (80)	5 (45)	1.3 (5)	3	1.4	—

Protein Selections: Emphasize In Meals 1–3

FOOD	SERVING SIZE	PROTEIN (g)	FAT (g)	CARBOHYDRATE (g)	CALCIUM (mg)	IRON (mg)	VITAMIN E (mg)
			Number in parentheses is the number of calories from that source per serving.				
Meat, Poultry, Related Products							
Lamb shoulder (lean only, roasted)	2.3 oz	17 (68)	6 (54)	2 (8)	8	1.0	—
Liver, beef (fried)	2 oz	15 (60)	6 (54)	4 (16)	6	6.0	15
Pork (cured, cooked)	3 oz	18 (72)	19 (171)	0.8 (3)	8	2.2	—
Pork roast (oven-cooked, lean only)	2.4 oz	20 (80)	10 (90)	1.3 (5)	9	2.6	—
Steak (lean, broiled)	2.4 oz	21 (84)	4 (36)	—	9	2.5	—
Veal cutlet	3 oz	23 (92)	9 (81)	3 (12)	9	2.7	—
Fish							
Bluefish (baked)	3 oz	22 (88)	4 (36)	2.8 (11)	25	0.6	—
Crabmeat (canned)	3 oz	15 (60)	2 (18)	1.8 (7)	38	0.7	—
Oysters (raw, meat only)	1 cup	20 (80)	4 (36)	11 (44)	226	13.2	—
Sardine (Atlantic, canned in oil)	3 oz	20 (80)	9 (81)	3.5 (14)	372	2.5	—
Shrimp (canned)	3 oz	21 (84)	1 (9)	1.8 (7)	98	2.6	—
Swordfish (in butter)	3 oz	24 (96)	5 (45)	2.3 (9)	23	1.1	—
Tuna (canned, oil)	3 oz	24 (96)	7 (63)	2.8 (12)	7	1.6	—

Dry Legumes							
Bean, lima	1 cup	16 (64)	1.1 (10)	47 (188)	55	5.9	—
Black-eyed pea (cowpea)	1 cup	13 (52)	0.8 (7)	33 (132)	43	3.3	—
Miscellaneous Items							
Gelatin (plain, dry powder)	1 envelope	6 (24)	—	—	—	—	—

Vitamin and Mineral Selections

FOOD	SERVING SIZE	PROTEIN (g)	FAT (g)	CARBOHYDRATE (g)	CALCIUM (mg)	IRON (mg)	VITAMIN C (mg)
		Number in parentheses is the number of calories from that source per serving.					
Dry Legumes							
Bean, navy	1 cup	15 (60)	1 (9)	40 (160)	95	5.1	—
Black bean (cooked)	1 cup	22 (88)	1.4 (13)	25 (100)	140	7.9	—
Black-eyed pea (cowpea) (cooked)	1 cup	13 (52)	0.8 (7)	33 (132)	43	3.3	—
Garbanzo bean (chick-pea) (cooked)	1 cup	20 (80)	4.6 (41)	54 (216)	150	6.9	—
Great northern bean (cooked)	1 cup	14 (56)	1.1 (10)	37 (148)	90	4.9	—
Lentil (cooked)	1 cup	16 (64)	—	37 (148)	50	4.2	—
Mung bean (cooked)	1 cup	25 (100)	1.3 (12)	61 (244)	120	8.1	—
Pea (whole, cooked)	1 cup	24 (96)	1.2 (11)	58 (232)	64	5.1	—
Pea (split, cooked)	1 cup	16 (64)	0.6 (5)	40 (160)	22	3.4	—
Pinto, calico bean (cooked)	1 cup	22 (88)	1.1 (10)	58 (232)	130	6.1	—
Vegetables and Vegetable Products							
Asparagus (canned)	1 cup	5 (20)	1 (9)	4 (16)	44	4.1	37
Bean, lima	1 cup	13 (52)	1 (9)	32.3 (129)	80	4.3	29
Beet	1 cup	2 (8)	—	11.8 (47)	24	0.9	10
Broccoli	1 stalk	6 (24)	1 (9)	3 (12)	158	1.4	162

Brussels sprout	1 cup	7 (28)	1 (9)	4.5 (18)	50	1.7	135
Cabbage (raw)	1 cup	1 (4)	—	4 (16)	34	0.3	33
Carrot (raw)	1	1 (4)	—	4 (16)	18	0.4	4
Cauliflower	1 cup	3 (12)	—	3.3 (13)	25	0.8	66
Corn	1 ear	3 (12)	1 (9)	12.3 (49)	2	0.5	7
Cucumber	1 10-oz	1 (4)	—	8.8 (35)	35	0.6	23
Dandelion green	1 cup	4 (16)	1 (9)	8.8 (35)	252	3.2	32
Kale (cooked)	1 cup	4 (16)	1 (9)	1.3 (5)	147	1.3	68
Lettuce (iceberg)	1 head	4 (16)	—	11 (44)	91	2.3	29
Mushroom (canned)	1 cup	5 (20)	—	5 (20)	15	1.2	4
Parsnip (cooked)	1 cup	2 (8)	1 (9)	21 (84)	70	0.9	16
Spinach (cooked)	1 cup	5 (20)	1 (9)	2.8 (11)	167	4.0	50
Squash (winter) (cooked)	1 cup	4 (16)	1 (9)	26.3 (105)	57	1.6	27
Sweet potato (cooked)	16-oz	2 (8)	1 (9)	94.5 (138)	44	1.0	24
Tomato	1	2 (8)	—	8 (32)	24	0.9	50
Tomato juice (canned)	1 cup	2 (8)	—	9.3 (37)	17	2.2	39
Turnip green (cooked)	1 cup	3 (12)	—	4.5 (18)	252	1.5	68
Fruit and Fruit Products							
Apple	1	—	—	17.5 (70)	8	0.4	3
Applesauce (sweetened)	1 cup	1 (4)	—	56.5 (226)	20	1.3	3

Vitamin and Mineral Selections

Number in parentheses is the number of calories from that source per serving.

FOOD	SERVING SIZE	PROTEIN (g)	FAT (g)	CARBOHYDRATE (g)	CALCIUM (mg)	IRON (mg)	VITAMIN C (mg)
Apricot (dried)	1 cup	8 (32)	1 (9)	87.3 (349)	100	8.2	19
Blackberry (raw)	1 cup	2 (8)	1 (9)	17.0 (68)	46	1.3	30
Blueberry (raw)	1 cup	2 (4)	1 (9)	18.0 (72)	21	1.4	20
Cantaloupe	½	1 (4)	—	14.0 (56)	27	0.8	63
Grapefruit (pink/red)	½	1 (4)	—	11.5 (46)	20	0.5	44
Grapefruit juice (canned, unsweetened)	1 cup	1 (4)	—	24.0 (96)	20	1.0	84
Grapefruit juice (fresh)	1 cup	1 (4)	1 (9)	22.8 (91)	22	0.5	92
Grape	1 cup	1 (4)	1 (9)	13.0 (52)	15	0.4	3
Orange	1	1 (4)	—	15.3 (61)	54	0.5	66
Orange juice (fresh)	1 cup	2 (8)	1 (9)	23.3 (93)	27	0.5	124
Papaya	1 cup	1 (4)	—	16.5 (66)	36	0.5	102
Peach	1	1 (4)	—	7.8 (31)	9	0.5	7
Pineapple (raw)	1 cup	1 (4)	—	17.8 (71)	24	0.7	24
Prune (dried) (Cooked, unsweetened)	1 cup	2 (8)	1 (9)	69.5 (278)	60	4.5	2
Prune juice	1 cup	9 (4)	—	49.0 (196)	36	10.5	5
Strawberry (raw)	1 cup	1 (4)	1 (9)	10.5 (42)	31	1.5	88

Grains and Flours

Bran flakes (with raisins)	1 cup	4 (16)	1 (9)	30.0 (120)	28	13.5	—
Potato flour	1 cup	15 (60)	1.5 (13)	143.13 (573)	61	32.0	35
Spaghetti (with meatballs, tomato sauce)	1 cup	19 (76)	12 (108)	36.5 (146)	124	9.7	22

Carbohydrate Selections: Emphasize in Meals 4, 5, and 6

FOOD	SERVING SIZE	PROTEIN (g)	FAT (g)	CARBOHYDRATE (g)	CALCIUM (mg)	IRON (mg)	VITAMIN E (mg)
		Number in parentheses is the number of calories from that source per serving.					
Meat, Related Products							
Beef pot pie	8 oz	23 (92)	33 (297)	43.0 (172)	32	4.1	7
Chili con carne (canned, with beans)	1 cup	26 (104)	38 (342)	16.0 (64)	97	3.6	—
Vegetables and Vegetable Products							
Pea (green, cooked)	1 cup	9 (36)	1 (9)	17.5 (70)	37	2.9	33
Potato (boiled, peeled after boiling)	1 medium	3 (12)	—	23.3 (93)	10	0.8	22
Potato (mashed, milk added)	1 cup	4 (16)	1 (9)	25.0 (100)	47	0.8	19
Fruit and Fruit Products							
Apricot nectar (canned)	1 cup	1 (4)	—	34.0 (136)	23	0.5	8
Banana (raw)	1 medium	1 (4)	—	24.0 (96)	10	0.8	12
Cranberry juice cocktail (canned)	1 cup	—	—	41.0 (164)	13	0.8	40
Cranberry sauce (sweetened canned)	1 cup	— (9)	1 (9)	99.0 (396)	17	0.6	6
Date (pitted)	1 cup	4 (16)	1 (9)	116.3 (465)	105	5.3	—
Fruit cocktail (canned in heavy syrup)	1 cup	1 (4)	—	47.8 (191)	23	1.0	5

Grape juice (canned, bottled)	1 cup	1 (4)	—	40.3 (161)	28	0.8	—
Pear (raw)	1	1 (4)	1 (9)	21.8 (87)	13	0.5	7
Raisin (seedless)	½-oz pack	—	1 (9)	10.0 (40)	9	0.5	—
Raspberry (red, raw)	1 cup	1 (4)	1 (9)	14.3 (57)	27	1.1	31
Rhubarb (cooked, sugar added)	1 cup	1 (4)	—	95.3 (381)	212	1.6	17
Watermelon (4×8″ wedge)	1 wedge	2 (8)	1 (9)	24.5 (98)	30	2.1	30
Grains and Flours							
Bagel	1 3-in	6 (24)	2 (18)	30.8 (123)	9	1.2	—
Barley (pearl, light)	1 cup	16 (64)	2 (18)	154.0 (616)	32	4.0	—
Bread, white	1 slice	2 (8)	1 (9)	13.3 (53)	21	0.6	—
Angel food cake	1 piece	3 (12)	—	30.8 (123)	50	0.2	—
Cornflakes (plain)	1 cup	2 (8)	—	23.0 (92)	4	0.4	—
Cornflakes (sugar-covered)	1 cup	2 (8)	—	36.8 (147)	5	0.4	—
Macaroni (enriched)	1 cup	6 (24)	1 (9)	39.3 (157)	14	1.4	—
Noodles (egg, enriched)	1 cup	7 (28)	2 (18)	38.5 (154)	16	1.4	—
Oats, puffed (with added nutrients)	1 cup	3 (12)	1 (9)	19.8 (79)	44	1.2	—
Pancake, wheat (enriched flour)	1 4-in cake	2 (8)	2 (18)	8.5 (34)	27	0.4	—
Pizza (cheese)	1 slice	7 (28)	6 (54)	25.8 (103)	107	0.7	4

Carbohydrate Selections: Emphasize in Meals 4, 5, and 6

Number in parentheses is the number of calories from that source per serving.

FOOD	SERVING SIZE	PROTEIN (g)	FAT (g)	CARBOHYDRATE (g)	CALCIUM (mg)	IRON (mg)	VITAMIN E (mg)
Popcorn (oil, salt)	1 cup	1 (4)	2 (18)	4.5 (18)	1	0.2	—
Pretzels (Dutch, twisted)	1	2 (8)	1 (9)	10.8 (43)	4	0.2	—
Rice (white, enriched)	1 cup	4 (16)	—	52.3 (209)	31	1.8	—
Rolls (hamburger, frankfurter)	1 roll	3 (12)	2 (18)	20.3 (81)	30	0.8	—
wheat, puffed	1 cup	2 (8)	—	11.8 (47)	4	0.6	—
Sugars and sweets							
Candy: chocolate, milk, plain	1 oz	2 (8)	9 (81)	14.0 (112)	65	0.3	—
Gum drop	1 oz	—	—	25 (100)	2	0.1	—
Hard	1 oz	—	—	27 (108)	6	0.5	—
Marshmallow	1 oz	1 (4)	—	21 (84)	5	0.5	—
Honey	1 tbsp	—	—	16 (64)	1	0.1	—
Jam, preserve	1 tbsp	—	—	13 (52)	4	0.2	—
Jelly	1 tbsp	—	—	12.5 (50)	4	0.3	1
Sugar (brown)	1 cup	—	—	205 (820)	187	7.5	—
Sugar (white)	1 tbsp	—	—	10 (40)	—	—	—
Miscellaneous Items							
Cola drink	12 fl oz	—	—	36.9 (147)	—	—	—

Fruit-flavored soda and Tom Collins mix	12 fl oz	—	—	44.6 (178)	—	—	—
Sherbet	1 cup	2 (8)	2 (18)	58.5 (294)	31	—	4
Soup (canned)							
Clam chowder (Manhattan)	1 cup	2 (8)	3 (27)	11.2 (45)	34	1.0	—
Split pea	1 cup	9 (36)	3 (27)	20.5 (82)	29	1.0	1
Tomato	1 cup	2 (8)	3 (27)	13.75 (55)	15	0.7	12
Vegetable beef	1 cup	5 (20)	2 (18)	10.5 (42)	12	0.7	—
Tapioca	1 cup	1 (4)	—	132 (528)	15	0.6	—

ing yourself any longer. Even the most carbohydrate-crazed hibernator won't have the slightest urge to eat anything more. If she simply eats slowly, she can go on eating all day and night.

But don't expect the Antihibernation Diet to help you lose weight. We confess—with embarrassment—that some people actually have lost pounds while following it, even during the winter, when typical hibernators usually gain ten to fifteen pounds. The sample menu shows how, for those days the dieters have used up four hundred more calories than they've taken in. Even if their metabolisms remain stable and they get no additional exercise, within nine days they'll lose one pound. But that's not supposed to happen. It's a mistake, a fluke. This is a weight *control* diet. People with four-hundred-calorie credits at the end of the day should spend it on a couple of glasses of wine with someone they love, and postpone losing weight until March.

Sample Menu
Menu Planner

Total Calories 2,300

MEAL	FOOD	PROTEIN Calories (20%) Total Daily 460	FAT Calories	CARBOHYDRATE Calories (50%) Total Daily 1,150	CALCIUM RDA: 800–1200 mg	IRON RDA: 18 mg	VITAMIN C RDA: 60 mg
1	Chicken, 3 ounces, skinless	80	27	8	8	1.4	—
	Cantaloupe, one-half	4	—	56	27	0.8	63
	Coffee or tea	—	—	—	—	—	—
2	Grapefruit juice	4	—	91	22	0.5	92
	Swordfish, 3 ounces	96	63	92	23	1.1	—
	Broccoli, one stalk	24	9	12	158	1.4	162
	Low-calorie beverage	—	—	—	—	—	—
3	Skim milk, 1 cup	36	36	52	879	0.4	5
	Veal cutlet, 3 ounces	92	81	12	9	2.7	—
	Peas, 1 cup	36	9	129	50	4.2	22

MEAL	FOOD	PROTEIN Calories (20%) Total Daily 460	FAT Calories	CARBOHYDRATE Calories (50%) Total Daily 1,150	CALCIUM RDA: 800–1200 mg	IRON RDA: 18 mg	VITAMIN C RDA: 60 mg
	Low-calorie beverage	—	—	—	—	—	—
4	Pizza, 1 slice	28	54	103	107	0.7	4
	Candy, 1 ounce, gumdrops	—	—	100	—	—	—
	Coffee or tea	—	—	—	—	—	—
5	Macaroni, 1 cup	24	9	157	14	1.4	—
	Spinach, 1 cup	20	9	11	167	4.0	50
	Sherbet, 1 cup	8	18	234	31	—	4
6	Blackberries, 1 cup	8	9	8	46	1.3	30
	TOTAL	460	324	1,116	1,541	19.9	432
	GRAND TOTAL	1,900					

Menu Planner

Total Calories _____

MEAL	FOOD	PROTEIN Calories (20%) Total Daily ___	FAT Calories	CARBOHYDRATE Calories (50%) Total Daily ___	CALCIUM RDA: 800–1200 mg	IRON RDA: 18 mg	VITAMIN C RDA: 60 mg
1							
2							
3							

Menu Planner

Total Calories ____

MEAL	FOOD	PROTEIN Calories (20%) Total Daily ___	FAT Calories	CARBOHYDRATE Calories (50%) Total Daily ___	CALCIUM RDA: 800—1200 mg	IRON RDA: 18 mg	VITAMIN C RDA: 60 mg
4							
5							
6							

1983 Metropolitan "Desirable" Height and Weight Tables

		Men		
HEIGHT (Without Shoes)	**SMALL FRAME**	**MEDIUM FRAME**	**LARGE FRAME**	
Feet Inches		Weight in Pounds (Without Clothing)		
5 1	123–129	126–136	153–145	
5 2	125–131	128–138	135–148	
5 3	127–133	130–140	137–151	
5 4	129–135	132–143	139–155	
5 5	131–137	134–146	141–159	
5 6	133–140	137–149	144–163	
5 7	135–143	140–152	147–167	
5 8	137–146	143–155	150–171	
5 9	139–149	146–158	153–175	
5 10	141–152	149–161	156–179	
5 11	144–155	152–165	159–183	
6 0	147–159	155–169	163–187	
6 1	150–163	159–173	167–192	
6 2	153–167	162–177	171–197	
6 3	157–171	166–182	176–202	

1983 Metropolitan "Desirable" Height and Weight Tables

Women

HEIGHT (Without Shoes)		SMALL FRAME	MEDIUM FRAME	LARGE FRAME
Feet	Inches	Weight in Pounds (Without Clothing)		
4	9	99–108	106–118	115–128
4	10	100–110	108–120	117–131
4	11	101–112	110–123	119–134
5	0	103–115	112–126	122–137
5	1	105–118	115–129	125–140
5	2	108–121	118–132	128–144
5	3	111–124	121–135	131–148
5	4	114–127	124–138	134–152
5	5	117–130	127–141	137–156
5	6	120–133	130–144	140–160
5	7	123–136	133–147	143–164
5	8	126–139	136–150	146–167
5	9	129–142	139–153	149–170
5	10	132–145	142–156	152–173

Note: Prepared by Metropolitan Life Insurance Company.

Source of basic data: Build Study, 1979, and Build and Blood Pressure Study, 1959, Society of Actuaries and Association of Life Insurance Medical Directors of America.

These figures are averages based on the fact that 19 percent of body weight is typically fat. Since muscle weighs three times as much as fat, a physically well-conditioned individual will appear thin while weighing considerably more than his or her "desirable" weight.

Planning the Great Escape: Why, When, and Where to Go

Change of soil and climate
has in it much that is pleasurable.
        —PLINY THE YOUNGER

Before phototherapy for the hibernation response, there was . . . Jamaica.

"People who don't go through this seasonal thing just can't understand it," says Kathy D. of Baltimore. Kathy's in her mid-forties, married, with two adult sons. Every winter for almost twenty years, this soft-spoken, self-effacing woman has dragged her husband off for a two-week vacation on the Negril coast of Jamaica.

These days she simply drops a hint, and they're off. It wasn't like that the first time. When she suggested that first trip, her husband, Tom, insisted that work and other commitments made a vacation impossible. So Kathy's suggestions became demands and finally a continuous ranting so uncharacteristic of her that Tom acquiesced.

"I was utterly ashamed of how I'd acted," Kathy admits. "It wasn't that I *wanted* to go south. I *had* to. Now I know why."

Today Kathy uses synthetic sunshine throughout the winter. She's converted one room in her house to a Spring Room, and she makes an effort to acclimatize to the cold, which is usually not severe in Baltimore. During the past two winters since she's taken these steps, Kathy hasn't felt a compulsion to travel south. Yet she and her husband still take a two-week southern vacation every year. The only thing that has changed is the timing. In the past they vacationed in late December or early January. Now they leave right after Thanksgiving.

Vacation Timing, the Personal Touch

Kathy's special gift is her self-awareness. She consciously recognizes her instinctive feelings, and instead of ignoring them or relegating them to the unconscious, she acts on them deliberately. Kathy didn't know anything about annual rhythm charts, but she did recognize that in her particular case she'd benefit most from a southern vacation in late autumn. Look at the composite graph of Kathy's energy and mood levels from October to March based on her recalled experiences previous to using synthetic sunshine.

Kathy's Chart

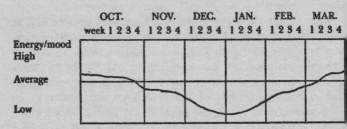

Kathy's chart tells us a couple of important things in terms of her vacation planning. First, her mood improves slightly during the latter part of January and throughout

February, the coldest months of the year in the north-eastern part of the United States. That means that in her case the hibernation symptoms are caused not by the cold but by the shorter days. Although Jamaica was a fine choice for extending the photoperiod, she didn't need the warm temperature. In fact, going from a cold environment to a hot one and back to the cold can play havoc with the body's ability to acclimatize to northern winters. The point is that Kathy recognizes when she can anticipate the onset of the hibernation response. There are always a couple of weeks in which she feels, in her own words, "just out of sorts."

Says Kathy, "I actually resist using the lights—I don't know why." Perhaps it's an example of the den-building impulse we discussed in Chapter 7, the instinct to retreat from light and activity and prepare for hibernation. Kathy's clever solution is to take her southern vacation at precisely that time—in her case, the end of November—then come roaring back to her Spring Room and artificial light.

But not everyone will benefit from a vacation in late November. Check the chart of a young northern New Jersey man—we'll call him Bill—whose hibernation response is triggered by temperature more profoundly than by photoperiod.

Bill's Chart

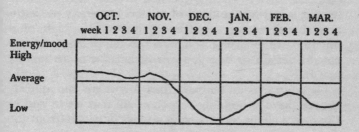

Both his first decline in mood and energy levels (which happens to coincide with the sudden onset of frigid temperatures) and a second downturn in mood during March (as temperatures rebound) strongly suggest a close relationship between mood/energy and temperature. This young man takes no vacations during the winter because his job doesn't permit them, but he should actually take two. According to his chart, the first should be at the end of November—*not to a warm climate, but to a cold one*, with an extended photoperiod. Albuquerque, New Mexico, with typically clear, sunny skies yet a normal daily minimum temperature in November of 30.8°F, would be a good choice. A couple of weeks in that environment will give a person of normal good health the boost needed to get the acclimatization process under way. Ideally this man ought to remain away until the wide temperature fluctuations of northern autumns have yielded to a stable cold climate.

Bill should schedule his second vacation for the end of February or early March when once again temperatures begin fluctuating. This time he should head to a warm climate and stay there until the temperature back home has taken on some stability.

Timing your own great escape depends entirely on your individual hibernation response pattern. If you're using synthetic sunshine and you've acclimatized to the cold, the period when a vacation is *least* likely to be of benefit is during the dead of winter. Generally the vacation should act as a buffer, maintaining a high photoperiod while easing you into the temperature of the coming season so that you can acclimatize more rapidly and fully.

Of course, cold temperatures anywhere can quickly trigger the den-building response. All that we've said in Chapter 5 about acclimatizing applies here. Confront the cold face-to-face early on. Get the blood pumping and the juices flowing at the outset, and you'll find you feel great all winter back home under your new lights. This isn't the time to run from the enemy, but to challenge and defeat it.

Destinations

Now you know how to use your annual rhythm charts to learn *when* to make your great escape. The next question is *where to go.*

In the absence of hard research to determine the length of the daily photoperiod required to eliminate the hibernation response—or, to put it another way, the north and south latitudes between which people rarely experience the response—we must fall back on an educated guess based on the information available.

One important piece of information comes from researchers at the University of California in San Diego, who have been trying to study seasonal affective disorder there but have been frustrated because, as of mid-1986, they haven't been able to find any SAD patients. San Diego, of course, has mild temperatures all year. Throughout the winter the coldest it normally gets is from 48° to 52°F, on average. Daily highs average in the sixties. That's important, of course, since cold temperatures can trigger the hibernation response among those who fail to acclimatize.

But San Diego is blessed with two more climatic advantages. In January there's an average of 10.2 hours between sunrise and sunset. That in itself means little—it tells us only the amount of sunshine available to the area—but equally important is what meteorologists call the "average percentage of possible sunshine" which actually reaches the city. The rest is blocked by clouds, air pollution, precipitation, and such. San Diego has one of the highest ratings in the United States. It receives 71 percent of possible sunshine. Or we might say that it has 7.2 hours of actual sunshine on average each day in January.

San Francisco is only eight to ten degrees cooler than San Diego. Yet the hibernation response is far from rare there. The days are about a half hour shorter in January—9.6 hours from sunrise to sunset—and that's a factor, no doubt. But much more important in this particular example is the percentage of possible sunlight reaching the city. It's only 56 percent. That means San Francisco's average daily sunshine in January is 5.4 hours—almost 2 hours less each day than San Diego's—and that's highly significant.

San Diego is at latitude 34 degrees north and actually receives more than 70 percent of possible sunlight. Those are the two major criteria we'll use in planning destinations for the great escape: a latitude of 34 degrees north or south and roughly 70 percent or more of potential sunlight. Those living in this swath around the globe seem to be completely free from the hibernation response.

That's not to say that there are no wonderful vacation spots above latitude 34 degrees. The latitude of the French Riviera is in the forties. So are much of Italy, the beautiful beaches of Yugoslavia, the island of Corsica. Each boasts a wonderful climate, especially throughout the fall and spring seasons. One reason, of course, is the high percentage of available sunlight penetrating the often cloudless, pollution-free atmosphere. But length of photoperiod is just one of several factors which create climate.

Another is the great winds, born of the earth's spinning and the sun's heat. Both reach extremes at the equator, and there, in the blister of rising air, the lazy undulations of convection, the great winds are created. The deserts and seas in that torrid zone may seem as still as death; in fact, everything, including the air, is moving at a thousand miles an hour, the speed of the earth's rotation.

Rising into the troposphere, the layer of atmosphere nearest the earth, the warm air spills from the equatorial zone to the north and south. To the north, it passes over Jacksonville and New Orleans, Cairo and Shanghai, where the earth's circumference is half that of the equator, its rotation only five hundred miles an hour. Yet seven miles above those cities, the equatorial air continues northward at a speed only slightly less than that at the equator. That's how the winds begin.

Continuing its journey toward the poles, the warm, lightweight air, referred to as a low-pressure system, grows cool, the atmospheric molecules now compressing into high pressure. Like an inflated balloon, this densely packed air of the polar regions constantly presses out toward low-pressure areas into which it can expand. In the winter, when it is most frigid, these mountains of heavy air may expand as far south as Quebec. Now low-pressure pockets developing in Buffalo or Chicago—and sometimes as far south as Florida—will attract chunks of that polar mass like a vacuum. The air will rush from north to south as though escaping an inflated balloon, from high pressure to low, creating more wind. As it cools the moist air of the low-pressure system, condensation takes place in the form of rain or snow, creating a winter storm or blizzard.

But the winds don't move freely around the globe. They meet obstacles. In Europe the polar winds plunge across Denmark and the Germanys, bringing them winters similar to those of the northern United States. Yet Rome, at a latitude nearly that of Buffalo, averages a high of 54°F during January, while Buffalo's highs are 31°F. That's because the polar winds never get to Italy; they're deflected by the Alps. The Himalayas do the same for northern India.

Ocean currents also play a major role in world climates. "In recent years, the role of the oceans in transporting heat has been more fully recognized," writes climatologist Louis J. Battan in *Weather*. "This is accomplished through the action of warm ocean currents traveling poleward while cold ocean currents move equatorward. The warm water moving under colder air gives off energy in the form of . . . heat which directly warms the air. . . . Overall ocean currents may account for 20 to 25 percent of the total meridional heat transfer."

That's why you can vacation from Ecuador to Chile on the west coast of South America at any time of the year and probably be more comfortable than you'd be in New York or Atlanta. The Humboldt Current from Antarctica chills the wind off the coast, and the wind cools the land.

Much of southern Europe owes its mild climate to the Gulf Stream as well as to the Alps. This current absorbs heat near the coast of northern Africa, crosses the Atlantic to the Gulf of Mexico, continues northeastward, heating the air of the Carolinas. Crossing the Atlantic again, it warms the breezes of the Mediterranean, bringing balm to the beaches of Spain and France. So great is its reservoir of heat that it continues northward still, making Iceland green while Greenland remains icy.

That, to answer a simple question in a roundabout way, is why you can enjoy bathing on the coast of southern Europe in January while the folks back home in Rochester and Detroit, which are at the same latitude, are digging out of a snowstorm in temperatures below 20°F.

All this is of importance to you in selecting an ideal vacation spot. What you *need* is an extended photoperiod.

Depending upon your acclimatization capacity, you may also require a cool environment—or a warm one.

Check the chart of representative United States cities, some at the northern border of the Antihibernation Belt (italicized) and others north or south of latitude 34 degrees, so that you can compare your winter photoperiod with that of the Antihibernation Belt. The hibernation response is mild or absent in some but not all of these italicized cities, and you'll recognize quickly which of them offer tourist attractions you *don't* want to enjoy during the winter. It's a wonder, for example, that Minneapolis—one of the most wonderful cities in the nation—hasn't gotten around to relocating itself by now, considering that half of its January days are completely overcast, a third of them are snowy, and a heat wave means the temperature has risen into the twenties.

You can easily see that several cities with adequate winter photoperiods are too overcast during the winter for hibernators. They include Raleigh, Chattanooga, Little Rock, and Oklahoma City.

Alamosa, Colorado, on the other hand, boasts thirteen clear days during January, and only eight cloudy ones. Surrounded by lovely mountains and open desert, it's among the most scenic areas in America. Unfortunately January temperatures average between minus 1° and 34°F.

Barrow, Alaska, has only two cloudy days in January, and only two partly cloudy ones. The rest are perfectly clear—all three of them. There are only seven long days in Barrow during January.

We humans have already discovered many of the ideal winter migration areas. That is why they've become so popular. The chart covering January lists a few of them.

American Cities

Month of January

City	Oct. 21 Hr	Oct. 21 Min	Nov. 21 Hr	Nov. 21 Min	Dec. 21 Hr	Dec. 21 Min	Jan. 21 Hr	Jan. 21 Min	Feb. 21 Hr	Feb. 21 Min	Mar. 21 Hr	Mar. 21 Min	Avg. Percent of Possible Sunshine	Daily Avg. Temp. Max.	Daily Avg. Temp. Min.	Days with Rain/Snow of 0.01 Inches or More	Clear	Partly Cloudy	Cloudy
Albuquerque, NM	11	8	10	11	9	47	10	12	11	9	12	10	72	46	24	4	14	7	10
Boston, MA	10	49	9	36	9	5	9	36	10	51	12	10	53	36	23	4	9	7	15
Chattanooga, TN	11	7	10	11	9	48	10	11	12	8	12	9	43	48	29	12	7	7	17
Chicago, IL	10	52	9	39	9	9	9	40	10	53	12	11	45	29	14	2	7	6	18
Little Rock, AR	11	8	10	13	9	50	10	13	11	9	12	9	46	50	30	10	9	6	16
Los Angeles, CA	11	9	10	15	9	53	10	15	11	10	12	9	69	64	45	6	14	8	9
Minneapolis, MN	10	43	9	21	8	46	9	21	10	44	12	12	52	20	2	9	9	7	15
New York, NY	10	53	9	44	9	15	9	45	10	56	12	9	50	38	26	9	8	9	14
Oklahoma City, OK	11	6	10	10	9	45	10	10	11	7	12	10	59	46	28	5	10	6	15
Philadelphia, PA	10	55	10	18	9	20	9	49	10	58	12	11	50	39	24	3	7	8	16
Phoenix, AZ	11	11	10	18	9	56	10	19	11	12	12	9	78	64	35	4	14	7	10
Raleigh, NC	11	5	10	8	9	43	10	8	11	6	12	10	54	50	29	10	9	7	15
Seattle, WA	10	35	9	5	8	27	9	6	10	37	12	12	25	45	36	6	3	5	23
San Juan, PR	11	39	11	12	11	2	11	13	11	38	12	7	67	83	70	16	8	19	4
Washington, D.C.	10	59	9	54	9	27	9	54	11	00	12	10	48	41	22	3	8	7	16

Source: *Comparative Climatic Data for the United States Through 1983*
National Oceanic and Atmospheric Administration

Month of January

CITY	CLEAR	PARTLY CLOUDY	CLOUDY	MAX. TEMP.	MIN. TEMP.
Las Vegas, NV	14	6	11	56	33
Key West, FL	11	12	8	72	66
Miami, FL	10	13	8	75	59
Fort Myers, FL	11	12	8	74	52
Orlando, FL	9	11	11	72	49
Amarillo, TX	12	7	12	49	22
San Juan, PR	8	19	4	83	70

Vacation Abroad

If you're planning a vacation to another country, here are some guidelines for selecting those areas which will be most effective in combating the hibernation response:

—Temperatures increase as you approach both the equator and sea level. They decrease with altitude, the reason that Quito, Ecuador, 8 degrees south of the equator but high in the Andes, has an average annual temperature of only 44°F and falls into the twenties during December. These two factors—altitude and proximity to the equator—explain why you can find any climate you wish, from subtropical to temperate, throughout Mexico and Central America.

—Areas on the windward side of mountain ranges, usually to the west and north, are likely to be wet and snowy during certain seasons. Check to see if

217

your destination has a rainy season, and when, before firming up vacation plans.

—The key criterion for the great escape is duration of daylight. During winter in the Northern Hemisphere the days are longest south of the equator. In fact, the sun never sets on Antarctica during that time (and there's never a crowd at the beach either).

The most intense sunlight during the Northern Hemisphere's winter falls between the equator and the Tropic of Capricorn, so if heat is what you're after, that's where you'll find it: in the lowlands and coastal areas of Brazil, southern Africa, Madagascar, the Seychelles and Mauritius islands, Indonesia, northern Australia, and New Guinea.

This includes paradise: the Solomon Islands, the New Hebrides, Tonga, Tahiti, and the rest of the Society Islands.

Even the Fiji Islands have their celebrated Blue Lagoon in the Antihibernation Belt.

Those are the hot spots, yet in many of those areas you can also find cooler temperatures simply by increasing the elevation. Primitive, sophisticated, crowded, desolate, cold, hot, dry, rainy—it's all right there, along with the brightest sunshine on earth. Use the temperature and precipitation table to find the destination best suited to your needs.

Temperature and Precipitation Data

Country, City	Latitude	Elevation	Temperature Average Daily F°						Precipitation Average		
			January		July		October		January	July	October
			Max.	Min.	Max.	Min.	Max.	Min.	Inches	Inches	Inches
MEXICO											
Acapulco	15°50'N	10	85	70	89	75	88	74	0.3	9.1	6.7
Guadalajara	20°41'N	5,194	73	45	79	60	78	56	0.4	9.4	2.2
Mexico City	19°26'N	7,340	66	42	74	54	70	50	0.2	4.5	1.6
CENTRAL AMERICA											
Belize, British Honduras	17°31'N	17	81	67	87	75	86	72	5.4	6.4	12.0
San José, Costa Rica	09°56'N	3,760	75	58	77	62	77	60	0.6	8.3	11.8
Guatemala City, Guatemala	14°37'N	4,855	73	63	78	60	76	60	0.3	8.0	6.8
WEST INDIES											
Bridgetown, Barbados	13°08'N	181	83	70	86	74	86	73	2.6	5.8	7.0
Camp Jacob, Guadeloupe	16°01'N	1,750	77	64	81	68	81	68	9.2	17.6	12.4
Ciudad Trujillo, Dom. Rep.	18°29'N	57	84	66	88	72	87	72	2.4	6.4	6.0
Fort-de-France, Martinique	14°37'N	13	83	69	86	74	87	73	4.7	9.4	9.7
Hamilton, Bermuda	32°17'N	151	68	58	85	73	79	69	4.4	4.5	5.8

Country, City	Latitude	Elevation	Temperature Average Daily F°						Precipitation Average		
			January		July		October		January	July	October
			Max.	Min.	Max.	Min.	Max.	Min.	Inches	Inches	Inches
Havana, Cuba	23°08'N	80	79	65	89	75	85	73	2.8	4.9	6.8
Kingston, Jamaica	17°58'N	110	86	67	90	73	88	73	0.9	1.5	7.1
La Guerite, St. Kitts	17°20'N	157	80	71	86	76	85	75	4.1	4.4	5.4
Nassau, Bahamas	25°05'N	12	77	65	88	75	85	73	1.4	5.8	6.5
Port-au-Prince, Haiti	18°33'N	121	87	68	94	74	90	72	1.3	2.9	6.7
St. Clair, Trinidad	10°40'N	67	87	69	88	71	89	71	2.7	8.6	6.7
St. Thomas, Virgin Is.	18°20'N	11	82	71	88	77	87	76	2.5	3.2	5.6
SOUTH AMERICA											
Buenos Aires, Argentina	34°35'S	89	85	63	57	42	69	50	3.1	2.2	3.4
Rio de Janeiro, Brazil	22°55'S	201	84	73	75	63	77	66	4.9	1.6	3.1
Salvador, Brazil	13°00'S	154	86	74	79	69	88	71	2.6	7.2	4.0
São Paulo, Brazil	23°37'S	2,628	77	63	66	53	68	57	8.8	1.5	4.6
Santiago, Chile	33°27'S	1,706	85	53	59	37	72	45	0.1	3.0	0.6
Bogotá, Colombia	04°42'N	8,355	67	48	64	50	66	50	2.3	2.0	6.3
Bahía Negra, Paraguay	20°14'S	318	92	74	79	61	90	69	5.4	1.5	4.2
Lima, Peru	12°05'S	394	82	66	67	57	71	58	0.1	0.3	0.1

Montevideo, Uruguay	34°52'S	72	83	62	58	43	68	49	2.9	2.9	2.9
Caracas, Venezuela	10°30'N	3,418	75	56	78	61	79	61	0.9	4.3	3.7
Ciudad Bolívar, Venezuela	08°07'N	197	90	72	90	75	93	75	1.4	6.3	2.8
Easter Island, Chile	27°10'S	98	77	64	70	58	73	58	4.8	3.5	4.6
EUROPE											
Nicosia, Cyprus	35°09'N	716	58	42	97	69	81	58	2.9	*	0.9
Corsica, France	41°52'N	243	56	40	85	64	72	55	3.0	2.8	3.8
Marseilles, France	43°18'N	246	53	38	78	58	76	57	1.9	0.6	3.7
Windmill Hill, Gibraltar	36°06'N	400	58	50	77	66	70	61	4.6	*	3.5
Athens, Greece	37°58'N	351	54	42	90	72	74	60	2.2	0.2	1.7
Crete, Greece	35°20'N	98	60	48	85	72	77	62	3.7	*	1.7
Rhodes, Greece	36°26'N	289	59	51	83	74	76	68	5.7	0.0	1.7
Salonika, Greece	40°37'N	78	49	37	90	70	73	56	1.5	1.0	2.4
Sardinia, Italy	39°15'N	3	56	43	86	67	72	58	2.2	0.1	3.0
Naples, Italy	40°51'N	82	54	40	84	70	71	60	3.7	0.6	5.1
Palermo, Sicily, Italy	38°07'N	354	58	47	86	71	75	62	3.8	0.2	3.7
Rome, Italy	41°48'N	377	54	39	88	64	73	53	3.3	0.4	4.3
Monaco	43°44'N	180	54	46	77	70	67	60	2.4	0.7	4.7
Lisbon, Portugal	38°43'N	313	56	46	79	63	69	57	3.3	0.2	3.1
Almería, Spain	36°51'N	213	61	47	85	69	76	62	0.9	*	0.9
Barcelona, Spain	41°24'N	312	56	42	81	69	71	58	1.2	1.2	3.4
Madrid, Spain	40°25'N	2,188	47	33	87	62	66	48	1.1	0.4	1.9
Valencia, Spain	39°28'N	79	58	41	83	68	73	57	0.9	0.4	1.6

Country, City	Latitude	Elevation	Temperature Average Daily F°						Precipitation Average		
			January		July		October		January	July	October
			Max.	Min.	Max.	Min.	Max.	Min.	Inches	Inches	Inches
AFRICA											
Nairobi, Kenya	01°16'S	5,971	77	54	69	51	76	55	1.5	0.6	2.1
Casablanca, Morocco	33°35'N	164	63	45	79	65	76	58	2.1	0.0	1.5
Cape Town, South Africa	33°54'S	56	78	60	63	45	70	52	0.6	3.5	1.2
Las Palmas, Canary Is.	28°11'N	20	70	58	77	67	79	67	1.4	*	1.1
Port Victoria, Seychelles	04°37'S	15	83	76	81	75	83	75	15.2	3.3	6.1
ASIA, FAR EAST											
Canton, China	23°10'N	59	65	49	91	77	85	67	0.9	8.1	3.4
Shanghai, China	31°12'N	16	47	32	91	75	75	56	1.9	5.8	2.9
Hong Kong	22°18'N	109	64	56	87	78	81	73	1.3	15.0	4.5
Tokyo, Japan	35°41'N	19	47	29	83	70	69	54	1.9	5.6	8.2
Tainan, Taiwan	22°57'N	53	72	55	89	77	86	70	0.7	16.0	1.2
ASIA, SOUTHEAST											
Davao, Philippines	07°07'N	88	87	72	88	73	89	73	4.8	6.5	7.9
Manila, Philippines	14°31'N	49	86	69	88	75	88	74	0.9	17.0	7.6
Bangkok, Thailand	13°44'N	53	89	67	90	76	88	76	0.2	6.9	9.9

Bangalore, India	12°57'N	2,937	80	57	81	66	82	65	0.2	3.9	5.9
Bombay, India	19°06'N	27	88	62	88	75	93	73	0.1	24.3	2.5
Calcutta, India	22°52'N	21	80	55	90	79	89	74	0.4	12.8	4.5
Jerusalem, Israel	31°47'N	2,654	55	41	87	63	81	59	5.1	0.0	0.3
Tel Aviv, Israel	32°06'N	33	64	50	82	72	79	65	4.9	0.0	0.4
Amman, Jordan	31°58'N	2,547	54	39	89	65	81	57	2.7	0.0	0.2
Riyadh, Saudi Arabia	24°39'N	1,938	70	46	107	78	94	61	0.1	0.0	0.0

AUSTRALIA, PACIFIC ISLANDS

Adelaide, Australia	34°57'S	20	86	61	59	45	73	51	0.8	2.6	1.7
Brisbane, Australia	27°25'S	17	85	69	68	49	80	60	6.4	2.2	2.5
Canberra, Australia	35°18'S	1,896	82	55	52	33	68	43	1.9	1.8	2.2
Melbourne, Australia	37°49'S	115	78	57	56	42	67	48	1.9	1.9	2.6
Sydney, Australia	33°52'S	62	78	65	60	46	71	56	3.5	4.6	2.8
Auckland, New Zealand	37°00'S	23	73	60	56	45	63	52	3.1	5.7	4.0
Wellington, New Zealand	41°17'S	415	69	56	53	42	60	48	3.2	5.4	4.0
Guam, Marianas Is.	13°38'N	361	84	72	87	72	86	73	4.6	9.0	13.1
Honolulu, Hawaii	21°20'N	7	79	66	85	73	84	72	3.8	0.4	1.8
Nouméa, New Caledonia	22°16'S	246	86	72	76	62	80	65	3.7	3.6	2.0
Suva, Fiji Is.	18°08'S	20	86	74	79	68	81	70	11.4	4.9	8.3
Tahiti, Society Is.	17°33'S	7	89	72	86	68	87	70	13.2	2.6	3.4
Tulagi, Solomón Is.	09°05'S	8	88	76	86	76	87	76	14.3	7.6	8.7

The U.S. Department of Commerce publication *Climates of the World* gives temperature and precipitation data for many additional locations around the world. The booklet is for sale by the Superintendent of Documents, U.S. Government Printing Office, Washington, D.C. 20402, for thirty-five cents.

The Divine Sun: Showing Some Respect

The lamp of the world, light of this universe.
— JOSHUA SYLVESTER

In the predawn darkness the massive doors of the temple at Cuzco, Peru, stood wide upon the eastern dawn. The reflection of blazing torches along the walls gleamed from the gold-plated ceiling like distant stars. The worshipers, as silent and motionless as the great stone statues towering over them, knelt facing the west wall and the huge altar. Beside the altar the yearlong fire burned in the sacred brazier, and behind it, on thrones arranged in a crescent, sat the mummified patriarchs, their faces animated in the flickering flames and shadows.

From out of the darkness the high priest ascended the steps to the altar, a young llama in his arms. In the silence he tied the animal securely, then turned his back to the supplicants. As one the worshipers followed his gaze to the great disk with radiating waves of gold, now all but lost in darkness.

In the stillness anticipation mounted. Beyond the temple doors the horizon remained a misty blue-gray, but now the gold image of the sun high on the temple wall began to flush with life. Within seconds it grew brightly pink, then burst into blinding brilliance, its rays shimmering with fire, reflecting the sun below the horizon.

Whispering prayers of thanksgiving, the mass turned silently toward the great doors to watch the sun itself rise in its full glory. On this day, once again, the supreme god would bestow his bountiful blessings. The mummies on their golden thrones would bathe in the sun's benevolence. The sun-god's subjects would thrive.

Just as the sun rose full on the horizon, the priest turned the llama's eyes toward it. Swiftly he tore open its chest, extracted the heart, lungs, and viscera, and placed them on the flaming brazier. Bursting into cries of exultation, the worshipers proceeded to the foot of the altar with their gifts of flowers, incense, vegetables, fruits, and beverages in cups of gold.

This was no annual festival among the Peruvians. It was not a monthly communion or a weekly sabbath, but a daily ritual in recognition of their utter dependency upon the sun-god. Indeed, the sun permeated all aspects of Peruvian life. The populace built entire towns facing east, enabling every citizen to greet the sun the instant it appeared each morning. They constructed great "columns of the sun" in every village, their tops leveled so that the sun-god would have a place to sit if he grew weary wandering across the sky each day. All major feasts were held in his honor, and the four great holidays of the year—the winter and summer solstices, the spring and autumn equinoxes—were keyed to celebrating aspects of the sun's relation to the earth. On such occasions gold thrones were placed on the tops of the columns so that the sun-god could recline in luxury while watching the festivities.

All that existed derived from the sun. Gold nuggets were its tears, fire its intimate gift; annually the chief priest kindled a fire by using a concave golden mirror to reflect the sun's heat to tinder. The flame was kept alive continuously in the temple and in the abode of the Virgins of the Sun until the following year. The populace even worshiped thunder, a servant of the sun.

The Peruvians worshiped joyfully, through chants and hymns, occasional fasting, and celebrations. They organized elaborate parades, the grand marshal being the Inca chief, followed by dignitaries and marchers in masks and costumes. Unlike contemporary parades, these began long before dawn and ended not at city hall but at an elevation overlooking the eastern horizon. As the sun rose, the celebrants fell to their knees and threw it kisses. The Inca chief poured the sun a sacred beverage, then drank the remainder himself.

Dancing, too, was an act of worship, and these people worshiped robustly at every festival. In fact, so abandoned was their dancing that outsiders of the day described it as madness.

Homage to the Sun

In Mexico the ancient Aztecs actually called themselves the "children of the sun," and every morning they welcomed it with trumpet peals and hymns. Eight times a day its priests held devotional services to the sun. The Aztecs did not worship through dance as much as the Peruvians did. They expressed their devotion by sacrificing many thousands of men, women, and children.

There is painful logic in the Aztec eagerness to offer only the best—human lives—to the deity that in an instant could annihilate everything and everyone in fire or ice. It was a bargain that even the saintly Abraham was willing to strike as he raised his dagger above the naked chest of his firstborn, Isaac. Likewise, the God/Father of

Christianity sacrificed his son that he might forgive those for whom the death atoned.

But the sun's divinity is unique in this respect: It has been recognized through all the earth, even in prehistory. It's a safe bet that no god has come close to competing with Old Sol, either in sheer numbers of devotees throughout history or in the excesses of their fervor. In Sumeria he was Utu; in Syria, Shemesh; in Egypt, Ra. The earliest humans, the Phoenicians, worshiped the sun, which they called Baal of Heaven.

The Babylonians credited the sun with so many attributes that they finally apportioned them among several gods. The kindly and supreme god was Shamash, whom they worshiped nude. To Shamash the poet-king Nebuchadnezzar wrote several poems.

The Egyptians built the Heliopolis in honor of the sun. In Japan the early dynasties traced their lineage directly from it. Native North American tribes, including the Sioux and Natahex, worshiped the sun and performed sun dances.

The sun is a rare god in that he is often portrayed without human attributes, a mere disk, sometimes with wings, from which radiate shimmering beams of light. He is an incomprehensible god, without physical form, an advanced theological concept among ancient people.

Very early we humans recognized the sun's centrality to our existence. We hailed it as the source of our very life, of fertility. In some way we comprehended its role in the creation of clouds and rain, for the sun-god is often depicted as drawing water to himself and bathing the earth in fish-laden rivers and streams which flow from his own body.

Our ancestors hailed the sun as champion of truth and uprightness, the giver of laws and oracles, punisher of evildoers, the source of life and death, supreme judge, bestower of health, lord of all lands, author of birth, creator even of other gods. Some tribes of India felt that it was the paradise where dwelled departed souls. Certain Hindus chanted a hymn referring to the sun by 108 names. One sect in southern India still declares a holiday in honor of the sun every February 4.

"In all the seven worlds," writes the poet of the Hindu *Bhagavad-Gita,* "and all the *brahma*-worlds, there is nothing superior to the sun."

The Fallen God

We of an enlightened time and culture no longer stand in awe of the sun. We do not worship it. (That is true for the most part, although the Pueblo tribes of the American Southwest still make offerings to a sun image in all-night ceremonies every December 22 to greet the return of gradually lengthening days. And modern-day Druids gather in Amesbury, England, every June 21 to worship the sun on the longest day of the year.) As a species we have grown smarter. We understand the sun, even entertain theories of its origin. Just as we have climbed Sinai and Olympus and found no God or gods there, as we've learned that lightning is a natural electrical phenomenon and that witch doctors perform no miracles beyond the laws of nature, so we have discovered that the sun, too, can be explained according to the laws of science. We have lost our sense of awe, and without awe there can be no gods.

It is one rather puny star among millions, but it is just right for us. Should it shine a fraction more or less intensely than it does, all life on earth would cease to exist. It has a weight of two billion billion billion tons, an incomprehensible figure surpassing even the national debt. And it achieves that weight without sprawling mountain ranges, vast continents, or great oceans—virtually no solids or liquids at all. The sun is composed entirely of gases which are drawn and held together just as the earth is—through gravity.

Among those gases, hydrogen is predominant. That's lucky for us, for hydrogen is the key to solar radiation. Not that the sun burns hydrogen the way a bonfire burns wood (if that were so, it would have run out of fuel a long time ago). The sun doesn't burn at all in the usual sense. It explodes. It's the original hydrogen bomb.

The larger a solar body, the greater its gravity. Compared with the earth, the sun is large indeed; it has a diameter of 864,400 miles, while the earth's is 7,900 miles. The sun's gravity is so great that zillions of hydrogen atoms plunge to its core at tremendous speeds every instant, smash into each other, and break apart, forming new configurations—helium atoms. Part of the original atoms escapes in violent bursts of heat and light. The temperature in the photosphere, the blazing surface of sun, reaches 13 million degrees K, more than 24 million degrees F.

About one-billionth of the sun's energy reaches us, flashing across ninety-three million miles of space in just eight minutes, fresh from the oven. It is a very small fraction of the sun's rays, but it still has the potential to destroy all life. The sun radiates its energy in the form of electromagnetism. This radiation seems to act both as separate packets of energy, known as quanta, and as waves of varying lengths. Some of those rays or waves are more than a thousand meters long, some as short as one ten-trillionth of a meter. The shorter wavelengths—cosmic rays, gamma rays, X rays, and one of three ultraviolet waves (UVC)—are deadly to the cells of living creatures. No life could exist were they to reach the earth.

We are protected from them by an unstable gas so rare that if compressed, it would form a shell only a tenth of an inch thick around the globe. Actually, ozone exists as a fraction of the atmosphere from six to thirty miles above the earth, where it absorbs virtually all of the sun's shortest rays and many of the medium-short ones. This fragile intermediary shelters us from the wrath of the sun-god.

Sunshine, Life, and Health

The radiation which does reach the earth creates life. It sustains life. Moment by moment, season by season, it manipulates both the external and internal environment of all living organisms. It does so not through the waves that give us light and color, not only through those infrared waves that warm the earth, but substantially by its ultraviolet spectrum.

Without ultraviolet radiation (UVR) the populations of many underdeveloped countries would be chronically sick and dying, poisoned by their drinking water. UVR purifies the water, penetrating to a depth of about twelve feet and killing many of the harmful microorganisms that breed in warm, static water. So efficient is the process that ultraviolet water purification systems are a growing industry, and some experts believe they may someday replace chlorine as the preferred means of treating major water supplies.

What UVR does in the water it also does in the air and on the skin. That may explain in part why we have fewer colds in the summer, when we spend a good deal of time out of doors under intense sunlight.

UVR also improves wound healing, sometimes dramatically, a fact recognized by both ancient Greek physicians and most of our grandparents, who preferred to leave cuts and scrapes unbandaged in order that they might "get the air." Only with the advent of antibiotics did we come to ignore the sun's healing powers.

The sun's ultraviolet rays are an internal antibiotic of sorts. Longer ultraviolet waves penetrate deeply enough to reach the blood supply, where they aid in destroying germs causing infection.

The sun's ultraviolet rays help keep the heart beating rhythmically, the muscles contracting when you want them to, the blood coagulating, the body's cells intact, and the bones from getting soft and brittle. UVR's role in these processes is a bit complex.

Your body requires calcium to perform those functions, as we discussed briefly earlier. Like all hormones, calciferol, the useful form of vitamin D, is manufactured in the body. We get some vitamin D in our diets, especially because we eat oily fish, liver, eggs, cheese, and butter, all of which can also be high in fats and cholesterol. We can get vitamin D from supplements and enriched milk and cereals. But according to a survey published in the prestigious scientific journal *Nature*, these sources provide only 10 to 20 percent of the vitamin D in our bodies. The rest is formed in the skin. Technically UVR converts cholesterol to prohormone 25-hydroxyvitamin D, which is converted to calciferol in the kidneys.

Most of us get more than enough sunlight to meet our vitamin D needs—from ten to twenty minutes' exposure daily on our hands and face. Yet apparently there are many millions who do not, usually because of certain illnesses and physiological problems. The reduced estrogen production of postmenopausal women interferes with the conversion of vitamin D to calciferol. The same is true among those suffering liver, kidney, or parathyroid disease. Pregnant and nursing women require significantly greater amounts of vitamin D and calcium than does the general population. So do people taking such anticonvulsive drugs as phenobarbital.

A survey of elderly residents of Albuquerque, New Mexico, in 1982 showed that 60 percent were getting less than 100 international units (IU) of vitamin D daily from all sources, and that's only one-fourth of the Food and Drug Administration's recommended daily allowance. That was true in spite of Albuquerque's abundant sunshine and was attributed in part to the conscious effort among those surveyed to avoid sunshine.

We can always increase our vitamin D levels through supplements, and among those whose bodies fail to process the nutrient normally, that's often the only reliable approach. But there's a fascinating point to be made here: In extremely excessive amounts—thousands of IU daily—vitamin D becomes toxic and can cause dangerous health problems. That's rare but possible. You can't get too much vitamin D from the sun, however. Your body responds to abundant vitamin D levels by reducing production. According to Hector DeLuca, Ph.D., chairman of the Department of Biochemistry at the University of Wisconsin, "Sunshine is the way you are meant to get your vitamin D."

As long ago as 1938 the U.S. Public Health Service found a direct correlation between the number of cavities children developed and their annual amount of sun exposure. In locations with more than three thousand hours of sunshine per year, researchers found an average of 290 cavities per hundred children. Where sunshine was less than twenty-two hundred hours per year, cavities increased to 487 per hundred youngsters.

Finally, a speculation. UVR changes cholesterol, more abundant in the skin than in any other tissues, into provitamin D, and that suggests a fascinating question: Might there be a relationship between the abnormally low amount of exposure to the sun until recently among most citizens of the United States and their abnormally high cholesterol levels? In recent years the increased interest in fitness and exercise has led millions of men and women to spend more time out of doors—and deaths from heart disease have substantially decreased. Certainly, improved diets have played a major role, but what has the increased exposure to sunshine contributed? To our knowledge the possible link between sunlight and low cholesterol levels has yet to be examined.

The Sun Is Deadly, Too

We owe our survival as much to the ultraviolet waves of the sun as to any other part of the solar spectrum, but as the ancients philosophized, only a fool approaches too close to the divine. Among those who, like Icarus, have confronted the sun with arrogance, millions have fallen in tragedy. Excessive exposure can cause potentially fatal skin cancer, a possibility that's much less remote than most people realize.

Skin cancer in the United States is skyrocketing to near epidemic proportions. Approximately one in seven Americans will develop skin cancer at some point in life. Squamous cell and basal cell skin cancers are slow to develop and almost always curable. But the most severe form, malignant melanoma, kills 25 percent of its victims.

That melanoma is the real problem. This year more than twenty-five thousand Americans will develop it. They are a small fraction of the half million skin cancer victims that will be diagnosed, but those twenty-five thousand represent an increase of 1,000 percent between 1930 and 1980.

According to dermatologists, there's no debating the issue: Ninety percent of skin cancers are triggered by excessive exposure to the sun. Because most citizens of advanced societies have enjoyed an increase in leisure time during the past fifty years, many have spent more hours out of doors under intense sunlight oblivious of the sun's power. As a result, we can chart the increased leisure time in terms of melanoma cases.

At least four factors determine the degree of damage UVR will cause. The first is the length of the ultraviolet waves reaching our skin.

The sun's radiation—all of it, not just the ultraviolet— reaches us as waves of greatly varying lengths. The length of a solar ray makes all the difference in the world. The shortest waves—the cosmic, X rays, and gamma rays—are too fragile to penetrate the earth's atmosphere. They're reflected back into space or are absorbed by the ozone layer. Slightly larger are the ultraviolet C waves. They're between 100 and 286 nanometers long. (A nanometer is abbreviated nm, and is one-billionth of a meter—pretty small.) UVC waves also fail to penetrate the atmosphere in any significant numbers.

UVB waves are from 286 to 320 nm in length, and UVA waves are 320 to 400 nm long. These are the waves that affect us for both good and ill, and we have much to say about them. They're followed in length by waves which are visible to humans. We can see only those which are from 400 to 720 nm in length, and as the lengths vary within that range, we see them reflected as varying colors.

Finally, the infrared waves are from 1,000 nanometers to 1 millimeter in length. These are the sun's heat waves. Ultraviolet and infrared waves are not the same. Most people know that. The good news: You can sit at your

Spring Room windows and swelter safely in the heat because the infrared waves penetrate the glass while 95 percent of UVR doesn't. The bad news: You can be out of doors on a cool, overcast day and get a serious burn because the clouds absorb much of the heat and light waves while ultraviolet radiation penetrates to the earth—and your skin.

As you've probably already discovered, you can also get burned in the shade. That's because UVR can be reflected from the sky (skylight) and from the surface of objects and the earth itself. Bright objects, such as cement and the sand of a beach, reflect a great deal more UVR than do darker surfaces such as grass (what you see as white, remember, is actually the reflection of all the waves of the entire color spectrum). All factors being equal, you're more likely to be burned at the shore than in the country. And here's something that may surprise you: You have a greater chance of getting burned during a humid afternoon at the Riis Park beach in New York City than in the Arizona desert, especially if you're in the shade at both locations. Once again, it's the reflection of UVR—by humidity—that greatly increases the amount of radiation bombarding you.

In fact, high humidity or spotty clouds through which direct sunlight penetrates can actually raise UVR exposure above that of a bright, sunny day.

Contrary to popular opinion, bodies of water—swimming pools, lakes, oceans—absorb the sun's rays rather than reflect them, thereby reducing our risk of burning if we're sitting in the shade in a boat on the water. But swimming involves two risks. First, the water keeps us cool, lulling us into the mistaken belief that we're not being burned. Secondly, UVR can burn our submerged bodies to a depth of several feet.

In addition to immediate environmental conditions, at

least three other factors play major roles in determining how much UVR exposure we get. The first is latitude. UVR increases as we travel closer to the equator. For example, Atlanta, Georgia, receives three times the UVR that Manitoba, Canada, does.

Solar radiation increases roughly 3 to 5 percent every three hundred miles closer to the equator, all other factors remaining constant. But if you're in a hurry to get that extra 4 or 5 percent of UVR (and of course, you shouldn't be), you can do it by traveling just a thousand feet—straight up. That's because the atmosphere grows increasingly thin as we move higher from sea level. You might easily suffer severe sunburn while freezing to death in the Andes! The amount of the most harmful ultraviolet rays, UVB, can increase by ten times in high mountains as compared with flatlands at the same latitude. Even UVC waves have been recorded at very high altitudes.

The Art of Prudent Sun Worship

Ultimately your genes will determine how you'll respond to UVR. Some people burn immediately in just minutes. They're often redheads or people with freckles or those who can trace their ancestry to England, Ireland, Scotland, or Wales. They simply lack the pigment necessary to darken the skin. That pigment, melanin, is an excellent sunscreen. It's the reason black people are black and brown people are brown, and it's the reason they can be out of doors all day beneath the African or Indian sun and be less likely to burn than fair-skinned people would. These are the people who have lived long and intimately with the sun and, having learned to pay homage to its power to bring bounty and famine, need not fear it in their bodies. Most of us fit between the two extremes.

The way melanin functions to protect us touches on the miraculous. The moment we step out the door into sunlight, UVA, the longest ultraviolet ray, begins to give us an instant tan. In fact, even the visible rays, the sunlight itself, can stimulate the darkening of the melanin pigment already in our skin. This is a first-aid measure, the body's attempt to prevent or reduce burning, which it "recognizes" as potentially very dangerous.

But most of us don't have a great deal of pigment in our skin, so when we get that first exposure to sun in the spring, we're not going to tan much. If we push our luck, we'll simply burn. What's more, this instant tan doesn't last long, a few hours to perhaps a day and a half. Fortunately another process is already under way. Both UVA and UVB waves stimulate the production of additional melanin pigment. It takes about five days for the new pigment to reach the skin, darkening it. If you're a sensible sunbather, you've probably noticed the process. A few hours after you've been in the sun briefly, your skin color changed very little, perhaps growing a shade darker. By the following day it was back to its usual color, but after a few more days you discover yourself tan again and darker than on the first day. This long-term tan is accompanied by thickening of the skin and is a much more effective protection from sunburn than is the immediate tan. It lasts until the layers of pigmented skin flake off. It can be maintained by continued sunbathing.[15]

Because the process which leads to tanning involves damage to skin cells similar to that which produces cancer, some dermatologists believe that there is no such thing as a "safe" tan. At a recent symposium of the American Academy of Dermatology and the American Academy of Pediatrics, some researchers warned against virtually any exposure to the sun, noting in a news release, "skin damage can occur whenever you're exposed to the sun, for any amount of time—not just when you're sunbathing. This includes walking, driving, picnicking, playing a sport or doing yard work."

The one surefire solution, according to the release, is the habitual use of commercial sunscreens from infancy on: "It is important that parents and physicians . . . protect children from the sun beginning with infancy." (This meeting, incidentally, was supported by a grant from the Johnson & Johnson baby products company.)

But the idea of chronically hiding behind sunscreens has a lot not going for it. First of all, none of us is going to do it. It's a good bet the dermatologists themselves don't. Before driving to work? Walking to work? From the office to a restaurant for lunch? According to these experts, we're risking skin damage during these brief interludes. Even while working in the yard for an hour or so, or sitting under a tree in a park, the majority of us aren't going to bother with sunscreens. We're going to save them for serious sunbathing.

That being the case, an alternate approach is to recognize that, as Dr. Howard Stoll of the Roswell Park Memorial Institute's Dermatology Section puts it, "The sun is not man's enemy." Obviously exposure to the sun has not created an epidemic of skin cancer, or the epidemic would have existed for as long as the sun has been shining on humanity. It's the *excess* exposure needed for a deep tan—the gaudy brand name status symbol that says, "I have money and leisure and do nothing but lie on a tropical beach all day"—that's the culprit. Gradual, moderate tanning is one of those adaptational miracles to which we humans owe our survival. The damaging of skin cells is basic to the process, just as our immune defenses are triggered by the destruction of some cells.

That's the way it's supposed to happen, and it does, and it has, keeping us from being burned to a crisp since the beginning. It's normal and natural.

The same can't be said for lying in a skimpy bathing suit in the broiling sun, sweating for hours in order to become a different color. The most ardent ancient sun worshiper would certainly find this practice bizarre in the extreme and purposeless apart from the pleasantries of mild exhibitionism and voyeurism.

While we're at it, we may as well say a word about sunlamps and tanning salons. First the lamps. In 1981 Food and Drug Administration researchers Kenneth Krell and Elizabeth D. Jacobson compared various sources of radiation to see how quickly they could make mouse cells mutate or die. The sources included the sun, fluorescent and incandescent lights, and a sunlamp. While the other sources were only fractionally as potent as the sun, the sunlamp was four times as deadly to the cells and created eight times as many deformities in a given period of time as the sun itself. These lamps are extremely potent sources of ultraviolet radiation.

Tanning boxes have a Plexiglas sheet on which the user lies. When the tanner pulls the lid down, he or she is surrounded by as many as twenty-eight ultraviolet tubes. They bombard the tanner with, primarily, UVA radiation. This is the wavelength that penetrates deeply into the skin, producing short-term tanning, and helps stimulate the body's production of additional melanin for long-term tanning. It's the least harmful UVR and by itself isn't likely to cause severe burning, although it has been implicated in skin wrinkling. Reputable operators insist that users start slowly, no more than five to ten minutes of exposure at a session. Once a tan is developed, it can be maintained with two thirty-minute sessions per week.

Apart from rare allergic and other reactions people have to the sun, the tanning booths appear to be safe. In fact, they can play a vital part in helping you prepare for a warm-climate vacation, especially if it's to be a short one—a week or two. That's because, almost invariably, no matter how dedicated you are to not doing so, you'll probably get too much sun during the first few days and spend the next few feeling miserable. It takes more willpower than most of us hibernators have to travel from Christmas trees to palm trees and not surrender to a day in the sun.

Of course, that's the perfect time to use a sunscreen. "The sun screen you select," writes Dr. Stoll, "should contain a combination of benzophenone and para-amino benzoic acid (PABA)." Benzophenone blocks UVA and other radiation, while PABA protects against UVB waves. Those UVB waves are the most dangerous ones, the major cause of sunburning. On the other hand, they're also primarily responsible for triggering the body's production of additional melanin for long-term tanning.

Sunscreens are now rated according to a sun protection factor (SPF) scale from two to twenty-three. The higher the number, the greater the protection. As the number decreases, you'll have more opportunity to tan—or burn. If you *do* want to develop that long-term melanin protection, look for a product with an intermediate SPF and limit your exposure until the tan develops.

Please let us not have any hibernator flying from the cold to the equator and running off to the beach without using a high SPF sunscreen over *all* exposed skin or spending a couple of months visiting a tanning facility regularly. During the winter the amount of ultraviolet light reaching us, even when we're out of doors frequently, is much less than that of the summer. We're not stimulated to produce melanin pigment, and we don't. Consequently, when exposed to tropical sun for the first time, our bodies can't perform the first aid of an immediate tan. Instead, we burn, often badly.

The ideal way to prepare yourself for the summer sun of the temperate zone is the natural way: by spending time out of doors as early in the season as possible, while the sun still remains low in the southern sky. At that time of year—late winter—the dangerous UVB radiation is reduced in intensity by a factor of forty as it travels through the increased atmosphere resulting from the sun's angle to the earth, but the UVA rays, which stimulate more safely a protective tan, are reduced by only 50 percent. This is the best time of year to begin tanning without burning.

This gradual exposure, incidentally, is the one followed by dedicated nudists and naturists, those folks who begin their volleyball season as soon as the temperature allows them out of doors without risking frostbite of vital appendages. They remain in the sun throughout the summer and often into late fall, a good many of them without the protection of sunscreens. If exposure to the sun in itself were the cause of skin cancer, it ought to exist in epidemic proportions among this group. This has not been found the case, according to spokespeople for the American Sunbathing Association. Even sunburn appears to be extremely rare since these people tan gradually, in step with the sun's increasing seasonal intensity.

By late spring follow this sun exposure program offered by Dr. Stoll: As the days grow longer, and you can fit some sunbathing in before or after work or on the weekends, begin with only ten minutes of sunning if you're fair-skinned, fifteen minutes if your skin is medium. If you're swimming, count that as exposure time.

241

And if you plan to be outside longer, use a sunscreen after the allotted time. Increase your exposure gradually but regularly—and at the same time each day. That's more important than you may think. For example, at the latitude of Minneapolis, Minnesota, you'll get twice as much radiation sunbathing at 11:00 A.M. as you will at 9:00 P.M. By casually shifting your sunbathing two hours later one morning, you'll be getting a lot more than a gradual increase in exposure.

In fact, until you've developed an effective tan, Dr. Stoll recommends avoiding direct exposure between 10:00 A.M. and 3:00 P.M.

Of course, the most important guideline of all is common sense. As we've said, it's possible—even easy—to receive damaging amounts of UVR, even when atmospheric conditions block the infrared heat waves and a fresh breeze makes you feel cool and comfortable. Don't rely on comfort. On the other hand, *discomfort* is always a dependable warning sign. If you're sweating and your skin feels hot and remaining in the sun is an act of masochism, however pleasant, you're doing a microwave number on your body. If the visible waves are there along with the infrared, so is the UVR. The very *instant* you begin to feel any discomfort from the sun, even if you have a tan, put on a good sunscreen, or get out of the sun.

Common sense is also the best guide to dressing for a warm environment. Medical climatologist F. P. Ellis, after studying the deterioration of servicemen in the tropics during the Second World War, concluded, "Man is a tropical animal and if he is able to discard the clothing conventions imposed on him, as the war prisoners did at Changi, he will tolerate the climate with ease, for he is better equipped than horses or cattle with a comparatively hairless skin and a more effective sweating mechanism."

You can protect yourself from the sun's infrared and ultraviolet waves to some degree by wearing a white broad-brimmed hat and a white, long-sleeved, porous, and loosely fitting shirt of lightweight material. But if the temperature rather than the sun is the problem, wear as little as possible.

Finally, a word about protecting your eyes. There's no question that continual exposure to bright sun can produce cataracts, a clouding of the eye lens that can cause partial or total blindness. Take this danger seriously. There's no pain to warn of damage as with sunburn and, apart from an eye exam, little evidence of the problem until your eyes begin to fail. By then it's too late for prevention.

The answer is to wear sunglasses whenever you're out of doors in sunlight. Ordinary sunglasses won't help much, though. Most optical stores also sell "UV-treated" sunglasses beginning at about twenty dollars—more, of course, if you want prescription glasses. It's an investment you shouldn't think twice about.

To summarize, in planning your great escape to the Antihibernation Belt, take the sun seriously into consideration. If you seek a hot climate, look for sea-level spots with plenty of shade. If you're fair-skinned and want moderate temperatures, avoid the high mountains in favor of more northern latitudes. Plan ahead to avoid too much sun, or to adapt your body to the sun through a preescape tanning program. And be sure to bring along—and *use*—both a good sunscreen and a pair of sunglasses designed to prevent ultraviolet penetration.

That way you'll return home not just a happy hibernator but a healthy one.

Coping with the Seasons: Adaptation Through the Year

*Whoever wishes to investigate medicine properly
should proceed thus: in the first place, consider
the seasons of the year, and what effect each of
them produces. . . .*
                              —HIPPOCRATES

In deciding to add this chapter, we're reminded of a
medical journal report some years ago describing a new
surgical procedure. The surgeons summarized the results
with their first patient in these words: "The operation was
entirely successful. Unfortunately the patient expired."

We're confident that no one who applies the information he or she has read in this book need ever again suffer the crippling slowdown of the hibernation response.
There need be no more months-long bouts of hope-
lessness, fatigue, and sorrow; abandonment to out-
of-control weight gain; the inability, through fatigue, to
accomplish even the simplest physical or mental chores.
We haven't given pep talks in these pages or a program
for merely enduring the inevitable. Our approach is a
comprehensive plan to eliminate every symptom of the
hibernation response while dealing with the fundamental
causes of the response. If it's autumn as you read this
book, and if you've been applying our advice, you've

probably already discovered that the operation has been a complete success.

We realize, however, that while triumphing over the hibernation response, you may yet fall victim to other climatic factors during the four seasons common in temperate zones—indeed, even other aspects of the winter which we haven't yet discussed. According to psychologist James Rotton, up to 20 percent of us are extremely sensitive to the weather. Women are more so than men, and it's a pretty safe bet that hibernators, who are so profoundly affected by the onset of winter, are also particularly responsive to other changes of season and weather. We'll talk about some of these changes, how they influence us and what we can do to cope, in this chapter. We'll simply not have our patients survive the operation only to succumb to related ailments.

Summer

Apart from increased photoperiods and the germ-killing effects of ultraviolet radiation, the warm temperature of summer days in itself helps us stay healthy. Researchers have long sought to understand why we suffer significantly fewer colds and respiratory infections in summer than in winter. One popular theory was that microorganisms become more virulent during the winter, but strong evidence opposes this theory.

In 1959 researchers at the Institute of Hygiene at the University of Utrecht in the Netherlands studied the effects of temperature on the influence of streptococci and staphylococci viruses, along with other microorganisms. They found that, as the temperature rises from 50° to 85°F, these microorganisms begin dying. And their death rates soar by a factor of two to four for every twelve degrees of temperature increase.

We've already seen how the sun itself—the UV rays—is a germicide, but the warm temperature of summer works in another way as well to kill harmful microorganisms that have set up housekeeping on your skin: It gets you to sweating. Ordinarily the pH, or alkalinity, of the skin is four to six, but evaporated sweat leaves behind an acid coating of three to five pH. That's deadly to most bacteria.

Warm temperatures also lower blood pressure. Although it's been suggested that there may be a psychological component to this phenomenon—pleasant temperatures help us relax, reducing stress and blood pressure—a major factor is physiological. The heat generated by the metabolism of the internal organs must be carried to the skin surface and dissipated into the air in order to maintain normal body temperature. When the air itself is warm, both the heat radiation and the convection processes by which body heat is released to the air are slowed. To compensate for that, the blood vessels relax and dilate in order to distribute the blood more thoroughly at the body's surface. Pumping the same quantity of blood through what amounts to larger vessels in a given time span reduces the pressure on those vessels.

That's true in warm, not hot, temperatures. It's the scorching days of summer that place high adaptational demands upon us. We've already discussed one of these—sunburn—in a previous chapter. Beyond that, excess heat forces the body to work harder to maintain normal core temperature. Those demands, particularly on the heart and circulatory system, can be very severe—too severe for some people.

A heat wave in July 1966, among the greatest to strike the United States in this century, led to 7,000 more deaths than the average for that month in the eleven states studied. According to L. A. Helfand, of the Illinois

Environmental Protection Agency, and Clyde Bridger, chief statistician for the Illinois Department of Public Health, stroke caused 1,041 of those deaths, while heart attacks triggered most of the others.

In fact, the annual peak for heart attacks doesn't occur in the winter, when unacclimatized and poorly conditioned people go on their snow-shoveling binges, although there *is* a secondary high then. The major heart attack season comes during the hottest months of summer. Dr. George E. Burch, an expert on health and weather, has found that being out of doors during the dog days of summer demands an increase in cardiac output of 57 percent compared with that of air-conditioned surroundings.

Dr. Burch and T. D. Giles report that people with ischemic heart disease, caused by inadequate blood supply to the heart tissue, are particularly vulnerable to angina pectoris during the summer months. They write, "When patients are exposed to high environmental temperatures and humidities, tremendous increases in cardiac output are necessary to transport heat to the body surface to be lost to the atmosphere. Such demands for an increase in cardiac output (by increasing heart rate and at times stroke volume) stress the already diseased myocardium and provide a mechanism for the production of angina pectoris in such patients."

Excessive heat affects both body and mind. Typically there's a definite limit beyond which most of us are unable to function. Investigators at the New South Wales Division of Occupational Health in Sydney, Australia, were asked to find that limit some years ago by a mines rescue station. The goal was to learn how long rescuers could endure exposure to the heat of the mines while working feverishly to save trapped miners.

The victims who volunteered for the study earned

247

whatever they were paid, and then some. They were placed in a heat chamber and asked to do two minutes of work, then to rest for three. By work the researchers meant walking on treadmills while carrying heavy loads and lifting weights.

This cycle continued, with body temperatures being monitored as they increased, until the volunteers could no longer continue.

The temperature in the chamber was 102°F. All but one of the five men worked until their core temperatures reached 101°F. At that point pulse rates were as high as 170 beats per minute. Some of the men felt giddy; others, nauseated and weak.

That, in the extreme, is what the heat of summer can do to your body. Another study, this one into the causes of psychiatric breakdown among Navy personnel during the Second World War, found these problems among sailors stationed in tropical climates. According to investigator R. K. MacPherson, in a symposium on fatigue,

> Men were irritable, less inclined to exert themselves, and less amenable than in other climates. Their work was slower, they lounged instead of walking, their dress was slovenly, their quarters were unnecessarily untidy, their courtesies were neglected, there was a lack of energy and enthusiasm. On every possible occasion a man would lie down when, in other climates, he would be content to sit. Early rising was practically unknown. It was not unusual to find officers still in bed at 0800 hours [8:00 A.M.]. Many of them breakfasted in bed. Most personnel took to their bunks for as long as possible during the midday recess. This siesta was often unduly prolonged.

In serious cases the heat-stressed victims lost weight, suffered insomnia and depression. In severe cases victims might suffer amnesia and anxiety and might even doubt their sanity.

Accuracy also falls with excessively high temperatures. We make more errors; we have more mishaps. Accidents in factories are at a minimum at temperatures between 65° and 69°F. They increase by 23 percent when the temperatures rise above 75°F. (Cold temperatures also lead to more accidents; below 55°F they increase by up to 35 percent.)

Add humidity to the heat—as nature does throughout much of the eastern portion of the United States, from Mississippi to Connecticut—and the effects of the high temperature on the body are compounded. That's because sweat can't evaporate in air that's already water-laden. Sweating is the body's primary means of keeping core temperatures down; organ heat is taken up by the blood and carried to the skin, where it's cooled through sweat evaporation. If, because of high humidity, the sweat fails to evaporate, we sweat even more in order to speed the cooling process.

That's why you'll produce more sweat and feel more discomfort on a steamy July in Philadelphia than you will in the Arizona desert.

There's just one advantage to high humidity: It kills the influenza virus. That's why we don't have flu outbreaks until the air becomes cool and dry. But there are numerous other microbial pathogens that thrive in moist air—those which cause tropical diseases.

The key to adapting to summer heat and humidity, like that of winter cold, is acclimatization. But heed this warning: *People with severe heart disease cannot acclimatize to heat,* any more than they can to cold. If you know that you have a heart condition, make sure that your doctor approves any acclimatization program before undertaking it. He may rule it out altogether or work with you in developing one suitable to your capabilities. If you don't know the health status of your cardiovascular system, get a thorough examination before you begin.

Acclimatizing to the Heat

John Maher, research biologist at the Army Research Institute of Environmental Medicine in Natick, Massachusetts, has developed a program capable of acclimatizing people in good physical shape in four to seven days. Its major emphasis is to increase cardiovascular strength, which means it'll make your heart stronger and your blood circulation more efficient, and that'll increase your ability to keep cool when the heat's on.

Begin in the spring, when the temperatures are cool, with eight days of walking for at least half an hour. Maher's volunteers stuck to a moderately brisk pace of three and a half miles per hour.

Step two in Maher's program requires equipment not available outside the laboratory; he had his volunteers ride stationary bicycles in a special cylinder heated to 120°F. By the second day the men had begun to acclimatize, their body temperatures dropping and their endurance increasing. They began sweating more efficiently.

You can reap the same results through any exercise that, while you wear an exercise suit, increases your heart, respiratory, and temperature levels above those of the walking level. Choose a suit made of a porous material such as cotton rather than airtight nylon or rubber. Jogging, bicycling, or even rapid walking will do the trick.

Don't push hard, just enough to keep your pulse rate in the *target area* for at least twenty minutes.

Your target area is easy to calculate. Simply subtract your age from 220. That will give your maximum heart rate. For example, if you're forty years old, your maximum rate is 180 beats per minute (plus or minus 10). It's not necessary to push for your maximum, however, and it can be dangerous. Instead, a good conditioning rate is 70 percent of the maximum—that's .70 × 180, or 126 beats per minute.

In fact, exercising at that rate for twenty minutes every other day will not only thoroughly acclimatize you to the heat in seven to fourteen days but condition you physically as well. Probably by the end of the first week you'll discover that although on the first day you might have reached the pulse target area with a brisk walk, by the second week you'll have to begin jogging to get there, yet you won't feel any more stress than you did walking the week before.

Why? Your heart has already grown stronger. Your blood vessels are enlarging, and you are acquiring new ones to supply the vital organs. You're using oxygen more efficiently. Your fitness will continue to improve dramatically but never so much as in these first weeks, when you need the encouragement most. And those are precisely the improvements your body needs to reach its maximum efficiency in the blood-cooling process. You'll notice the improvement within days. Studies have shown that during the first exercise period in high temperature, subjects have high core temperatures and pulse rate and low sweat loss. When people are pushed to extremes—as you won't be—they become extremely uncomfortable. But within four to six days both temperature and discomfort decrease, along with heart rate, while sweating increases significantly.

Two points: (1) Don't push yourself to the point of serious discomfort. Stop every four or five minutes, and take your pulse for fifteen seconds. Multiply your pulse rate by 4. If the figure is above your target area, slow down. (2) Once you begin to sweat easily, remove the exercise suit so that evaporation can take place.

Here are some additional pointers to keep in mind both during the acclimatization process and throughout the summer:

—Let your instincts be your guide regarding water consumption. You can lose three quarts of water through sweat and exhaled moisture from your lungs in ninety minutes of activity in the summer heat, and they have to be replaced. Otherwise, your body will absorb water from your blood, reducing blood volume and thickening it. Drink whenever you're thirsty. If you don't think that's often enough, a good rule of thumb when you are active is: eight ounces of water every twenty minutes in temperatures above 80°F and 60 percent humidity.

—Sweating consumes two important minerals: potassium and sodium chloride, or salt, the reason that sweat tastes salty. Salt tablets are no longer considered necessary, even by servicemen in basic training. Instead, eat such salt- and potassium-rich foods as celery, seafood, raisins, spinach, prunes, and bananas and such leafy vegetables as broccoli and cauliflower. And if you have a sudden craving to use more salt as a seasoning, do so. Although we've come a long way since the days when, like mice, we instinctively sought foods which gave us the nutrients needed to offset temporary deficiencies, there's evidence that such a capacity still exists in humans. Many pregnant women attest to compulsive cravings for foods that they've never liked before but that provide specific vitamins and minerals their bodies require. To a lesser degree we all go through such "irrational" cravings. They vanish as quickly as they came when we fill specific nutritional needs.

Chances are you'll find yourself seeking out potassium- and salt-rich foods during the summer as your need for them increases.

—Just as too warm an environment combats acclimatization to cold, so a cool environment disrupts adaptation to heat. Air conditioning becomes essential only when the humidity becomes intolerable. Depending upon the humidity, acclimatized persons can be comfortable in temperatures well above 100°F.

Whether at work or at home, air conditioners, when used, should be kept at 78°F or above if they're not to wreak havoc with your hard-earned ability to handle the summer heat and humidity. The primary function of an air conditioner should be to remove moisture from the air, not to refrigerate it, and that can also be achieved with a less expensive dehumidifier.

—Never exercise when the relative humidity exceeds 97 percent. Regardless of your level of fitness and acclimatization, you can't alter the basic laws of thermal regulation. When sweat can't evaporate, there's no stopping the potentially fatal rise in body temperature.

—Encourage sweat evaporation. We humans are a species bent on denying the animal in us, and that's nowhere more obvious than in our disgust with sweat. We turn up our noses at its odor, banish it from our underarms as though it were a curse, and wipe it from our face even before it forms there. "Just don't let them see you sweat" was part of the language even before Madison Avenue adopted it.[16]

Sweat that's stifled or wiped away doesn't help cool the body. Nor can sweat evaporate if it's absorbed by soggy shirts and trousers. Some exercise suits can prove downright dangerous during the summer if they prevent air circulation and evaporation.

When exercising in the heat, there should be as little as possible between your skin and the atmosphere. What you do wear should be loose or porous enough to allow ample air circulation.

Even when all precautions seem to have been taken, there remains the possibility—it is hoped, remote—of a heat-related crisis. Recognizing the symptoms could save your life.

Heat exhaustion involves profuse sweating, a moist skin, and a rapid pulse. Victims feel very uncomfortable, gasp for breath, and may even collapse.

The condition is often caused by a sudden exposure to very hot air—for example, spending the day in an excessively cool office and stepping outside into sweltering heat. The blood rushes quickly to the surface of the body, causing a dramatic drop in blood pressure. That causes the fainting. Core temperature increases, and water is taken from the blood to be used as sweat. That causes a decrease in blood volume, causing blood pressure to drop even further.

If you feel heat exhaustion coming on, drink plenty of liquids and get to a cool environment.

Heat stroke occurs among those doing extremely strenuous exercise in hot weather. The body can lose as many as eight quarts of water in an hour and a half of such activity, and it's impossible to replace it that quickly.

The first symptoms of heat stroke are the same as those of exhaustion. Eventually the body runs out of moisture. Sweating ceases; the skin becomes dry; body temperature soars.

By then things are serious indeed. If the core temperature is not lowered promptly, the victim will suffer brain damage and probably death.

Autumn

While many people love autumn—its brilliantly colored leaves, clean and brisk air, the bright, almost eerie sunlight and long shadows, the swift turbulence of contrasting white and gray clouds—we hibernators find little to celebrate during the fall. While others are happily thankful on November 25, we're thankful and grumpy. To the TV newscaster's annually expressed concern for the plight of turkeys everywhere, we respond, "To hell with the turkeys—what about me?"

But we who are conscious of our hibernation response aren't alone in bemoaning autumn. During this period of gray, cloudy, drizzly days, the sudden chill in the air, many people become troubled emotionally and develop physical ailments. A European telephone counseling service has reported a great increase in calls from both men and women, but to a greater extent from women, about problems with their spouses as the weather turns bad. Calls concerning health problems also increase significantly during the bad weather of autumn and reach their peak in winter.

Autumn, like spring, is a period of maximum atmo-

Heat Stress Chart

ACTUAL TEMP.	HUMIDITY						
	40%	50%	60%	70%	80%	90%	100%
	Apparent Temperature					(1)	(2)
67	66	66	67	67	69	69	69
69	67	67	69	69	71	71	73
71	69	69	71	71	73	73	75
73	71	73	73	75	75	75	76
75	73	75	75	76	76	78	78
76	75	76	76	78	80	80	82
78	78	78	80	80	82	84	85
80	80	80	82	84	85	87	91
82	82	84	84	87	89	93	96
84	84	85	87	91	94	98	103
85	85	87	91	94	98	103	112
87	87	91	94	98	103	112	
89	91	94	98	103	111	123	
91	93	96	102	109	120		
93	96	100	102	116			
94	98	103	112	123			
96	102	109	120				
98	105	114					
100	111	120					

(1) Drink more fluids and avoid prolonged heavy exertion.

(2) Avoid strenuous activity completely.

spheric turbulence in temperate zones, as arctic air sweeps southward to clash with northward-moving subtropical low-pressure pockets. Hurricanes form. TV weather maps become cluttered with high- and low-pressure fronts. The approach of these fronts, particularly as temperatures rise and pressure falls, have been associated with increased death rates.

First, it seems clear that those suffering serious ailments should avoid the harsh extremes of this season completely. Those who can afford it should simply set up housekeeping in a more mild and stable environment. Others might create such an environment in their homes according to the advice presented in Chapter 7. Synthetic sunlight alone can go a long way toward offsetting many of the negative aspects of autumn. So can plants, adequate humidity, cheerful colors, and such. Keep in mind that emotional state has a clear-cut and significant influence on physical well-being, in part through the release of various hormones into the bloodstream. The trick here is to manipulate your mood into a pleasant, positive, upbeat one through the methods already given in this book, as well as others you might have discovered for yourself.

Secondly, perhaps the majority of people who suffer mood disorders and minor physical complaints in the fall are actually unconscious hibernators. They, like those who recognize a frank hibernation response, can best be helped by putting into practice the recommendations we've discussed throughout these pages.

Winter

There are actually some good things about the winter, as your annual chart will show. Just as excessive heat reduces efficiency, accuracy, and productivity, so William F. Petersen, M.D., has reported that his subjects did faster, more accurate work on days when the outside temperature was cool. He also found that cold air masses led to "a greater imaginative reaction." Winter is the best time for detail work and continued creative activity—that is, if you aren't laid low by infection or the hibernation response.

Still, there's no escaping it: Winter is the worst season for physical health. The cold breezes lead to a constriction of blood vessels, which can lead to high blood pressure and heart attacks. Although throughout the United States as a whole most heart attacks occur in the summer, they occur most frequently during the winter in northern climates.

Microbial infections increase significantly in the winter partly because the cold, dry air outside our homes and the artificially heated, dry air inside often eliminate the moisture in our mucous membranes. Ordinarily these membranes, particularly those in the nasal passages, trap and destroy airborne organisms. When the mucus is too dry, however, these organisms reach our lungs to create the common winter colds, flu, and pneumonia. Dry air also contributes to congestion. We deal with it by taking antihistamines, which dry our mucous membranes even more, temporarily eliminating the symptom by compounding the cause. The wiser approach is to buy humidistats for the bedroom and main living areas of the house, along with humidifiers for those rooms, and make sure you maintain a relative humidity level of 45 to 55 percent.

Having read Chapter 7, you already know that. And by acclimatizing, you've taken another major step toward avoiding winter disease. If animal research is applicable to humans, then we can conclude that adapting to lower temperatures somehow increases our resistance to infections. Researchers at the Laboratory for Experimental Medicine in Cincinnati placed two groups of mice in separate rooms, one at 90°F and the other at 64°F. Three weeks later they subjected all the animals to various types of infections. Those that had not acclimatized to the cold had less ability to resist the diseases. In fact, the nonacclimatized rodents died after being exposed to only one-fourth the dose of streptococcus required to kill the mice that had adapted to the cold.

Finally, a word about cabin fever, one of the classic complaints of winter months. Some of the symptoms once ascribed to cabin fever are in reality those of the hibernation response: sleepiness; depression; lack of energy. The primary characteristic of true cabin fever is a restlessness and impatience that sometimes approaches panic. Its primary cause is a conscious or unconscious feeling of confinement, imprisonment, even claustrophobia. It's rather common in areas where people are restricted to their homes during particular seasons. For example, Paul Rosenblatt, a social scientist at the University of Minnesota, has found through surveys that cabin fever hits at least half of all Minnesotans during a typical winter there.

Chances are, if you've already overcome the hibernation response, you needn't worry about cabin fever—especially if you've also followed the advice in Chapter 7 concerning the eternal springtime home. To repeat, interior colors ought to be light, cheerful, and spacious, and bright, dark, or heavy colors should be used only as accents, but used to some extent to relieve the monotony and capture the essence of springtime.

Bright lighting is absolutely essential. The ideal is probably the full-spectrum bulbs discussed in Chapter 3, but an alternative is to combine incandescent bulbs for the "warm" part of the spectrum and fluorescent ones for the "cold." They produce a spectrum of color waves that come closer to that of the sun than either type of bulb alone.

Those suffering cabin fever also need to get out of the house. That will take an act of will, no doubt, and for some it may be impossible. Some suggestions:

—Start exercising with a friend. It's very possible that you know someone who suffers cabin fever as you do and will be particularly grateful to meet with another human being regularly for any excuse. And the exercise won't do you any harm.

—Start a hobby that involves you with others: the church choir; an arts and crafts club; skydiving.

—Organize a supper club so that each week you have a commitment, whether you feel like it or not, to be somewhere or have guests over.

—When you feel like absolutely *not* going outside, when you feel that nothing in the world could get you to walk through the door, even though staying inside is driving you mad, go out for a walk. Simply do it. You'll be more surprised than you can imagine at how therapeutic that walk will be.

When you began this book, you may have felt that autumn was the most dreaded season. Now, as you put what you've learned into practice, you'll find that you no longer need to withdraw from those last months of the year. You may even begin to find some beauty and pleasure in them. Who knows but you might begin to look forward to winter itself and take up skiing or ice skating or at least building snowmen (and women). If the advice in these pages is implemented, you'll move serenely through every fall and winter to come, detached from the unpleasant aspects of the external environment, embracing the positive, and patiently looking forward to . . .

. . . Spring

The sun was warm, but the wind was chill,
you know how it is with an April day
when the sun is out and the wind is still,
you're one month on in the middle of May.
But if you so much as dare to speak,
that cloud comes over the sunlit arch,
a wind comes off a frozen peak,
and you're two months back in the middle of March.
—ROBERT FROST

The signs are subtle and inconclusive. Mornings come earlier, and by mid-March the afternoons seem warmer than they were a month before. But the nights are cold, and just when we think we have it figured out, the last blizzard of the season buries us under a couple of feet of snow. In it is the moisture that, within a day or two, will begin nourishing the roots of plants and trees. The rhythmic frost of the late-winter night and the warmth of the noonday sun are the heartbeat thrusting the sap into the trees.

The earth is stirring. In their dens and burrows, hibernating animals, in complete darkness and surrounded by the same temperatures they've endured all winter, spontaneously begin their listless arousal. They gasp for breath. Their heartbeats soar. Minutes or hours later they stretch and move, and with an obvious lack of enthusiasm, they eventually stumble forth to confront the day.

The songs of birds greet them—not only the screams of blue jays and peeps of chickadees and starlings but the lilt of rock doves and cardinals, those whose lush fluff of feathers and rapid heartbeat and skill at finding nourishment even in the snow have allowed them to survive the winter rather than escape it. Joining them in defending territories and attracting mates are the migrants, primarily the insect eaters. Robins tug soggy worms from the mud. Wild ducks hunt tadpoles along the banks of chilly ponds.

Red-winged blackbirds return to the cattail swamps, and Canadian geese honk their way northward. By March 19 the northern cliff swallows are back in San Juan Capistrano. The white-throated sparrow begins the flight from the eastern United States to upper New York and Canada.

The sun continues its struggle with the frozen earth and wins. Ugliness and inconvenience descend for a week or two; New Englanders call it mud time. As snow dissolves into mud, snowshoe rabbits and ermines change their camouflage coats from white to brown.

Then, almost suddenly, the earth surrenders its liquid form. The first flowers spring from it in softly colored blossoms. At first tentatively, then with explosive enthusiasm, life declares itself. Snakes and lizards, their bodies warmed by the sun, find their way from beneath rocks. The rising temperature of the bay stirs the turtle into sluggish mobility. Hormones surge through rodents and birds and mammals, through humans. Raccoons come into heat. The earth teems with vitality.

By the middle of April the extended daylight, not the warmth, has begun to stimulate the red clover, black-eyed Susan, larkspur, radish, dill, sugar beet, rose of Sharon. The spinach plant bolts, or goes to seed. Strawberry plants begin sending out their runners.

We grow strong yet remain lazy and light-headed. It is no time for introspection—we've had enough of that—yet during the most beautiful of these days, soft in mist-filtered sunlight, fragrant with moist earth, we might just ponder whether ours is not, after all, the best of all possible worlds.

There is a sense each spring of renewal, of rebirth, of having one more chance to start over, and, for those of us who are of an emotional disposition, a feeling of hope and gratitude. Such feelings are not easily stirred in climates of monotonous days, even when such days are perfect in their beauty. In the words of Thomas Moore, "Spring would be but gloomy weather if we had nothing else but spring."

But there is more to it than that. David Gates writes in *Man and His Environment: Climate,* "One suspects that a climate with constant weather conditions would not be advantageous to man and that a certain amount of variability is desirable. Changing conditions act as physiological and psychological stimuli. The tropics represent those parts of the world with the least seasonal thermal variation. The people living there have a greater incidence of disease and seem to have less vitality and vigor than those living in other climates."

Ellsworth Huntington, a Yale University geographer, has argued that the strongest civilizations have emerged in parts of the world which have the most stimulating climates.

We've already seen that we reach our creative and intellectual peaks during the fall and winter months—that is, if we're not freezing to death. And there's evidence to explain why. In order to maintain normal body temperature, as we've learned, thyroid and adrenal hormones are secreted. They increase metabolism and circulation, which boost the availability of oxygen and other nutrients to the brain. That in itself can enhance our capacity to think, feel, and create.

What's more, those adrenal and thyroid hormones are nature's pep pills. They give us more energy, make us more alert.

"It would appear," writes Gates, "that the optimum temperature for physical comfort is definitely greater than the optimum temperature for mental vigor, so the theory of climatic determinism would indicate a more rapid evolution of thought and inventiveness as man moved into the temperate regions of the world."

It also has been argued that the capacity to respond to stressors—and the changing seasons certainly trigger stress—can be beneficial to us. Perhaps you already know that stress in itself isn't a dirty word. In fact, it's usually downright positive. It's the reason we enjoy sports and video games and sex and good books and films and TV dramas. Stress, another word for the response to challenge is what makes life worth living.

The next time you swelter in the July heat, shiver in the December chill, slop your way through an unexpected April downpour, or chase your hat along a blustery boulevard in October, smile and say a prayer of gratitude. Like the weak muscle that grows strong with use, your adaptational capacities grow robust as they're placed under stress. Feel free to grow arrogant in the knowledge that you can probably survive a much greater spectrum of climatic variation than the brawniest Amazonians. They, after all, have adapted to mere heat and humidity.

You might brazenly hurl a challenge at the Siberians as well. Like their South American counterparts, they're highly adapted to a particular climate. We of a temperate climate are more versatile. If you've handled a typical

Chicago summer and winter, you'll probably get by any-where, given the proper equipment. In terms of climate we're among the most highly stress-ridden people on earth, and we've adapted to it. To put it plainly, we are the World Champions of Climatic Endurance. Our trophies:

—Freedom from the boredom of a static climate
—The cleansing, penetrating warmth of summer
—The beauty, turbulence, and euphoria of autumn
—The refreshing, mind-clearing, flesh-piercing cold of winter
—The new birth of spring

So some final advice in this final chapter about how to maintain your sense of humor while getting through winter and mud time and on into the glorious promise of spring.

Planning for Winter Survival

1. Choose your parents very carefully. If you're going to live in a climate with cold winters, select fairly short, stocky people; hairy, if possible.
2. Try to be female; there is evidence, all other things being equal, that you will survive better in the cold.
3. Keep the number of fleshy appendages to a minimum to avoid frostbite.

As Winter Begins

1. Don't wrap up too soon; continue enjoying the out-of-doors with as few garments or lack thereof

as you wear during the summer. That helps promote physiological adaptation to the cold. It will also enhance your reputation as an eccentric. Also, no heat in the house until December 1—or until pipes freeze.

2. Try to keep a sense of humor. Hang mirrors in every room, and make faces at yourself when you are in a sour mood.

As Winter Progresses

1. Reflect on past glories. Remember it was an ice age that gave us supremacy.

2. Develop as many daily rituals as possible. They are valuable in preoccupying the mind. Buying a wood stove as a pet can provide more rituals than most people wish to acquire.

When Spring and Mud Season Arrive

1. Avoid at all costs totaling up the winter heating bills. That can lead to a depression not subject to the seasons.

2. As the young man's thoughts begin turning to what the young woman has been thinking about all winter, restraint is required. Confine all expressions of sexual desire to a platonic level—an exchange of poems and flowers, for example. Mating season among humans is in the fall, and all overt sexual activity should be reserved until then.

Continuing in Harmony

We have stressed repeatedly in these pages human-kind's awesome capacity to adapt. We are rare in the animal kingdom in being able to survive on an equatorial island or a polar ice floe. We can flourish and bear young on a diet of berries and vegetation or whale flesh and blubber. We can get by in the shelter of a cave, an igloo, a thatched hut, a tin shack, or a palace. We have thrived in the asphalt jungles of inner cities and in tiny outriggers skimming a thousand miles of Pacific Ocean. We have conquered ice ages and searing heat and famine. We have done so very slowly, at a cost of untold lives, by changing what we were to what we had to be. We can no longer count on that.

In the words of Warren Weaver, vice-president of the Alfred P. Sloan Foundation:

> We know that over long periods of time evolution adjusted man slowly to his environment and furnished for him a set of physiological and other properties which put him into reasonable balance with nature about him. . . . And then, over the last few hundred years came Science, and over the last 50 years, in a mad rush—Science and Technology. And the result is that we now live under scientific and technological rates of change which are so rapid that they completely outstrip the mutation rate. We can no longer hope that evolution will succeed in keeping man in balance with his environment. And since we can no longer accomplish this with our genes, we have only one recourse—we must do it with our brain.

That is what we have attempted to do with regard to the hibernation response. But we have done it, we trust, with deep humility, recognizing that we and all that naturally surrounds us are a continuum. In preventing the hibernation response, we've shown how to lengthen the photoperiod as our sun and planet do; we've shown how to create as natural a spring environment as possible.

In these pages we've discovered that one aspect of nature, the climate—particularly the deepening cold and the shortening days of autumn and winter—profoundly affects our lives. In recognizing that, we can learn to heal ourselves. But there is more. The tides, the orbits of planets, the laws governing gravity, electromagnetic energy—all are a part of us. We did not know awhile ago that invisible rays from the sun could kill bacteria in our blood and turn cholesterol into a hormone that would make our bones stronger.

We did not know, and for that reason, many would have thought the suggestion that the sun showered us with invisible rays a foolish flight of fancy.

We didn't know that spraying aerosols under our arms and using chlorofluorocarbons in industry would someday help destroy food crops and human beings around the world. Today we know that. It will happen, if we allow it to, by erasing from the sky that fragile pencil line of ozone currently protecting us from those deadly invisible rays.[17]

And we can continue to learn. As Bette Davis's character says in the film *The Petrified Forest*, "We've been fighting nature and we thought we had it licked. But that's where we're wrong. We've got to admit that nature can't (and shouldn't) be beaten." One hopes that we have learned that at least. The only way to win is to play the game nature's way and to use some of the adaptive strength which nature has given us to work in harmony with our environment. That's what we hope we have helped you do here in the pages of *The Hibernation Response*. So let's recognize it, maximize our coping with the challenge it reflects, and use our human intelligence to change the toil of winter to an eternal springtime. For many of us it's an adaptation worth mastering.

Notes

1. Peter R. Oeltgen of the Veterans Administration Medical Center in Lexington, Kentucky, has found that the final phase of deep hibernation in animals is induced by an opiatelike substance which he calls the hibernation induction trigger. He and others have injected plasma from the blood of hibernating woodchucks into active woodchucks and squirrels during the summer and turned them into hibernators within minutes. Oeltgen produced a similar effect with a rhesus monkey, which normally does not hibernate. Within fifteen minutes after the injection, the animal had begun to sink into a deep sleep. Body temperature dropped by several degrees, and the heartbeat plummeted by 50 percent.

2. This tiny reddish brown globular structure has intrigued scientists and philosophers for centuries. Its position, deep between the two cortical hemispheres of brain and in close proximity to the cerebellum, has stimulated intriguing speculation regarding its function. One theory was that it acted as a valve controlling the emotions that move from the larger hemispheres to the cerebellum and other parts of the brain. Descartes considered it the seat of the soul.

Actually the pineal gland lies outside the brain, although it does originate from neuronal tissue in the embryo. Information concerning light reaches the gland through a complex series of nerves that run from the eye into the brain past a very important nucleus called the supercharismatic nucleus, or SCN (so named because it lies over the intersection of the nerves coming from the eye). These nerves continue into the neck, where they connect with the sympathetic nervous system before they track up some of the main vessels in the neck to the pineal gland. All along the way there are synapses and other junctures where chemical messengers are necessary to relay the information coming from the eye.

3. As with most scientific breakthroughs, research pointing to the cause of seasonal affective disorder was already being undertaken in 1980 by, among others, Daniel F. Kripke of the Department of Psychiatry at the University of California, San Diego. Kripke had made some insightful observations having to do with both hamsters and humans. Writing in *Biological Psychiatry 1981*, he observed, "There is evidence for human seasonal rhythms in mania, depression, suicide, and various endocrine and neurotransmitter functions. Oddly enough, seasonal rhythms in births and deaths are related to the seasonal rhythms of sunlight intensity. Melatonin in humans, as in rodents, is suppressed by light, but in humans, only bright light is effective. These results suggest that human seasonal responses may be sensitive to light of particularly bright intensity. Perhaps depression in humans is to some extent analogous to animal hibernation.…"

Kripke even went so far as to treat seven depressed patients with dim red light for an hour on one morning and bright white light for an hour on the morning after. The result was only mildly positive. We now realize that the bright light exposure period was too brief.

4. The most frequent symptoms of SAD (the emotional aspect of our hibernation response) among children, as ranked by the parents of sufferers, occur in the following order of severity: irritability, fatigue, school difficulties, sadness, sleep change (primarily difficulty in awakening in the morning), headaches, increased appetite, carbohydrates craving, decreased activity, crying spells, anxiety, withdrawal from friends and relatives, and temper tantrums.

Generally the symptoms are milder in youngsters than in adults, and youngsters rarely recognize the relationship between the environment and their problems.

In some cases phototherapy produces dramatic results. Norman Rosenthal of NIMH tells of two competitive swimmers whose performances typically dropped each winter but who were able to maintain their levels of achievement while undergoing the therapy described in Chapter 3. One twelve-year-old boy reached the honor roll for the first time while using the lights. Within two to three days after not using them, he became depressed again but improved after just a day of renewed treatment. These changes are often so dramatic that teachers and others who come into contact with the children comment spontaneously upon the remarkable improvement.

It seems certain that a great many youngsters suffer each year from the hibernation response but that adults dismiss the problem as the tribulations of adolescence, the normal moodiness of teenagers and such. Considering the simplicity of treatment and the potential for dramatically positive improvement, we might expect the hibernation response to be given routine consideration in the diagnosing of any child brought to a physician with a complaint of sadness, anxiety, irritability, lethargy, fatigue, or depression during the autumn and winter. A family clinic for the diagnosis and treatment of such difficulties has recently been established at the University of Pennsylvania by William Sonis, M.D., a child psychiatrist, and Steven James, M.D., a psychiatrist and sleep researcher.

5. The people of the Soviet Union, located in extreme northern latitudes, apparently are more susceptible than those from more southern countries to symptoms of the hibernation response. As a result, their scientists have been using phototherapy since the 1950's and probably have done more research on the subject than those of any other nation.

Writing in *Applied Optics*, N. M. Dantsig of the Institute of General and Municipal Hygiene, the Academy of Medicine, in Moscow, states: "Clinical and physiological observations suggest that limitation or deprivation of sunlight results in disturbances of physiologic equilibrium in the human body that lead to the development of pathologic symptoms which are known as sunlight deficiency [starvation]....Sunlight deficiency is most pronounced in people living in the extreme north and beyond the polar circle, as well as in those working in mines or in buildings deprived of natural light, i.e., in the so-called windowless and lanternless industrial interiors. This also applies, to a degree, to residents of big industrial cities."

The Russians long have treated the hibernation response by building photaria, health-clublike installations of bright full-spectrum lights. The national health code requires that such facilities be made available to persons working in mines, industrial buildings deprived of natural light, and all industrial establishments north of the polar circle.

Similar lighting exists in many workplaces and schools. Some years ago, when experiments with artificial lighting were first conducted, the positive results were immediately apparent, according to Dantsig. "Among other things, this was indicated by positive clinical and physiological changes in children, by the data on their physical development, by blood counts, by indices of the organic phosphorus content and activity of alkaline phosphotase in the blood, and by other variables. Especially marked was the reduction in the incidence of diseases and the increase in the overall immunological responsiveness of children living in the northern regions."

The Russian scientists have brought creativity to bear in designing the photaria. Some are winding corridors through which the users stroll as through a park. The walls are lined with evenly spaced bulbs. There are even artificial beaches, the synthetic sun shining from the "sky" and "horizon."

Perhaps because of the extreme intensity of the light, exposure rarely lasts longer than half an hour daily or every other day.

6. Although we know a good deal about melatonin, its exact role, direct or indirect, in the hibernation response continues to evade many researchers. It seems that virtually every new finding contradicts previous ones, until efforts to discern melatonin's precise role in the hibernation response come to resemble driving out of a mud puddle. The harder you work at it, the deeper down you go.

Some readers may be interested in this research, however, and for their amusement we'll present it here. But we're reminded of the student who was assigned a term paper on Abraham Lincoln. During the semester he read thirty books and seventy-five articles on the great leader and turned in an admirable paper. It included, as required, a final paragraph answering the question "What have you learned about Abraham Lincoln?" The student wrote, "More than I wished to know."

Here are some of the paradoxes:

- While it's true that blood levels of melatonin increase with the onset of darkness by five times, that melatonin triggers the symptoms of the hibernation response in animals (and presumably in humans), and that light, which suppresses melatonin levels, alleviates those symptoms, light administered during the day—which does not extend the photoperiod—also decreases the symptoms. Perhaps some people have "leaky" pineals, which continue to secrete melatonin unless an additional dose of light shuts them off. But light which apparently is not bright enough to decrease melatonin levels also has improved moods in some subjects.

- Drugs which block the pineal's secretion of melatonin are not particularly effective in controlling the hibernation response. It's possible that since the pineal secretes many other chemicals, one or more of those might modify the effects of melatonin. What's more, the pineal manufactures melatonin from another body hormone, serotonin, and the availability of that substance may influence melatonin production. Research is now under way to determine this role of serotonin in the hibernation response. We have more to say about serotonin in Chapter 9.

- Steven P. James and others have suggested that it may be the total *amount* of light—or the number of photons—to which we're exposed during a twenty-four-hour period, not the number of *hours* of light, that regulates melatonin secretions.

Although there are many unanswered questions concerning melatonin, sunlight, and the hibernation response—and even some paradoxical findings—much of the confusion probably results from individual differences among those studied. Few of us are definitive examples of hibernation responders. Larry Pressman probably is. On the last night of his therapeutic regimen in 1980 Dr. Lewy awakened him not at the usual 6:00 A.M., but at 2:00 A.M. and exposed him for two hours to the same light as during the previous ten days. Lewy had been taking blood samples through a catheter from his volunteer throughout the night, and he discovered that Pressman's blood melatonin levels promptly dropped by 88 percent during light exposure—"to approximately those of daytime levels." Ordinarily those levels would have remained high for two more hours. Synthetic sunlight had made all the difference.

What we do know is that when you are awake and light is entering the eyes, the neuronal pathway is activated. This in turn inhibits the producton of melatonin. The SCN, the middle nucleus in the brain above the optic junction, regulates the timing of the production of melatonin, but the precise daily release is dictated by the actual amount of sunlight you get—and when. This very sophisticated mechanism has basically two components to it: One controls a daily rhythm of melatonin release, something which the brain has had programmed in it over many generations of evolution. The second component precisely times melatonin secretion to the real environment in which we live. The two components make it possible, for example, for mammals to have their young at times of the year when they are most likely to survive. Similarly, it is this mechanism that generates the phenomenon of jet lag, in which our internal clocks are out of phase for a while with external environmental cues resulting from the changed photoperiod of the new place in which we find ourselves.

Melatonin itself is a rather delicate hormone in that it is rapidly changed by the liver and excreted out of the body. This mechanism ensures that there is a rapid on-and-off mechanism, which again allows for more precise timing of the functions that the pineal oversees and integrates with environmental cues.

For each twenty-four-hour period there is a production of melatonin which occurs as darkness falls in the evening. The rise of melatonin occurs a few hours after dusk and exists for six to eight hours in the human being regardless of the length of the night. It is shut off very dramatically and quickly in the morning when a strong pulse of light enters the retina. That process has been shown clearly to be related to the intensity of the light; the light itself behaves rather like a drug. Varying doses of the drug have varying effects. Thus, if you live in a very dark environment, the switching off of the melatonin in the early morning will not be precise. The problem is compounded in the winter when sunlight is not as intense.

7. Dr. Daniel Kripke, who first linked animal hibernation with the hibernation response in humans, proposed long before anyone had ever heard about seasonal affective disorder that mornings were the critical time to administer effective light therapy. His argument is based on research with the hamster. He says, "It is not the duration of light exposure in itself but rather the time relationship of the critical interval to the time when light is

present which regulates hamster seasonal responses." In other words, if light is present during a critical early evening or morning hour—as it is in the summer months—the hamster will not enter phase one of the hibernation process. Only when that period is reached in darkness does hibernation begin.

Kripke draws on research by Thomas A. Wehr and Anna Wirz-Justice which suggests that humans, too, have a critical photosensitivity period which normally occurs soon after the time of awakening during the lengthening days of spring. If that period arrives during darkness, it could trigger the depression associated with the hibernation response. For that reason, Kripke suggests that artifical light exposure is most effective two hours before most of us usually awaken in the fall and winter.

8. Practically the instant you step out of doors into the cold, your body surges into action. The thermostat is the brain's hypothalamus. Its front part responds to excess heat by triggering changes in the body that increase heat loss, and the rear portion senses the cold and stimulates heat conservation.

How does the hypothalamus recognize external temperature changes? By monitoring the blood reaching it through vessels near the skin surface in the neck. Even slight external temperature changes can warm or chill the blood flowing through these vessels sufficiently for the hypothalamus to detect them and respond. By cooling the hypothalamus of baboons for one or two hours while keeping the rest of their bodies warm, researchers have stimulated increased oxygen consumption, a measure of general body metabolism, by about 50 percent and have quickly produced constriction of blood vessels in the skin and shivering—all responses to cold.

9. Many animals not discussed in this chapter are at the mercy of the environment when it comes to their body temperatures. They're called cold-blooded, or poikilothermic, animals. "Poikilothermic" means "labile in temperature."

Some of these creatures can help influence their temperatures by behavior. The lizard darts in and out of the sun to warm up or cool down. Others, particularly some fish, can usually keep their body temperatures slightly above freezing by secreting into the tissues a glycoprotein which acts as an anti-freeze.

No animals are as efficient in regulating their body temperatures as a small group called homoiotherms, which includes us humans. We warm-blooded animals maintain a remarkably narrow range of body temperature; humans around the globe, regardless of climate, body build, and other factors, have a normal temperature of between 97° and 99.5°F, although during the course of twenty-four hours that figure may fluctuate by a maximum of two degrees.

We maintain that relatively constant body temperature by (1) producing body heat, (2) conserving that heat, and (3) transferring heat into the environment when we need to lower body temperature. That capacity to transfer heat is as essential as generating it in the first place; comfortably, at rest, our body core temperature would increase almost 2°F every hour if we were unable to get rid of it. As it happens, heat escapes our bodies in three ways: through convection, conduction into the cooler surfaces of clothing and the furniture we touch as well as the air around us, and radiation.

Many homoiotherms also have the ability to change the setting of their physiological thermostats, dramatically decreasing their normal body temperature during periods of lethargy and hibernation. Yet even then that lower temperature is being very precisely regulated.

Mammals, the group of animals that give birth to live offspring and feed them with milk during their infancy, have very highly developed temperature regulatory mechanisms. After a hundred and fifty million years or so of tinkering with the mechanism, they've developed a capacity to be highly adaptable. We humans are mammals, and it's probably because of our robust independence from the physical environment and the ingenuity of our brains in controlling our immediate surroundings that we have become the most successful of all creatures in adapting to this changing planet.

10. Thyroxine becomes eight times more potent when converted to triiodothyronine (T_3) by means of an enzyme called 5'-deiodinase. The enzyme is found in the liver, kidney, and brain. It's also found in brown fat, which has received attention in recent years as a result of some controversial diet plans. Brown fat was first described in the sixteenth century. Those early researchers noted that it occurs in curious places: around the main arteries and between the two shoulder blades.

Actually there is so little brown fat in the body that it would be impossible to lose much weight even if we *could* burn it preferentially for fuel as some diets suggest. And we probably ought not to try it in the first place. Richly vascularized as it is, which is probably why it has the brown color, it produces the enzyme 5'-deiodinase quite efficiently and is able to put it quickly into the blood, where it can trigger the conversion of thyroxine to T_3.

There is an interesting observation to be made here. Some mammals that are not considered true hibernators but exhibit so-called carnivore lethargy during the winter—the skunk, the raccoon, the badger, and probably the bear among them—do *not* have brown fat. Some *hibernating* animals do, along with humans.

11. As long ago as 1917 Herbert S. Swan and George W. Tuttle condemned the trend toward cities dominated by skyscrapers which blocked the sun and subjected most residents and workers to a life of comparative perpetual darkness. In their article "Planning Sunlight Cities," published in the *American City*, they argued that cities should be designed to permit every building, from ground level to roof, to receive sunlight on the shortest day of the year. To achieve that, they suggested constructing shorter buildings or wider streets. The dimensions would depend on latitude. In Winnipeg, Canada, for example, streets would have to be more than three times as wide as buildings are tall. A five-story building would require a street width of 210 feet—some twenty lanes with 10-foot-wide sidewalks on each side of the road.

12. E. Hribersek and his colleagues at the University of Louvain in Belgium recorded in the February 1987 issue of the *British Journal of Psychiatry* another interesting piece of evidence that human sexuality is cyclical. They analyzed about twenty-three thousand telephone calls made to a telephone counseling service, attempting to correlate particular problems with the weather and season. The researchers report "a remarkable increase in calls for masturbation from men during the summer...." For everything—including obscene phone calls—there is a season.

10. Dr. Robert Sack and others at the Department of Psychiatry, Oregon Health Sciences University, have offered an interesting theory about the relationship between melatonin and both sleep disorders and the hibernation response. They collected urine samples from many volunteers over three nights in late June, and then again about the third week in December, and found that

the amount of melatonin in the blood didn't increase during the winter. What changed was the length of time the hormone stayed in the blood. Melatonin remains in the blood longer during the extended darkness of winter. "Thus, in humans," writes Sack, "it is likely that the time of year affects the *timing* of MT [melatonin] secretion more than the *amplitude* [amount]." (Italics added.)

14. Most people recognize that emotional stress causes our bodies to grow tense, our muscles rigid. Those emotional pressures keep us from relaxing physically into sleep. We also know that making those muscles relax—for example, through massage—has the effect of calming us emotionally. What's good for the body is good for the mind.

Of course, muscular tension can develop completely apart from emotional stress. One very common source of tight muscles, particularly as we grow older, is their natural tendency to shorten if not stretched regularly. Normal full-range-of-movement exercise on a regular basis provides this stretching, or flexing, keeping muscles loose and tension-free. Perhaps that's why those who exercise regularly sleep more soundly than do those who are sedentary.

At any rate, stretch exercises are a potent sleeping aid among those whose insomnia results from muscular tension. Here are some exercises that will relax your body in just a few minutes each night. Do them just before bedtime, and you'll be surprised how quickly you fall asleep. NOTE THIS: These are *static* stretching exercises. That means that you reach a position in which you feel *mild* discomfort and hold it there until the muscles relax of their own accord. Jerking and forcing movements can tear a muscle, ligament, tendon—or all three. Don't go beyond mild discomfort. Be patient. In thirty seconds to a couple of minutes the pain will ease and you will be able to move a bit farther. You can't stretch back to normal in a single day muscles that have been shortening for years. The encouraging points: You can stretch them sufficiently the very first night to feel the relaxation, and you can restore to normal the flexibility lost to shortened muscles in fewer than two weeks.

Remember, you won't be able to complete these exercises if you're suffering from shortened muscles. The object is to progress little by little, day after day.

1. Interlace your fingers behind your back and, straightening

   your arms, lift your hands upward as far as you can. If your
   shoulders and your chest and arm muscles are flexible, you'll
   be able to stand tall and still raise your hands behind you to
   the same level as your navel.

2. While maintaining the above position, lower the side of your
   head to your shoulder. You're sufficiently flexible if your
   earlobe comes to within one finger width of touching your
   shoulder. Repeat with the opposite shoulder—and no fair
   lifting your shoulder to your ear.

3. Sit on the floor with your legs extended, your knees slightly
   bent, your toes pointing back toward your body. Lower your
   chin to your chest. Curl your back forward *without
   straining*. When you feel minor discomfort, stop and hold
   that position. Reach for your toes. You have no flexibility
   problems in your back, hamstring, or calf muscles if you can
   touch your forehead to your knees while grasping your toes.

4. Lie on your back with your legs straight, your arms
   outstretched pependicular to your body. Raise your right leg
   to form a ninety-degree angle with your body, your toes
   pointed toward the ceiling. Bring that leg across your body
   and downward while your shoulders remain flat on the floor.
   Try to touch your left hand with your right foot. Repeat with
   your left foot. This exercise stretches the hamstring, lower
   back, and upper buttock muscles.

5. Lying on your back, place the soles of your feet together, and
   spread your knees as far apart as possible. While tilting your
   pelvis forward, press your knees gently toward the floor.
   Unless you're extremely flexible, your knees won't touch the
   floor, but you'll certainly feel the adductor muscles of your
   inner thighs stretching. Be particularly careful not to force
   this position, or you risk long-term damage to tissues
   unused to being stretched.

6. This is a simple neck rotation, and for those who carry
   tension in their neck and shoulders, it can provide the
   most valuable relief. Go gingerly; it's the easiest thing
   in the world to get a sprained neck without having the
   slightest idea how it happened. Begin by simply shaking
   your head "no" slowly, increasing the extremes of the left-
   right movement and holding each position. If you feel a
   cramp coming on, turn your head in the opposite direction

immediately and discontinue the exercise.

Do a "yes" nod, chin to chest, then head back as far as comfortable. Now, after your neck muscles are sufficiently flexible in the yes and no movements, combine them into a complete rotation, both left and right. Not only do these exercises increase the flexibility of neck and shoulder muscles, but tense and aching back muscles can also be involved.

15. The body's protective mechanism against ultraviolet waves is complex. It begins when sunlight—not UVR—stimulates skin chromophores to form biologically inactive photoprotective substances. Thereafter keratin, a filamentous protein found in dead cells of surface skin, strongly absorbs the most dangerous UVB radiation. Since these skin cells are not biologically active, they cannot be damaged.

After that melanin is activated, first by UVA for short-term tanning, then by UVB for the long term. There are two types of melanin: Brown melanin, called eumelanin, is quite efficient; yellow melanins, on the other hand, not only are poor photoprotectors but are suspected of actually being photosensitizers, weakening the cells' ability to defend against radiation and leading to chronic cellular damage.

16. In fact, we should not in the *least* mind letting "them" see us sweat. It is one of our most highly developed physiological achievements. We sweat in three ways. You're almost certain to be sweating right now, regardless of the temperature, as water continuously passes through the skin and is absorbed by the air. *Insensible* perspiration is going on all the time, unless the humidity of the surrounding air is 100 percent. That's why when the humidity is high, we feel very uncomfortable and it's much more difficult to cool the body.

Specific sweat glands also produce sweat in order to *cool the body* from evaporation.

A third form of sweat gland, predominantly found in the palms and the soles of the feet, excretes moisture during excitement or emotional turmoil.

Ordinarily humans don't have nearly as efficient a means for adapting to cold. As we've already mentioned, our "zone of thermal neutrality" when naked is between 77° and 80°F, and when the temperature drops much below that, we become uncomfortable. Certain other animals have critical temperatures in the same ranges. They're all native to the tropics.

What's more, several studies have shown that humans living in temperate climates adapt much more rapidly and efficiently to warm climates than to cold ones. We belong where it's warm. Our bodies respond to that truth as quickly as our instincts do.

Says R. K. MacPherson, "Man is best suited to the warm, equable environment of a tropical forest, with its small diurnal variation in temperature and the protection it affords from heat gain from solar radiation during the day and the heat loss by radiation to a clear sky at night."

Indeed, there's little doubt that we began as a species in the savannas and hot tropical forests of the African continent; even today these latitudes of delightful warmth, while accounting for only 36 percent of the earth's landmass, still support some 40 percent of the human population.

17. In October 1987 scientists in Antarctica reported that an iceberg twice the size of Rhode Island had broken away from the continental ice shelf to form an island. The possibility arises that this phenomenon, unique in terms of size of the iceberg, points to a warming trend over our southernmost continent and that such a trend is, at least in part, directly related to another environmental phenomenon of the Antarctic, a gaping wound in the ozone layer.

We discussed in Chapter 12, in sufficient detail, the ease with which unfiltered UVR can cook our skin. We also said that UVB exposure can lead to cataracts, the third leading cause of blindness in the United States. It's been related to herpes and shingles attacks as well.

Presumably it would be possible, although highly inconvenient, to shelter ourselves from the more intense ultraviolet radiation of an ozone-depleted atmosphere, but we could not hope to shelter the entire globe. There is no question that at some point in the continuing destruction of the ozone layer, entire species of plants and animals will be annihilated. Our planet will become, especially in those areas in which the ultraviolet radiation is most intense, deserts populated primarily by nocturnal animals. Only those creatures protected by scales, exterior skeletons, and great quantities of body hair will be sure of survival beneath the sun.

Beyond that, weather patterns will change drastically worldwide. Those humans and other animals that have adapted over thousands of millennia to the cold might well be plunged into torrid heat throughout the year, and conceivably those who have learned to survive in the tropics might find themselves buffeted by blizzards. No one can predict with certainty the effect that dozens of giant icebergs, breaking free from Antarctica and drifting equatorward along the Humboldt and other currents, will have on the climates of such continents as South America.

This is no theoretical problem. Don Heath, Ph.D., a NASA scientist, has reported that between 1978 and 1986—after the United States had banned the use of chlorofluorocarbons (CFCs) in aerosol propellants—the ozone layer has continued to be depleted by up to 7.4 percent. Virtually all scientists not involved in the manufacture of CFCs believe they are the major culprits in ozone destruction. One CFC atom can destroy about a hundred thousand molecules of ozone, and it has an atmospheric lifetime of from 75 to 110 years. That means that if not a single CFC molecule entered the atmosphere from this moment on, we can still look forward to more than a century of ozone destruction.

But CFC production hasn't stopped. In the United States CFCs are used in air conditioners, in refrigerators, and in solvents that clean computer circuitry and as propellants of the foam in Styrofoam products. And many other nations still use them in aerosol spray cans; a million tons of CFCs have been released from these cans alone since 1974. While legislators plot slowly to harmonize the interests of major corporations with those of CFC opponents, and some manufacturers, such as Du Pont, promise to cease production, ordinary citizens have it within their power to make the difference. They can do it through their wallets, refusing to purchase fast-food products—any products for that matter—packaged in Styrofoam. Paper has served us well for a couple of millennia and has the advantages of being biodegradable and produced without seriously polluting the environment.

We can avoid buying cleaning products that contain carbon tetrachloride, methylchloroform, and methylchloride. We can also insist on alternatives to foam cushion fillers when possible. When traveling abroad, we can refuse to purchase CFC-propelled aerosols in cosmetics and other products.

And of course, we can raise hell with our congressional representatives.

Bibliography

Chapter 1: The Sleep That Never Comes

Bombeck, Erma. "At Wit's End." *Allentown* (Pennsylvania), *Morning Call*, January 15, 1986, section D, p. 4.

Davies, Robertson. *The Papers of Samuel Marchbanks: Comprising the Diary, the Table Talk, and a Garland of Miscellanea.* Toronto: Irwin Pub., 1985.

Frazer, A., and R. Brown. "Melatonin: A Link Between the Environment and Behavior?" *Integrative Psychiatry*, vol. 5 (March 1987), pp. 3–26.

Gonzalez, Elizabeth Rasche. "From Deep Cold to Deep Sleep." *Journal of the American Medical Association*, vol. 241 (June 15, 1979), pp. 2586–87; 2595.

Gunby, Phil. "Primitive Creature Holds a Metabolic Secret." *Journal of the American Medical Association*, vol. 239 (February 27, 1978), p. 817.

Klem, Daniel, Jr., associate professor of biology, Muhlenberg College, Allentown, Pennsylvania, Interview, October 19, 1987.

Kripke, Daniel F. "Photoperiodic Mechanisms for Depression and Its Treatment." *Biological Psychiatry 1981: Proceedings of the IIIrd World Congress of Biological Psychiatry*, ed. C. Perris, G. Struwe, and B. Jansson. New York: Elsevier-North Holland Biomedical Press, 1981.

Lyman, Charles P. *Hibernation and Torpor in Mammals and Birds.* New York: Academic Press, 1982.

Morris, Desmond. *The Naked Ape.* New York: McGraw-Hill, 1967.

Steinhart, Peter. "Sleeping on the Job." *National Wildlife*, vol. 20 (November 1982), pp. 46-47.

Woodbury, David O. *The Great White Mantle.* New York: Viking, 1962.

Chapter 2: Are You a Hibernator?

Akerstedt, Torbiorn; Mats Gillberg; and Lennart Wetterberg. "The Circadian Covariation of Fatigue and Urinary Melatonin." *Biological Psychiatry*, vol. 17 (May 1982), pp. 547–54.

Baker, Sherry. "Human Hibernation." *Omni*, vol. 6 (March 1984), pp. 69–74.

Hillard, James R.; Jacqueline M. Holland; and Dietlof Ramm. "Christmas and Psychopathology: Data from a Psychiatric Emergency Room Population." *Archives of General Psychiatry*, vol. 38 (December 1981), pp. 1377–81.

Kraepelin, Emil. *Manic-Depressive Insanity and Paranoia*, ed. G. M. Robertson and trans. R. M. Barclay. Edinburgh: E & S Livingstone, 1921.

Lewy, Alfred J.; H. A. Kern; N. E. Rosenthal; and T. A. Wehr. "Bright Artificial Light Treatment of a Manic-Depressive Patient with a Seasonal Mood Cycle." *American Journal of Psychiatry*, vol. 11 (November 1982), pp. 1496–98.

Lillyquist, Michael J. *Sunlight and Health.* New York: Dodd, Mead & Co., 1985.

Molello, Stephen A. Personal communication, February 25, 1987.

Rosenthal, Norman E. "Consensus and Controversy in Seasonal Affective Disorder and Phototherapy." Paper presented at the IVth World Congress of Biological Psychiatry, Philadelphia, September 1985.

———; D. A. Sack; J. C. Gillin; A. J. Lewy; F. K. Godwin; Y. Davenport; P. S. Mueller; D. A. Newsome; and T. A. Wehr. "Seasonal Affective Disorder: A Description of the Syndrome and Preliminary Findings with Light Therapy." *Archives of General Psychiatry*, vol. 41 (January 1984), pp. 72–80.

Chapter 3: Let There Be Light

Dietzel, M.; B. Saletu; O. M. Lesch; W. Sieghart; and M. Schjerve.

"Light Treatment in Depressive Illness: Polysomnographic, Psychometric and Neuroendocrinological Findings." *European Neurology*, vol. 25, supplementum 2 (1986) pp. 93–103.

Hellekson, Carla J.; Judith A. Cline; and Norman E. Rosenthal. "Phototherapy for Seasonal Affective Disorder in Alaska." *American Journal of Psychiatry*, vol. 143 (August 1986), pp. 1035–37.

Jacobsen, Frederick M.; T. A. Wehr; R. A. Skwerer; D. A. Sack; and N. E. Rosenthal. "Morning Versus Midday Phototherapy of Seasonal Affective Disorder." *American Journal of Psychiatry*, vol. 144 (October 1987), pp. 1301–5.

James, Steven P.; T. A. Wehr; D. A. Sack; B. L. Parry; and N. E. Rosenthal. "Treatment of Seasonal Affective Disorder with Light in the Evening." *British Journal of Psychiatry*, vol. 147 (October 1985), pp. 424–28.

Kripke, Daniel F. "Photoperiodic Mechanisms for Depression and Its Treatment." *Biological Psychiatry 1981: Proceedings of the IIIrd World Congress of Biological Psychiatry*, ed. C. Perris, G. Struwe, and B. Jansson. New York: Elsevier-North Holland Biomedical Press, 1981.

————; S. Craig Risch; and David S. Janowsky. "Lighting Up Depression." *Psychopharmacology Bulletin*, vol. 19 (1983), pp. 526–30.

Lewy, Alfred J.; H. A. Kern; N. E. Rosenthal; and T. A. Wehr. "Bright Artificial Light Treatment of a Manic-Depressive Patient with a Seasonal Mood Cycle." *American Journal of Psychiatry*, vol. 11 (November 1982), pp. 1496–98.

————; Robert L. Sack; and Clifford L. Singer. "Assessment and Treatment of Chronobiologic Disorders Using Plasma Melatonin Levels and Bright Light Exposure: The Clock-Gate Model and the Phase Response Curve." *Psychopharmacology Bulletin*, vol. 20 (Summer 1984), pp. 561–65.

Ridlehimber, Hugh, M.D. Interview, May 12, 1986.

Rosenthal, Norman E. "Seasonal Affective Disorder and Light Treatment in Children." Paper presented at the American Psychiatry Association Annual Convention, Dallas, May 18-24, 1987.

————; D. A. Sack; C. J. Carpenter; B. L. Parry; and W. B. Mendelson. "Antidepressant Effects of Light in Seasonal Affective Disorder." *American Journal of Psychiatry*, vol. 142

February 1985), pp. 163–69.

————; and Thomas A. Wehr. "Seasonal Affective Disorders." *Psychiatric Annals*, vol. 17 (October 1987), pp. 670–74.

————; A. J. Lewy; T. A. Wehr; H. A. Kern; and F. K. Goodwin. "Seasonal Cycling in a Bipolar Patient." *Psychiatric Research Reports*, vol. 8 (January 1983), pp. 25–31.

Terman, Michael. "Light Therapy for SAD: Dosing Regimens." Paper delivered at American Psychiatric Association Annual Convention, Washington, D.C., May 14, 1986.

U.S. Department of Commerce, National Oceanic and Atmospheric Administration. *Comparative Climatic Data for the United States Through 1985*. Washington, D.C.: Government Printing Office, 1986.

Wehr, Thomas A.; F. M. Jacobsen; D. A. Sack; J. Arendt; L. Tamarkin; and N. E. Rosenthal. "Phototherapy of Seasonal Affective Disorder: Time of Day and Suppression of Melatonin Are Not Critical for Antidepressant Effects." *Archives of General Psychiatry*, vol. 43 (September 1986), pp. 870–75.

Williams, Roger. *Biomedical Individuality*. Austin: University of Texas Press, 1974.

Wirz-Justice, Anna; C. Bucheli; A. C. Schmid; and P. Graw. "A Dose Relationship in Bright Light Treatment of Seasonal Depression." *American Journal of Psychiatry*, vol. 143 (July 1986), pp. 932–33.

Chapter 4: How Animals Survive the Cold

Allen, Joel A. "The Influence of Physical Conditions in the Genesis of Species." *Annual Report of the Board of Regents of the Smithsonian Institution, Report of the U.S. National Museum*. Washington, D.C.: Government Printing Office, 1906.

Folk, G. Edgar, Jr. *Introduction to Environmental Physiology*. Philadelphia: Lea & Febiger, 1966.

Gale, C. C. "Endocrine and Metabolic Responses to Cold in Baboons." *Research Activities at Regional Primate Centers in the Federation of the American Society for Experimental Biology Proceedings*. Washington, D.C.: n.p., 1975.

Gates, David. *Man and His Environment: Climate*. New York: Harper & Row, 1972.

Hanson, Peter G., and Robert E. Johnson. "Variation of Plasma

Ketones and Free Fatty Acids During Acute Cold Exposure in Man." *Journal of Applied Physiology*, vol. 20 (January 1965), pp. 56–60.

Jordan, Daniel; Francois Perrin; and René Mornex. "Circannual Variation of TSH Circadian Rhythm Parameters in the Rat." *Neuroendocrinology*, vol. 36 (January 1983), pp. 17–20.

Klem, Daniel, Jr., associate professor of biology, Muhlenberg College, Allentown, Pennsylvania. Personal communication, October 1987.

Konno, N. "Comparison Between the Thyrotropin Response to Thyrotropin-Releasing Hormone in Summer and That in Winter in Normal Subjects." *Endocrinologica Japon*, vol. 25 (December 1978), pp. 635–39.

Kopecky, Jan; L. Sigurdson; I. Park; and J. Himms-Hagen. "Thyroxine 5'-Deiodinase in Hamster and Rat Brown Adipose Tissue: Effect of Cold and Diet." *American Journal of Physiology*, vol. 251 (July 1986), pp. E1–E7.

Mather, John Russell. *Climatology: Fundamentals and Applications*. New York: McGraw-Hill, 1974.

Muzik, Katherine, and Michael Fedak. "Birds That Refuse to Freeze." *Sea Frontiers*, vol. 22 (July 1976), p. 223.

Scholander, P. F. "Evolution of Climatic Adaptation in Homeotherms." *Evolution*, vol. 9 (March 1955), pp. 15–26.

Smith, Robert E. "Cold Acclimatization—An Altered Steady State." *Journal of the American Medical Association*, vol. 179 (March 24, 1962), pp. 110–16.

Suzuki, Mitsuo. "Initial Response of Endocrine Functions to Cold Exposure." *Environmental Changes and Endocrine Functions*, ed. Mitsuo Suzuki. Tokyo: Tokyo Press Company, Ltd., 1971.

Vaughan, M. K. "The Influence of Natural Short Photoperiodic and Temperature Conditions on Plasma Thyroid Hormones and Cholesterol in Male Syrian Hamsters." *International Journal of Biometeorology*, vol. 28 (July 1984), pp. 201–10.

Chapter 5: Conquering the Cold

Butson, A. R. C. "Acclimatization to Cold in the Antarctic.' *Nature*, vol. 163 (January 22, 1949), pp. 132–33.

Cannon, Walter B. *Wisdom of the Body*. New York: W. W. Norton and Co., 1932.

Darwin, Charles. *Journal of Researches into the Natural History and Geology of the Countries Visited During the Voyage of H.M.S. Beagle Round the World.* London: John Murray, 1832.

Folk, G. Edgar. *Introduction to Environmental Physiology.* Philadelphia: Lea & Febiger, 1966.

Hefco, E.; L. Krulich; P. Illner; and P. R. Larsen. "Effect of Acute Exposure to Cold on the Activity of Hypothalamic-Pituitary-Thyroid System." *Endocrinology,* vol. 97 (November 1975), pp. 1185-95.

Joy, Robert J. T.; J. C. Matone; G. W. Newcomb; and W. C. Bradford. "Responses of Cold-Acclimatized Men to Infused Norepinephrine." *Journal of Applied Physiology,* vol. 18 (November 1963), pp. 1209-12.

Konno, Norimichi. "Comparison Between the Thyrotropin Response to Thyrotropin-Releasing Hormone in Summer and That in Winter in Normal Subjects." *Endocrinologica Japon,* vol. 25 (1978), pp. 635-39.

Sellers, E. A.; K. V. Flattery; A. Shum; and G. E. Johnson. "Thyroid Status in Relation to Catecholamines in Cold and Warm Environment." *Canadian Journal of Physiology and Pharmacology,* vol. 49 (April 1971), pp. 268-75.

Smith, Eleanor. "Winter in Antarctica: Health Despite Discomfort." *Psychology Today* (March 1987), pp. 60-61.

Talan, Jamie. "Adapting to the Cold." *Newsday,* December 9, 1986, "Discovery" section, p. 2.

Tromp, S. W., and V. Faust. "Influence of Weather and Climate on Mental Processes in General and Mental Diseases in Particular." *Progress in Biometeorology, Div. A, Vol. 1, Part II, Period 1963-1975,* ed. S. W. Tromp, Amsterdam: Swetz & Zeitlinger, 1977.

Yamada, T., and T. Onaya. "Studies on the Mechanism of Action of Cold in Producing an Increase of Thyroid Hormone Secretion." *Psychoneuroendocrinology, Workshop Conference of the International Society of Psychoneuroendocrinology, Mieken 1973.* Basel: Karger, 1974.

Chapter 6: Dressing for the Cold

Folk, G. Edgar, Jr. *Introduction to Environmental Physiology.* Philadelphia: Lea & Febiger, 1966.

Nicolson, Nigel. *Napoleon 1812.* New York: Harper & Row, 1985.

Siple, Paul A. "Clothing and Climate." *Physiology of Heat Regulation and the Science of Clothing*, ed. L. H. Newburgh. Philadelphia: W. B. Saunders Co., 1949.

Smith, Eleanor. "Winter in Antarctica: Health Despite Discomfort." *Psychology Today* (March 1987), pp. 60–61.

Chapter 7: Eternal Springtime in Your Home

Albers, Josef. *Interaction of Color*. New Haven: Yale University Press, 1963.

Bender, Bonnie. "Color Power—Make It Work for You." Pittsburgh Paints, Pittsburgh, n.d.

Birren, Faber. "Color and Man-Made Environments: Reactions of Body and Eye." No. 2 of a series. *American Institute of Architects Journal*, vol. 58 (September 1972), pp. 35–39.

————. *Light, Color and Environment*. New York: Van Nostrand Reinhold Co., 1969.

————, ed. *Munsell—A Grammar of Color*. New York: Van Nostrand Reinhold Co., 1969.

————. *New Horizons in Color*. New York: Reinhold Publishing Co., 1955.

Clark, Linda. *The Ancient Art of Color Therapy*. Old Greenwich, Conn.: Devin-Adair, 1975.

Dantsig, N. M.; D. N. Lazerev; and M. V. Sokolov. "Ultraviolet Installations of Beneficial Action." *Applied Optics*, vol. 6 (November 1967), pp. 1872–76.

Goldstein, Kurt. "Some Experimental Observations Concerning the Influence of Colors on the Function of the Organism." *Occupational Therapy*, vol. 21 (June 1942), pp. 147–51.

Hunt, Roland T. *Complete Color Prescription*. Los Angeles: Paramount, 1962.

"The Ion Story." *Executive Fitness Newsletter* (October 16, 1982), pp. 1–2.

Kunishima, Michiko, and Takuko Yanase. "Visual Effects of Wall Colours in Living Rooms." *Ergonomics*, vol. 28 (June 1985), pp. 869–82.

Longmore, J., and E. Ne'eman. "The Availability of Sunshine and Human Requirements for Sunlight in Buildings." *Journal of Architectural Research*, vol. 3 (May 1973), pp. 24–29.

Martin, Tovah. "January's Blossoms." *Country Journal* (January 1987), pp. 39–44.

Matthaei, Rupprecht, ed. *Goethe's Color Theory.* New York: Van Nostrand Reinhold Co., 1970.

Pacifica Community Hospital, Huntington Beach, California. Press Release #85447-10285 ("Color and Health"), November 22, 1985.

Ringle, Ken. "Conference Catches the Flavor of the Importance of Smell." *Allentown* (Pennsylvania), *Morning Call*, November 27, 1986, section D, p. 26.

Schwartz, Gary. "Subjective and Respiratory Differentiation of Fragrances: Interactions with Hedonics." Paper presented at the meeting of the Society for Psychophysiological Research, Montreal, October 17, 1986.

Swan, Herbert S., and George W. Tuttle. "Planning Sunlight Cities." *The American City*, vol. 17, no. 3 (September 1917), pp. 213-17.

Walter, Morton. "Are You Breathing Malnourished Air?" *Prevention* (July 1979), pp. 93-96.

Watson, Donald. *Designing and Building a Solar House.* Charlotte, Vt.: Garden Way Publishing, 1977.

Wilson, Robert F. *Color in Industry Today.* New York: Macmillan, 1960.

Wright, Jonathan V. "A Case of Air Ion Sensitivity." *Prevention* (November 1979), pp. 85-88.

Chapter 8: Charting the Ebb and Flow

Byers, S. W.; K. F. Dowsett; and T. D. Glover. "Seasonal and Circadian Changes of Testosterone Levels in the Peripheral Blood Plasma of Stallions and Their Relation to Semen Quality." *Journal of Endocrinology*, vol. 99 (October 1983), pp. 141-50.

Del Greco, Sandra. "Sex and the Sun." *Harper's Bazaar* (January 1980), pp. 121; 140.

Ehrenkranz, Joel R. L. "A Gland for All Seasons." *Natural History* (June 1983), pp. 18-23.

Hartung, John. "Light, Puberty, and Aggression: A Proximal Mechanism Hypothesis." *Human Ecology*, vol. 6 (September 1978), pp. 273-97.

Hibersek, E. "Influence of the Day of the Week and the Weather on People Using a Telephone Support System." *British Journal of Psychiatry*, vol. 15, no. 2 (February 1987), pp. 182-92.

Lagoguey, M., and A. Reinberg. "Circannual Rhythms in Plasma LH, FSH, and Testosterone and in the Sexual Activity of Healthy Young Parisian Males." Paper presented at the Proceedings of the Physiological Society, January 9–10, 1976.

Luce, Gay Gaer. *Biological Rhythms in Psychiatry and Medicine*. Bethesda, Md.: National Institute of Mental Health, 1970.

Parkes, A. S. "Seasonal Variation in Human Sexual Activity." *Eugenics Society Symposium*, vol. 4 (1964), pp. 238–45.

Reinberg, Alain; M. Lagoguey; F. Cesselin; Y. Touitou; J. Legrand; A. Delassalle; J. Antreassian; and A. Lagoguey. "Circadian and Circannual Rhythms in Plasma Hormones and Other Variables in Five Healthy Young Human Males." *Acta Endocrinologica*, vol. 88 (July 1978), pp. 417–27.

Rubin, Zick. "Seasonal Rhythms in Behavior." *Psychology Today* (December 1979), pp. 12–16.

Smolensky, Michael H.; A. Reinberg; A. Bicakova-Rocher; and J. Sanford. "Chronoepidemiological Search for Circannual Changes in the Sexual Activity of Human Males." *Chronobiologia*, vol. 8 (July-September 1980), pp. 217–30.

Swain, Roger B. "Reading the Signs of Spring." *New York Times Magazine* (April 25, 1982), pp. 53; 67–70.

Tromp, S. W., and V. Faust. "Influence of Weather and Climate on Mental Processes in General and Mental Diseases in Particular." *Progress in Biometeorology, Div. A, Vol. 1, Part II, Period 1963–1975*, ed. S. W. Tromp. Amsterdam: Swetz & Zeitlinger, 1977.

Udry, J. Richard, and Naomi M. Morris. "Seasonality of Coitus and Seasonality of Birth." *Demography*, vol. 4 (1967), pp. 673–79.

Waldhauser, Franz; H. Frisch; M. Waldhauser; G. Weiszenbachter; U. Zeitlhuber; and R. J. Wurtman. "Fall in Nocturnal Serum Melatonin During Prepuberty and Pubescence." *Lancet*, vol. 1 (February 18, 1984), pp. 362–65.

Chapter 9: The Harmony of Sleep

Czeisler, Charles A.; J. S. Allan; S. H. Strogatz; J. M. Ronda; R. Sánchez; C. D. Rios; W. O. Freitag; G. S. Richardson; and R. E. Kronauer. "Bright Light Resets the Human Circadian Pacemaker Independent of the Timing of the Sleep-Wake Cycle." *Science*, vol. 233 (August 8, 1986), pp. 667–71.

Dement, William C. "Medical Community Is Awakened to Seriousness of Sleep Disorders." Press release, Sleep Science Information Center, Upjohn Company, Kalamazoo, Michigan, January 1987.

"Graveyard Shift." *U.S. News and World Report* (June 9, 1986), p. 76.

Kripke, Daniel F. "Photoperiodic Mechanisms for Depression and Its Treatment." *Biological Psychiatry 1981: Proceedings of the IIIrd World Congress of Biological Psychiatry,* ed. C. Perris, G. Struwe, and B. Jansson. New York: Elsevier-North Holland Biomedical Press, 1981.

Lewy, Alfred J., and Robert L. Sack. "Light Therapy and Psychiatry." *Proceedings of the Society for Experimental Biology and Medicine,* vol. 183 (October 1986), pp. 11-18.

————; ————; and Clifford L. Singer. "Assessment and Treatment of Chronobiologic Disorders Using Plasma Melatonin Levels and Bright Light Exposure: The Clock-Gate Model and the Phase Response Curve." *Psychopharmacology Bulletin,* vol. 20 (Summer 1984), pp, 561-65.

Lyman, Charles P. *Hibernation and Torpor in Mammals and Birds.* New York: Academic Press, 1982.

Sack, Robert L.; A. J. Lewy; D. L. Erb; W. M. Vollmer; and C. M. Singer. "Human Melatonin Production Decreases with Age." *Journal of Pineal Research,* vol. 3 (1986), pp. 379-88.

Saletu, B.; M. Dietzel; O. M. Lesch; M. Musalek; H. Walter; and J. Grunberger. "Effect of Biologically Active Light and Partial Sleep Deprivation on Sleep, Awakening and Circadian Rhythms in Normals." *European Neurology,* vol. 25, supplementum 2 (1986), pp, 82-92.

Savides, Thomas J. "Natural Light Exposure of Young Adults." *Psychology and Behavior,* vol. 38 (1986), pp. 571-74.

Siwolop, Sana. "Helping Workers Stay Awake at the Switch." *Business Week* (December 8, 1986), p. 108.

Chapter 10: The Antihibernation Diet

Beard, John. Personal communication, August 13, 1987.

Burton, Alan C. *Man in a Cold Environment.* London: Edward Arnold, 1955.

Cannon, Walter B. *Wisdom of the Body.* New York: W. W. Norton and Co., 1932.

Edman, Marjorie. "Nutrition and Climate." *Medical Climatology*, ed. Sydney Licht. New Haven, Conn.: Elizabeth Licht, 1964.

————. "Effect of Nutrition on Bodily Resistance Against Meteorological Simuli." *Progress in Biometeorology, Div. A. Vol. 1, Part II, Period 1963-1975*, ed. S. W. Tromp. Amsterdam: Swetz & Zeitlinger, 1977.

Hay, Tina M. "Human Response to Cold." Human Development Research at the Pennsylvania State University, 1987.

Kuntzleman, Charles T. *Activetics*. New York: Peter H. Wyden, 1975.

Lyman, Charles P. *Hibernation and Torpor in Mammals and Birds*. New York: Academic Press, 1982.

Magnesium News Bureau. "Magnesium: What Consumers Should Know." Press release, Los Angeles, April 3, 1985.

Mitchell, H. H.; N. Glickman; E. G. Lambert; R. W. Keeton; and M. K. Fahnestock. "The Tolerance of Man to Cold as Affected by Dietary Modification: Carbohydrate Versus Fat and the Effect of the Frequency of Meals." *American Journal of Physiology*, vol. 146 (April 1946), pp. 84-96.

Pao, E. M., and S. J. Mickle. "Problem Nutrients in the United States." *Food Technology*, vol. 35 (September 1981), pp. 58-79.

"Rhythmic Method of Girth Control." *Next* (July/August 1980), p. 76.

Wurtman, Richard J. "Nutrients that Modify Brain Function." *Scientific American*, vol. 246, no. 4 (April 1982), pp. 50-59.

Chapter 11: Planning the Great Escape

Battan, Louis J. *Weather*. Englewood Cliffs, N.J.: Prentice-Hall, 1974.

Gates, David M. *Man and His Environment: Climate*. New York: Harper & Row, 1972.

Nautical Almanac Office, United States Naval Observatory. *Sunrise and Sunset Tables*. Washington, D.C.: Government Printing Office, 1965.

U.S. Department of Commerce, Environmental Science Services Administration. *Climates of the World*. Washington, D.C.: Government Printing Office, January 1969.

————, National Oceanic and Atmospheric Administration. *Comparative Climatic Data for the United States Through 1985*. Washington, D.C.: Government Printing Office, 1986.

Chapter 12: The Divine Sun

American Academy of Dermatology and American Academy of Pediatrics. "Making Children and Adolescents Sun Smart: The Importance of Sun Protection." News release, May 18, 1987.

Haddad, John G., Jr., and Theodore J. Hahn. "Natural and Synthetic Sources of Circulating 25-Hydroxyvitamin D in Man." *Nature*, vol. 244 (August 24, 1973), pp. 515-17.

Hersey, Peter; E. Hasic; A. Edwards; M. Bradley; G. Haran; and W. H. McCarthy. "Immunological Effects of Solarium Exposure." *Lancet*, vol. 1 (February 18, 1984), pp. 545-48.

Jackson, Samuel M., ed. *The New Schaff Herzog Encyclopedia of Religious Knowledge*. New York: Funk & Wagnalls, 1911.

Jastrow, Morris, Jr. *The Religion of Babylonia and Assyria*. Boston: Ginn & Co., 1898.

Kime, Zane R. *Sunlight Could Save Your Life*. Penryn, Calif.: World Health Publications, 1980.

Lillyquist, Michael J. *Sunlight and Health*. New York: Dodd, Mead & Co., 1985.

Meade, Jeff. "A Sunny Safeguard for Strong Bones." *Prevention* (December 1985), pp. 97-112.

North Atlantic Treaty Organization Advanced Study Institute. *Proceedings of the NATO Advanced Study Institute on Primary Photo-Processes in Biology and Medicine*. New York: Plenum Press, 1985.

Omdahl, John L.; P. J. Garry; L. A. Hunsaker; W. C. Hunt; and J. S. Goodwin. "Nutritional Status in a Healthy Elderly Population: Vitamin D." *American Journal of Clinical Nutrition*, vol. 36 (December 1982), pp. 1225-33.

Owens, Neal. The SunBox Company, 1037 Taft Street, Rockville, Md. 20850. Interview, July 31, 1987.

Petersen, W. F. *Man, Weather, and Sun*. Springfield, Ill.: Charles C. Thomas, 1947.

Reville, Albert D. D. *The Native Religions of Mexico and Peru*, trans. Philip Wicksteed. New York: Scribner's & Sons, 1884.

Roswell Park Memorial Institute. "Skin Cancer: A 'Hot' Topic for Dermatologists." Regional Clinical Cancer Report, Buffalo, N.Y., 1987.

Schmidt-Kessen, W. "Therapy in Natural Climates." *Progress in Biometeorology, Div. A, Vol. 1, Part II, Period 1963-1975*, ed. S. W. Tromp. Amsterdam: Swetz & Zeitlinger, 1977.

Tromp, S. W., and V. Faust. "Influence of Weather and Climate on Mental Processes in General and Mental Diseases in Particular." *Progress in Biometeorology, Div. A, Vol. 1, Part II, Period 1963-1975*, ed. S. W. Tromp. Amsterdam: Swetz & Zeitlinger, 1977.

U.S. Department of Health and Human Services, Food and Drug Administration. "Symposium on Biological Effects and Measurements of Light Sources." Rockville, Md., 1980.

Yoe, Mary Ruth. "Celebrating the Winter Solstice." *Johns Hopkins Magazine* (December 1980), pp, 23-28.

Chapter 13: Coping with the Seasons

Anastos, Chris. "Weather and the Patient." *Modern Medicine*, vol. 40 (April 17, 1972), pp. 27-31.

Bedford, Thomas. "Thermal Factors in the Environment Which Influence Fatigue." *Symposium on Fatigue*, ed. W. F. Floyd and A. T. Welford. London: H. K. Lewis and Co., 1953.

Burch, G. E., and T. D. Giles. "Influence of Weather and Climate on Cardiovascular Diseases. *Progress in Biometeorology, Div. A, vol. 1, Part II, Period 1963-1975*, ed. S. W. Tromp. Amsterdam: Swetz & Zeitlinger, 1977.

Ellis, F. P. "Tropical Fatigue." *Symposium on Fatigue*, ed. W. F. Floyd and A. T. Welford. London: H. K. Lewis and Co., 1953.

Gates, David. *Man and His Environment: Climate*. New York: Harper & Row, 1972.

Hribersek, E.; H. Van De Voorde; H. Poppe; and J. Casselman. "Influence of the Day of the Week and the Weather on People Using a Telephone Support System." *British Journal of Psychiatry*, vol. 150 (February 1987), pp. 189-92.

Lamprell, B. A. "Tropical Neurasthenia." *Medical Journal of Malaya*, vol. 3 (September 1949), pp. 34-40.

MacPherson, R. K. *Tropical Fatigue*. Brisbane: University of Queensland Press, 1949.

Petersen, William F. *Man, Weather, and Sun*. Springfield, Ill.: Charles C. Thomas, 1947.

Rotton, James. "Weather and Your Health." *Allentown* (Pennsylvania), *Morning Call*, August 1, 1983, section D, p. 3.

Welsh, R. B.; E. O. Longley; and O. Lomaev. "The Measurement of Fatigue in Hot Working Conditions." *Ergonomics*, vol. 14 (January 1971), pp. 85-90.

World Health Organization Scientific Group on Health. "Heat Stress and Heat Strain." *Industrial Medicine and Surgery*, vol. 41 (January 1972), pp. 31-34.

Chapter 14: ... Spring

Frost, Robert. "Two Tramps in Mudtime," in *The Road Not Taken: A Selection of Robert Frost's Poems*, ed. Louis Untermeyer. New York: Holt and Company, 1971.

Gates, David M. *Man and His Environment: Climate.* New York: Harper & Row, 1972.

Whybrow, P. C. "Where There's Mud There's Momentum." *Yankee Magazine* (April 1979), pp. 94-115.

Additional Sources

Lewy, A. J.; R. L. Sack; L. S. Miller; Tana M. Hoban; C. M. Singer; J. R. Samples; and G. L. Krauss. "The Use of Plasma Melatonin Levels and Light in the Assessment and Treatment of Chronobiologic Sleep and Mood Disorders." *Journal of Neural Transmission*, vol. 21 (1986 supplementum), pp. 311-22.

Parry, Barbara L.; N. E. Rosenthal; L. Tamarkin; and T. A. Wehr. "Treatment of a Patient with Seasonal Premenstrual Syndrome." *American Journal of Psychiatry*, vol. 144 (June 1987), pp. 762-65.

Rosenthal, N. E.; D. A. Sack; F. M. Jacobsen; S. P. James; Barbara L. Parry; Josephine Arendt; L. Tamarkin; and T. A. Wehr. "Melatonin in Seasonal Affective Disorder and Phototherapy." *Journal of Neural Transmission*, vol. 21 (1986 supplementum), pp. 256-67.

Wehr, Thomas A.; R. G. Skwerer; F. M. Jacobsen; D. A. Sack; and N. E. Rosenthal. "Eye Versus Skin Phototherapy of Seasonal Affective Disorder." *American Journal of Psychiatry*, vol. 144 (June 1987). pp. 753-57.

Whybrow, P. C; H. S. Akiskal; and W. T. McKinney. *Mood Disorders, Toward a New Psychobiology.* New York: Plenum Press, 1984.

Index

Index

Index